★ ★ ★ **ALL-OUT FOR VICTORY!**

ALL-OUT FOR

VICTORY!

MAGAZINE ADVERTISING
AND THE WORLD WAR II
HOME FRONT
JOHN BUSH JONES

BRANDEIS UNIVERSITY PRESS

Waltham, Massachusetts

Published by

UNIVERSITY PRESS OF NEW ENGLAND

Hanover & London

BRANDEIS UNIVERSITY PRESS

Published by University Press of New England,

One Court Street, Lebanon, NH 03766

www.upne.com

© 2009 by Brandeis University Press

Printed in the United States of America

5 4 3 2 1

Library of Congress Cataloging-in-Publication Data

Jones, John Bush.

All-out for victory! : magazine advertising and the World War II home
front / John Bush Jones. — 1st ed.

    p. cm

Includes bibliographical references and index.

ISBN 978-1-58465-768-2 (cloth : alk. paper)

1. Advertising, Magazine—United States—History—20th century.
I. Title

HF6105.U5J66 2009

940.53'1—dc22   2008055182

University Press of New England is a member
of the Green Press Initiative. The paper used
in this book meets their minimum requirement
for recycled paper.

8137

★★★ CONTENTS

What drew me to study wartime advertising—and wartime popular songs before that—are two personal passions of mine. First, as a child of the home front (I was born in 1940) I still carry with me vivid memories of those years and seem to have an innate affinity with home front culture and social history. Second, ever since graduate school I've had a penchant for doing original research using primary sources almost exclusively, especially on topics not before treated extensively or comprehensively. World War II war ads (as they were called then and I call them now) qualify on both counts.

The literature on World War II advertising is scant and fragmentary. Frank W. Fox's *Madison Avenue Goes to War* has some value as a book about the advertising *industry* during the war but less as a treatment of the actual ads. The small selection that Fox discusses he seemingly picked to advance his theory that Madison Avenue used the war to polish up advertising's reputation. Maureen Honey's *Creating Rosie the Riveter: Class, Gender and Propaganda during World War II* is not *about* wartime advertising per se. Rather, Honey uses magazine ads (and fiction) in only the *Saturday Evening Post* and *True Story* to examine images of women during the war, with results that do not fully represent those images. For example, Honey concludes from some ads in the *Post* alone that the homemaker with a husband overseas was portrayed as the "innocent, vulnerable mother" (131). Had she looked at ads in just one other magazine, *Ladies' Home Journal*, she would have seen strong, resilient homemakers capable of keeping not just the home but the whole home front together. From ads only in *Life*, Sue Hart's essay in *Visions of War: World War II in Popular Literature and Culture* edited by M. Paul Holsinger and Mary Anne Schofield, concludes that all wartime advertisers "were selling patriotism and promise first" (125). This conclusion is too narrow and also erroneous on the subject of patriotism, as discussed more fully in Chapter 1. Roland Marchand's splendid article "Suspended in Time: Mom-and-Pop Groceries, Chain Stores, and National Advertising during the World War II Interlude" in *Produce, Conserve, Share and Play Square: The Grocer and the Consumer on the Home-Front Battlefield during World War II* edited by Barbara McLean Ward only treats advertising and chain stores' impact on small independent grocers during the war and does not relate to the present study of war ads.

My own approach to the artifacts of cultural history is that of a narrative historian. In other words, as with wartime songs before, I simply set out to see what the ads would "say" to me, listened very carefully, and then attempted to tell their story as vividly and lucidly as possible. My research began with selecting which magazines I wanted to scour for war ads. Since upwards of six hundred national and regional magazines were published during the war, it would have been impossible to look at all of them (or even to *find* many of them), so I abandoned all thoughts of an exhaustive treatment of war ads in favor of an extensive or comprehensive treatment based on ads in a smaller but representative number of magazines. I decided on ten large-circulation general-interest and news magazines, including one women's magazine, one men's magazine, one aimed at the business community, and one with a readership primarily of farmers and other rural Americans: *Life, Look, Collier's, Saturday Evening Post, Ladies' Home Journal, Esquire, Time, Newsweek, Business Week*, and *Farm Journal and Farmer's Wife*. Nearly all these magazines had a subscriber base in the millions (even *Farm Journal*, with close to three million subscribers in the 1940s), so war ads in them had the best chance of being seen by the largest numbers of home front Americans in the widest possible geographic and demographic distribution.

Starting with *Life* since it consistently contained the most ads, for a solid year I turned every page of every issue of each magazine from January 1, 1942, through December 31, 1945. I photocopied almost every war ad and entered information about each one into a computer database: date, magazine, advertiser (company or product), and subject (War Bonds, rumor control, coping with rationing, etc.). At the end of my odyssey through the magazines, I had twenty-six three-inch ring binders full of photocopies and a database containing 5,143 ads, fewer than a hundred of which duplicate a single ad published in more than one magazine. With the photocopies, database, and wartime articles in *Business Week*, the advertising trade journals *Printers' Ink* and *Advertising & Selling*, and a few other magazines, I had all I needed strictly from primary sources to begin writing—supplemented by a little information from such secondary materials as standard histories of the home front, other books, and websites.

I said that I photocopied "almost" every war ad since I excluded some based on the book's focus on ads only by commercial advertisers. I did not photocopy and do not discuss ads prepared by or for any government agencies such as the Treasury Department or the Office of War Information unless they also had a commercial sponsor. But I do include ads by organizations like the American Meat Institute and the Cast Iron Pipe Research Association since these were trade associations that represented groups of commercial advertisers. I also exclude ads by commercial advertisers that merely show servicemen or women in the art when the ads themselves contain no war message and are just selling a product. Yet I include ads that exploited a wartime concern in order to sell something, such as those for toothpastes and deodorants in which getting rid of bad breath or body odor boosts a serviceman's or civilian girl's morale. Silly as they may be, these are kinds of war ads and have a place in the book, if only a small one.

★ ★ ★ A few aspects of the text perhaps need explanation. Instead of hundreds of footnotes leading only to the dates and page numbers of ads and citations of other sources, I employ the system of parenthetical documentation within the text as laid out in the *MLA Style Manual*. To keep some of their style and flavor when quoting from the ads, I have retained the *italics*, **boldface**, SMALL CAPS, and underscoring that occur in the original copy. In the 1940s many ads used the three separated periods (. . .) that we use for an ellipsis in a text as the equivalent of a dash (—) to indicate a shift in thought or a pause. I have retained these, and when needing to abbreviate a particularly long passage, I signal my doing so by placing the three ellipsis periods within square brackets [. . .]. Also, since I often cite percentages, instead of the formal convention of spelling them out (fifty-seven percent), I use the numeric system (57%) for brevity and to make the figures stand out. It perhaps goes without saying, but when I say "late in the war" it's meant from a postwar perspective since no one knew when "late" in the war would be while it was still going on. Rather than repeat cumbersome phrases like "according to the ads in the magazines examined here" I often say something like "according to most ads in the magazines," which should be understood to mean the ten magazines in this account, not all wartime magazines. Finally, following the common parlance of the day, I often refer to America's young men and women during the war, in the service or civilians, as boys and girls, rather than the more politically correct "men" and "women" by today's standards. To do otherwise would falsify the picture of the war years, the ads, and the way these boys and girls referred to themselves and were referred to by others.

★ ★ ★ My list of people and institutions to thank for helping make this book happen isn't very long, but all their contributions have been invaluable. Deservedly first, I begin with three people whose input and thought-provoking questions helped jump-start this project—Professors Susan Smulyan of the Department of American Civilization at Brown University, William O. Beeman, then at Brown and now of the Department of Anthropology at the University of Minnesota, and my long-time friend and former colleague at Brandeis University, Stephen J. Whitfield of the Department of American Studies.

I practically lived in libraries for the year I went through magazines, and my indebtedness to them for their collections and for the helpfulness of their staffs can't be measured. Once again I did most of my research in the libraries of Brown University, this time, because of its extensive collection of American magazines, mostly in the Rockefeller Library, where Edwin Hayslip, Steven Lavallee, Daniel P. O'Mahony, and Jennifer Martenson each gave me specialized kinds of assistance I could not have done without. Though I spent less time in Brown's John Hay Library, I am again indebted to the Hay's Rosemary Cullen, Ann Patrick, Peter Harrington, and Andy Moul for supporting the project in many varied ways. Splendid as the collections and personnel are in the Brown libraries, I had to range farther afield for some material, and accordingly I want to especially thank Mary Anne Sumner of the University of Rhode Island Library for unearthing from storage the run of *Farm Journal* for the war years and making it available to me. The Boston Public Library, the Providence Public Library, the Pawtucket (Rhode Island) Public Library, and the Goldfarb Library at Brandeis all filled in some holes in the runs of magazines at Brown or had some books unavailable there. Also, many thanks to home front enthusiast and lecturer Calvin Knickerbocker for extensive information on World War II posters.

Purely personally, I owe much to the encouragement and just plain "being there" of my son, Carson, and his wife, Dawn, my long-time friends Bob and Elva Mathiesen, Claudia Novack, former student Helen Lewis, attorney Jerry Cohen, and doctors Bruce Fischberg and Charles Sherman.

Finally, in a class by herself is my editor Phyllis Deutsch. From the start, Phyllis believed in the ads project, stood by it, and worked with me and my sometimes errant prose every step of the way, seeing it through to its conclusion. For this my debt to Phyllis is far more abundant than the words I have to express it.

J. B. J.
Providence, Rhode Island
January 4, 2009

★ ★ ★ **ALL-OUT FOR VICTORY!**

1

★ ★ ★ ★ ★ ★ ★
★ ★ ★ ★ ★ ★ ★
★ ★ ★ ★ ★ ★ ★
★ ★ ★ ★ ★ ★ ★

"ALL-OUTS" AND "DOUBLE-BARRELLEDS"

HOW TO ADVERTISE

A WAR

It took just one day—December 7, 1941—for Americans' perennial wrangling over isolationism versus interventionism to cease, and, in the words of *New York Times* columnist Arthur Krock, for national unity to "click into place" (*New York Times* 8 Dec. 1941: 6). Except for a handful of pacifists and conscientious objectors and approximately 15,000 so-called native fascists such as the members of the German-American Bund and Silver Shirts, as of that day roughly 130 million Americans stopped debating whether to enter the war. Pearl Harbor provided a clear answer.

The Japanese bombs that fell on Pearl Harbor also effectively detonated the biggest advertising explosion in this country's history. Nearly three years after that fateful Sunday in 1941, the advertising agency of Young & Rubicam placed an ad in *Newsweek* on September 18, 1944, stating with absolute accuracy, "**No product** in the world has ever received such advertising support as American business has put behind U. S. War Bonds" (26). It's equally accurate to say that nothing ever received such advertising support as civilian involvement in the war effort *generally*. The ensuing chapters examine systematically the varieties of home front support and the ways in which ads by commercial advertisers promoted them in national magazines. As background, the present chapter looks at prewar precursors to such war ads and the workings of the wartime advertising industry vis-à-vis national magazines.

National Unity and Advertising

It's become commonplace to declare that the four years comprising World War II were the longest period of sustained national unity in the American twentieth century—or, perhaps, in the entire history of the United States. But this commonplace is absolutely true. Both contemporary observers and later historians substantiate that this national unity was the real thing. The day after Arthur Krock reported from Washington that the new national unity "seemed visibly to arise from the wreckage at Honolulu," an unsigned *New York Times* editorial observed that "there are no party lines today in Congress," that leading Republicans like Herbert Hoover and Alf Landon had taken their place by the side of President Roosevelt, and that the far-right America First Committee and a far-left labor union had come together in a display of national unity (9 Dec. 1941: 30).

Writing more than three decades later, historian Ronald H. Bailey in *The Home Front: U.S.A.* corroborated those contemporary observations with statistics: "On December 10, [. . .] a public opinion poll found that only 2 per cent of Americans disapproved of the declaration of war against Japan" (23). And as if to show that the 98% in favor of the war was not just a product of the aftershock of Pearl Harbor, Bailey offers a statistic from much later: "Sociologists reported finding a widespread sense of 'unconscious well-being,' which they attributed to participation in civilian defense, scrap drives and the other efforts to bring the War home" (117). In *Days of Sadness, Years of Triumph*, Geoffrey Perrett concluded from his own research that national unity not only continued but intensified as the war went on. In early 1942 when things looked bad for the American forces in the Pacific, Perrett found that "The country was fused as it had never been before in living memory. Not all the defeats, setbacks and frustration could break down that sense of national union and purpose. It was a precious thing, a strong sense of genuine community. It sustained almost the entire country during the long, bitter months from December, 1941, to October, 1942" (215). Much later in the war "the country's participation in the war was accepted by almost everyone as a just and necessary act. If anything, it looked increasingly justified as it went on and the Nazi concentration camps fell into Allied hands" (441).

Among historians of the home front, only John Morton Blum asserted in *V Was for Victory* "that federal agencies and private institutions utilized techniques earlier developed by national advertising" to whip up national unity (16). This claim is simply inaccurate. Among the thousands of war ads in the leading magazines, national unity was central to a mere ten, and only two of those made an appeal for it. Very early in the war, Warner and Swasey Turret Lathes devoted its ad in *Newsweek* on January 5, 1942, to urging national unity: "The time has come—*now*—when every man and woman—workman, manager, politician, labor leader—is *all for* America or *all against* America. There can be no hyphenated loyalty to America and some private cause" (9). About a year and a half later the Hartford Fire Insurance Company in the *Saturday Evening Post* (hereafter shortened to "the *Post*") on July 3, 1943, urged people not to let slip the unity already in place: "Let's fight the enemy— not each other" (71). The remaining eight national unity ads (six published in the first year of the war) did not urge it but rather described how the unity that Pearl Harbor engendered had a salutary effect on everything from support for the war effort to bringing neighbors together to share old-fashioned American values.

This virtually unified stance in support of U.S. involvement made the home front receptive to ads plugging the many ways to actively participate in the war effort. Most admen during the war seem to have known or sensed unconsciously what Roland Marchand concisely articulated in *Advertising the American Dream*, namely, that most ads contain "ideas and images that reinforce and intensify existing patterns and conceptions" (xviii), the existing conception in this case being the home front's national unity. For admen this unity was a platform upon which to build their various campaigns for home front participation. And too, it was precisely this national unity that made the four-year blitz of war ads both possible and effective; without it the ad campaigns would have been doomed to failure. Because of Americans' divided and divisive feelings about every war the United States has fought in since World War II, similar saturation advertising for citizen support would not have been acceptable, let alone possible. The proof of this is self-evident: From Korea to Iraq, no such ad campaigns were ever tried.

Prewar War Ads

Days before Pearl Harbor, a peculiar national unity advertisement was prominently displayed inside the front cover of *Life* on December 1, 1941. At that moment in time the ad might have been seen as relevant social commentary, even raising a smile or two over the still ongoing dissension among Americans about whether or not the country should enter the war. The ad features a drawing of seven people walking toward the reader with linked arms, a sailor on the left, a soldier on the right, and five very well-dressed middle-class civilians (two men and three women) in between. Beneath the artwork and above a lot of copy in small type extolling the virtues of various Parker Pens is, in very large lettering, the caption "You Bet there's *National Unity* in the Gift We Want *This* Christmas." This wry look at national unity may have had some validity before December 7, but the ad appeared again *after* Pearl Harbor, in the *Post* on December 13, and in the January 1942 *Esquire*, which clearly hit the newsstands well before Christmas, judging by its plethora of Christmas-gift ads. The long lead time needed to create an ad and submit it to a magazine in time to meet the deadline for ad copy caused the Parker ads in the *Post* and *Esquire* to be obsolete the moment they appeared. After Pearl Harbor the effect of the ad's caption was to trivialize the national unity that by then was a very real thing.

Still, its first appearance before Pearl Harbor does not make the Parker ad an anomaly. War-related ads didn't just spring up overnight following the Japanese attack. There had, in fact, been war-related or, more precisely, defense-related ads as far back as 1939 with the buildup of America's defense industries, even though the general public never saw most of them. These were informational advertisements by manufacturing firms, known as institutional advertising in ad industry terminology. Such ads didn't sell anything. Just prior to and during the war, they simply described how one manufacturer or another was contributing to defense production. Institutional ads were published mostly in what the business and manufacturing communities referred to as business, trade, or industrial papers, which included such media as trade journals, informational booklets for specific industries, and house organs for individual manufacturers. Prior to Pearl Harbor informational or institutional ads also appeared in those national magazines with numerous readers in corporate and industrial America such as *Business Week* and *Fortune*, and even occasionally in the two most prominent weekly news magazines, *Time* and *Newsweek*, which had a similar readership. Some prewar institutional advertising even found its way into popular magazines like *Life, Collier's, Ladies' Home Journal*, the *Saturday Evening Post*, and *Farm Journal and Farmer's Wife*. Once the United States was in the war, institutional ads in general-interest magazines measurably increased. These were not just ads by companies that made something as familiar to consumers as automobiles or a particular brand of tire (neither of which could be bought for the duration), but even firms that produced things as arcane to most of the public as turret lathes or roller bearings (see Chapter 3 for more on wartime informational advertising).

The war ads published in national magazines during the month preceding Pearl Harbor and in the few weeks following it — also technically prewar ads since they had to have been written prior to December 7—were an eclectic bunch. The purely informational ads were the most straightforward. With virtually no products to sell, such an ad simply displayed a company's participation in the war effort while keeping its name and/or its products before the business community. An extended series of Inland Steel ads in *Time* between November 10 and December 15, 1941, proclaimed in their headlines everything from "Over a Million Soldiers Will Sleep on Cots of Inland Steel" to "At Inland 'Full Speed Ahead' Helps Build Our Two-Ocean Navy." Also in *Time* on November 10, the Lone Star Cement Company could boast that thanks to its product and construction services "850-ACRE QUONSET POINT AIR BASE COMPLETED WITHIN A YEAR" (39). Prior to and during the war most magazine ads of all kinds were so prosy and prolix that few twenty-first-century Americans would take the time to read them. But the rare ad stood out for the brevity of its copy and the vividness of its art. One such purely informational ad was the Douglas Aircraft Company's in *Time* on November 24, 1941. The entire message was that Douglas was building planes for the Allies, vividly expressed in a single line of copy, "Douglas Defends the Democracies," and in the ad's striking color illustration depicting airplanes in the already familiar and symbolic "V" for Victory formation (74; see fig. 1).

When informational ads appeared in the popular magazines, they often tacked on a sales pitch for whatever consumer goods the advertiser was still manufacturing or had in stock. In *Life* on December 22, 1941, an ad stated, "Defense takes full priority at Oldsmobile" since the company was making cannon for fighter planes and high-caliber shells for field artillery "at the rate of thousands a day" (35). But farther down the page the copy managed to hype the new Olds B44 with "Hydra-Matic Drive."

Other more specious prewar ads tried to draw analogies—often pointless and far-fetched—between the armed forces and a company's goods or services. "When the Army goes into the field [for maneuvers] the Mimeograph duplicator goes with it." The ad later informs readers that "your office or factory" could have "the same speed and accuracy" of a Mimeograph machine (*Life* 8 Dec. 1941: 34). In other words, if it's good enough for the Army, it's good enough for you. In *Newsweek* on November 10, 1941, an ad for the Chase National Bank featured a handsome drawing of the huge guns on a battleship and a quotation from Secretary of the Navy Frank Knox: "The Navy is always ready." The copy then

FIGURE I

declared, "Bank credit—like the U. S. Navy—also is always ready" to help finance defense industries (35). Ads for financial institutions were particularly prone to using absurd or gratuitous analogies. In the same issue of *Newsweek* as the Chase ad, the New England Mutual Life Insurance Company's half-page ad was largely taken up with a drawing of some marines, rifles above their heads, sloshing through water toward (presumably) a beach. After a brief opening about how marines are "always ready to go anywhere," the ad asks the reader, "Are you ready to meet *any* emergency—wherever and whenever it comes? Can you plunge into the uncertain years ahead as confidently as a Marine splashing shoreward through the surf?" (4). Once we were in the war there was a definite decline in analogy-based war ads. Initially, admen may have seen this approach as appealing to patriotism, but it must have eventually dawned on copywriters that such pointless, false analogies made little sense.

In the weeks just before and after Pearl Harbor, defense-associated magazine ads aimed at the general public, soon to be known as the home front, were comparatively few compared to the institutional advertising placed by large manufacturing firms. Some of these consumer-oriented ads continued to sell a product, but they were not what the advertising industry referred to as "business as usual" ads—ads devoted strictly to selling without taking any cognizance of the war at all. Two ads in *Ladies' Home Journal* for November 1941 are typical of defense and, later, war-oriented consumer advertising, each one important for prefiguring a major theme in war ads. An ad for S.O.S. scouring pads barely mentions the defense buildup. The closest it gets is in its headline, "Aluminum is getting scarce," after which the ad suggests ways to conserve aluminum pots and pans since no more will be readily available (82), adding that a primary means of conserving them is, of course, by cleaning them with S.O.S. In effect, then, the ad combines a plea for conserving a strategic material with selling the company's product. In the same issue of *LHJ*, under a cartoon of a marching double boiler, teakettle, and percolator, and the headline "We're in the Army Now," the Aluminum Goods Manufacturing Company, maker of Mirro cookware, explains, without selling anything, why aluminum is needed for defense work (154). Like many ads during the war itself, Mirro's patiently explains to the public why there is a shortage of something, tacitly asking for the public's patience. The closest the ad comes to selling is in the final sentence reminding the reader that once the "national emergency" is over, Mirro products will again be available. This promise of "future goods" occurs frequently in war ads, often in conjunction with an appeal for the public to buy War Bonds (see Epilogue).

Like the popular songs of the war years, advertising frequently employed either humor or sentiment, two of the most effective means of sustaining or boosting both civilian and military morale (see Jones 28–29). The use of both approaches in war ads began well before Pearl Harbor. When sentiment—an appeal to the emotions rather than the intellect—came into play in ads, it ran the gamut from the tasteful and understated to the tasteless, overproduced, and maudlin. A fine example of the former type, created though not published prior to our entry into the war, is a Kodak ad in *Life* on December 15, 1941, in which, as was often the case, the artwork carried much of the ad's sentimentality. Here (see fig. 2) in a living room decorated for Christmas, a soldier on leave stands with his mother, father, little sister, and the family dog. The caption reads, "Snapshots never meant so much as now." The rest of the ad is a straightforward sales pitch for Kodak film, but the visual image of the importance photos have for family members in a time of national crisis makes the ad vivid and memorable.

Like sentiment in war ads, humor came in all shapes and sizes, from the sort that raised just a wry smile to the kind that elicited out-loud belly laughs. Wonderful in the quiet subtlety of its joke is an ad for Monel Water Heater Tanks in the *Post* on November 22, 1941, weeks before the United States entered the war. The artwork's caption reads, in boldface, **"Portrait of Mrs. Whitlock's New Water Heater Tank,"** but instead of what one would logically expect, the "portrait" is of a rather ominous-looking *military* tank rumbling over rocky terrain. The rest of the ad, like so many during the war itself, explains how defense priorities and production have caused not just shortages but the total unavailability of certain consumer products—like hot water heater tanks. The philosophy behind such advertising was that the more civilians understood *why* they couldn't buy things they wanted or needed, the less they would grumble, a significant plus for home front morale. And if an ad could raise a smile, all the better.

In prewar ads, as in many more during the war itself, keeping up GI morale was often linked to folks on the home front buying certain products and sending them to the boys in stateside camps or overseas. With-

Snapshots never meant so much as now

CHRISTMAS, 1941—you are sure, by now, that it will have special meaning. As the family comes together for this day of peace and plenty, every scene and episode will be more than ever important . . . precious things for snapshots to capture and keep, fresh as the day they happen.

The timeliest gift of all . . . A bright new Gift Package filled with Kodak Film—for every camera owner on your Christmas list. An inexpensive gift—yet bright and early Christmas morning it will go to work . . . And through the day, and all the holiday season, this generous reserve supply of film will be on hand to keep the snapshot record. Get your gift packages of Kodak Film at your Kodak dealer's. Eastman Kodak Co., Rochester, N. Y.

Give a Kodak . . .   *Give Kodak Film*

SEE THE CHRISTMAS KODAKS AND BROWNIES AT YOUR KODAK DEALER'S

45

FIGURE 2. © Kodak 1941.

out question, next to letters from home, servicemen's preferred morale booster was cigarettes. In the 1940s most of adult America smoked, and in the picture magazines during the war years it's hard to find a photo of a GI without a cigarette except when in combat or on dress parade (see Jones 185). An early ad by Camel cigarettes (a profusion of Camels ads was yet to come) combined sustaining GIs' morale with using the armed forces as a kind of product endorsement in an ad whose main purpose clearly was to sell cigarettes. Published on the back cover of *Collier's* on December 27, 1941, and two days later in the same spot in *Life*, the ad featured drawings of the heads of a soldier, sailor, and marine, all smoking. Each declared that Camels were not only tops with him personally but with his entire branch of the service. Thus, the soldier says, "Give me camels every time. They're first with the men in the army." The copy below the artwork is headed "SEND THEM THE CIGARETTE THEY ASK FOR — SEND A CARTON OF CAMELS TODAY!" The ad also let readers know that "Camel cartons specially wrapped and ready for mailing to men in the service" were available.

The number of prewar war ads of the types described above would multiply a hundredfold or more once the United States was actually in the war, and advertising copy was usually able to meet the deadlines of national magazines in a timely fashion.

War Ads and the Magazines

The most famous advertising slogan of World War II never appeared in a magazine — or in a newspaper, on a billboard, poster, or any other print medium except the packaging of the product it was touting. But "Lucky Strike Green has gone to war!" was heard so often on the radio that listeners, including Luckies smokers, supposedly got very tired of it. Still, if people remember any ad slogan from the war years, it's almost certain to be this one. What it referred to, incidentally, was the change from forest green to white as the background for the big red bull's-eye on the Lucky Strike pack since the pigments used for the green were critical for military camouflage (see *Business Week* 28 Nov. 1942: 80).

Does this mean that radio was a more potent medium for war ads than print generally and magazines in particular? Not at all. Each medium had its virtues, and magazine ads stood up against radio ads very well. First, there was the matter of audience. There's no denying that the United States in the war years was a nation of radio listeners, but it was a nation of readers as well, notably readers of newspapers and popular magazines. There were over six hundred flourishing national and regional magazines published during the 1940s. Subscriptions to the major national magazines ran into the millions, not to mention the copies sent to American servicemen (and, later, servicewomen) both stateside and abroad. And while it is likely that the total number of war ads in newspapers was larger than in national magazines, their audience was not. Even such major-market papers as the *New York Times* and *Chicago Tribune* had what was essentially a local or regional audience, albeit quite a large one, while subscribers to popular magazines lived in every corner of the land. Even *Farm Journal and Farmer's Wife*, the only major magazine aimed exclusively at America's rural population, had a subscriber base of close to three million during the war. Indeed, far more then than now, the general public was a reading public. That Americans' media habits changed after the war with the advent of television is dramatically demonstrated by the postwar demise (mostly in the 1970s) of the original forms of such formerly popular and heavily subscribed magazines as *Look*, *Collier's*, *Life*, *Saturday Evening Post*, and *Esquire*, precisely half of the magazines examined for this present account of war ads.

Beyond an audience base that could stand up to that of radio, print ads in magazines had some distinct advantages over radio war ads. Given the time strictures of radio, each commercial announcement had to be necessarily brief, certainly no longer than a minute. Conversely, war ads in magazines could include all the copy that a page (or sometimes even a two-page spread) could hold. Advertisers took advantage of Americans' patience with and propensity for reading by packing their ads with column after column of small-print minutiae in quantities few twenty-first-century readers could tolerate. But back then no one apparently complained, since the practice continued throughout the war. Long copy was common both in explanatory ads about such matters as rationing and proper nutrition aimed at the home front public and, primarily, in informational ads addressed to the business and manufacturing community. (These institutional ads so central to magazine war advertising almost never appeared on radio because they weren't consumer-oriented.) A typically verbose ad is that of the Pullman-Standard Car Manufacturing Company on page 61 of *Newsweek* on May 24, 1943 (see fig. 3).

A total of 865 suppliers and sub-contractors contributed to the building of this tank. 407 were small manufacturers, 300 were medium-sized manufacturers, and only 158 would be considered large manufacturers. Many of Pullman-Standard's sub-contractors have also let sub-contracts. In one instance a medium-sized sub-contractor in turn drew on 300 suppliers and sub-contractors.

THE TANK THAT CAME OUT OF 865 PLANTS

Here's a deadly example of what well-disciplined teamwork can achieve — a stirring proof that a sub-contracting relationship can be the basis of truly democratic co-operation

Tough, merciless sluggers—these husky, vicious devils! Built to take it—outside. Built to keep everlastingly going—inside. We know, for we build them—here at Pullman-Standard—with the able co-operation of 865 suppliers and sub-contractors, large and small.

This smooth teamwork is the result of engineering—of patient planning and preparation. Even though Pullman-Standard's plants could have built practically the entire tank, yet was it clear that many manufacturers working together in a huge co-operative effort, utilizing investments already made, must surely build tanks and other essential war matériel a great deal faster than could any one plant alone.

* * *

Combing highway and byway, city and hamlet, Pullman-Standard sought capable, experienced team-mates for a vast share-the-work program; sought plants with management, men and facilities; sought and found them.

Brains worked together, pooled experience to develop sound methods, to perfect tool designs, to synchronize production schedules. In many instances Pullman-Standard loaned supervision to get the job going smoothly. And of every dollar received by Pullman-Standard for

a great fleet of 30-ton tanks, 80% is passed along to those suppliers and sub-contractors. Pullman-Standard itself—for coordination, painstaking engineering, exhaustive planning, manufacturing, assembly, rigid tests, and for assuming full responsibility for the tanks' unfailing performance—retains the remaining 20%, which in turn is distributed for labor, overhead, services and Federal taxes.

Participating in that tank program are 865 suppliers and sub-contractors, in 206 cities in 25 states—from a one-man shop to a great industry employing 150,000 workers—operating under 5432 contracts from Pullman-Standard.

* * *

Today, in addition to **TANKS,** Pullman-Standard has produced huge quantities of **HOWITZER CARRIAGES, TRENCH MORTARS, BOMBS, SHELLS** of various calibers and sizes, parts for **ANTI-AIRCRAFT GUN MOUNTS, AIR-CRAFT MAJOR SUB-ASSEMBLIES, FREIGHT CARS** for the Army, Navy, and Railroads, and **NAVAL PATROL CRAFT.**

Pullman-Standard is itself a sub-contractor—chosen to provide great quan-

tities of other war matériel; chosen because of particular fitness, long experience, ample facilities, and "know-how."

Eager to give "all-out" aid to the nation's war effort, Pullman-Standard opened its doors to all who sought to learn from its experience. Many came and still come—with the result that thousands of ordnance items are pouring forth faster in many plants, because alert manufacturers recognized methods for speeding production and adopted them.

* * *

Core and heart of this teamwork is Pullman-Standard's 84 years of varied and fruitful experience. Here, truly, are the endless resourcefulness of American industry and the stirring capacity to improve that are so characteristic of Democracy inspired to its ultimate best.

* * *

We long for peace—for a return to the kindly relationships of neighbors, to making things for pleasant, happy living. To those joyous tasks we shall bring new and better methods learned under the driving necessity of war! New comforts and conveniences of which we have not dreamed! Stirring proof that Democracy alone can make a world fit to live in!

BUY U. S. WAR BONDS and STAMPS

The Pullman-Standard plants at Butler, Pa. and Hammond, Ind. have both been awarded the Army and Navy "E" pennant for efficiency in production.

PULLMAN-STANDARD CAR MANUFACTURING COMPANY

Chicago, Illinois . . . Offices in seven cities . . . Manufacturing plants in six cities

© 1942, P. S. C. M. CO.

FIGURE 3

There's no question that radio had the aural advantage of an announcer's voice to lend immediacy to messages in war ads. Radio also had the capacity to broadcast entertaining songs and jingles pitching everything from scrap metal salvage to War Bonds, a number written by some of Tin Pan Alley's finest songwriters (see Jones 196–206). But even beyond allowing for seemingly interminable ad copy, magazines had the visual advantage of the artwork in the ads. This art for ads' sake ranged from meticulously executed paintings—often signed by the artist—to caricatures and cartoons. Many of the latter were drawn—and also signed—by some of the country's best and best known editorial cartoonists, or by eminent cartoonists for magazines like *Collier's*, *Saturday Evening Post*, *The New Yorker*, and *Esquire*. Very often, even more than the copy, the art provided a war ad's emotional clout. An extraordinary, yet typical, example of what might be called such visual persuasion is a full-page ad placed by the General Tire & Rubber Company on page 8 of the *Post* for December 11, 1943 (see fig. 4). Taking up most of the page is an illustration of a young boy looking straight at the reader; he wears the Congressional Medal of Honor on a ribbon around his neck and holds a soldier's cap; a single tear falls down one cheek. The picture's caption, which is the ad's entire copy, reads "He knows why this Christmas all of us should GIVE WAR BONDS."

Advertising art and copy also teamed up to produce a unique virtue of magazine war ads—series or serial advertising. This consisted of a sequence of ads produced by a single company that appeared over weeks and months either in one magazine or several, the individual ads in a series related to each other thematically or in some other way. Thanks to superb art in conjunction with engrossing copy, these series of ads had enough "entertainment value" to keep readers coming back to successive issues of a magazine for the latest installment. Serial ads were thus very effective for keeping the war before the public, a method virtually impossible to replicate on radio. The most prominent thematic serial ads (each discussed more fully in its appropriate chapter) include the Philco corporation's long series discussing industrial support for the war, each ad featuring an "Axis-bashing" cartoon by a different political cartoonist (see Chapter 3); the equally long Nash-Kelvinator series portraying GIs in combat ruminating on "What I'm Fighting For" (Chapter 2); Gripper Fasteners' seemingly endless string of silly comic strips in the service of selling War Bonds (Chapter 9); and SKF Ball and Roller Bearings' shorter

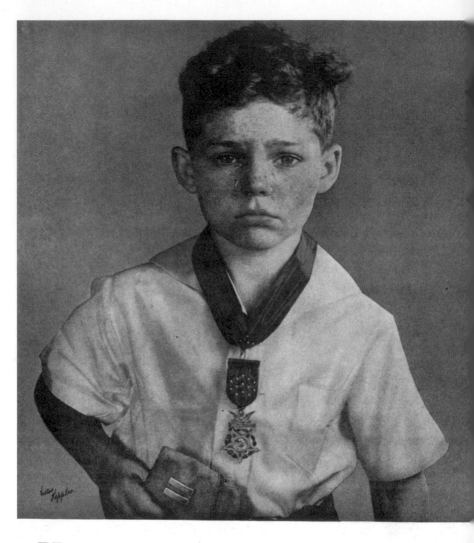

He knows why this Christmas
all of us should GIVE WAR BONDS

THE GENERAL TIRE & RUBBER COMPANY • AKRON, OHI

FIGURE 4

but equally effective series about the Bill of Rights, one Right per ad (Chapter 2).

Series ads not thematically tied usually addressed a different wartime issue in each succeeding ad—saving kitchen fats one week, squelching rumors another. What often linked these ads was their "cast of characters," some of which had become national icons before the war. The cute Scottish and West Highland White Terriers Blackie and Whitey had for some time promoted Black & White Blended Scotch Whisky [sic], always, appropriately, in black and white ads. During the war they turned their talents to showing the home front ways to support the war in no fewer than eighteen different ads between 1942 and 1945, typical of which was their pitch for Victory Gardens in *Time* on June 5, 1944 (49; see fig. 5). If the terriers were cute on behalf of the war effort, the Borden cows were nothing short of hilarious. Elsie the Cow, the unflappable voice of reason, shared ad space with her daughter, Beulah the Calf—eager, inquisitive, and a bit naive—and Elsie's husband, Elmer the Bull, a sort of bovine Archie Bunker—stubborn, bullheaded (pun intended), socially inept, sure his way is the only way, and usually proven wrong. Colorful comic art was partnered with equally funny copy in nearly thirty war ads featuring the cows, making reading about things like inflation, price controls, and proper nutrition very easy to take. A typical Borden cows ad is one late in the war in which an especially grumpy—and sleepy—Elmer can't fathom why, with all the Allied successes, reducing worker absenteeism and keeping up all-out war production are still so important (*Life* 5 Mar. 1945: 21; see fig. 6).

Some serial ads became collectibles even while the war was still on, encouraged by the advertisers themselves. By far the most collected serial ads were neither political nor patriotic, but charmingly personal and sentimental. The ads in the "Back Home for Keeps" series from Community Silverplate were so sought after that *Life* made them and their collectors the subject of its weekly "Speaking of Pictures" feature on May 14, 1945, pp. 12–13, under the headline "*SENTIMENTAL ADVERTISEMENTS START A NEW KIND OF PIN-UP CRAZE.*" Nominally these ads were of the future goods variety, explaining late in the copy that Oneida's Community Silverplate would be available again once the war was won. But what fed the imaginations of millions of women across America, and of a fair number of men as well, were the gorgeous color illustrations, each depicting, as *Life* described it, "the breathless meeting of a young wife and her

Dig for Victory!

Blackie: "Our master is growing a lot of food for freedom, Whitey!"

Whitey: "So is every patriotic American, Blackie — it means more food for those whose needs are greater than ours!"

How about you? Start a Victory garden! Grow more in '44. It will add to your supply of rationed foods — and give you more varied, balanced meals. *Equally important —* it will help insure a bigger reserve of food for everybody! Write to your State Agricultural Department for booklet on Victory Gardens.

"BLACK & WHITE"

The Scotch with Character

BLENDED SCOTCH WHISKY • 86.8 PROOF

THE FLEISCHMANN DISTILLING CORPORATION   NEW YORK, N.Y. • SOLE DISTRIBUTORS

FIGURE 5

"But, dear," protested Elsie, "real Americans are never satisfied with *pretty good*. They want the *best* in everything. When they want vitamins, for instance, they know that the kind that does the *best* for them comes in a *food*. That's why so many folks *insist* on *Hemo*, Borden's chocolate vitamin *food* drink!"

"Just *you* keep insisting," threatened Elmer, "and there *will* be a crisis. Not in Japan either—but right here in this room! Just one more sentence—"

"In just one sentence," interrupted Elsie blithely, "I can tell you all about *Borden's Homogenized Milk*. It's got cream in every sip, and a full day's supply of Vitamin D in every quart, and it's homogenized to make it easy to digest."

"Hold on!" bellowed Elmer. "What's my digestion got to do with a crisis? Stick to the subject!"

"One subject I could stick to for hours," chirped Elsie, "is delicious, delightful *Borden's Ice Cream* and *Borden's Milk Sherbets*. You should try them for pepping up your energy, dear. They're real foods as well as delightful refreshers. The boys in our armed forces eat tons and tons of ice cream every day. Now, if they *couldn't* get their good eats, and guns and—"

"Say!" cried Elmer jumping out of bed, "that *would* be a crisis! Get going! Pack me a lunch! Get breakfast on the table! We can't have this war dragging on! *Well?* What are you waiting for?"

"Just waiting to say what I always say," answered Elsie: "*if it's Borden's, it's GOT to be good!*".

"Mother warned me" sighed Elsie "you were no man for a crisis!"

"CRISIS? CRISIS?" mumbled Elmer, the bull, sleepily. "I don't want any crisis. Go 'way, woman, and let me sleep! I'm taking the day off."

"This is no time to take days off," said Elsie, the Borden Cow, firmly. "Our boys still have a tough fight on their hands. And you're going to get right to your war job and help them win!"

"Ah, those boys don't need any help," poo-pooed Elmer. "They'll get those bums in Europe and then clean up the Japs in no time! I don't see what difference it's going to make in winning the war if I take just one teeny, weenie, little day off."

"If everybody felt that way," commented Elsie, "where would the Army and Navy get the things they need *when* they need them—necessary things like guns

and food? Suppose, for instance, that the folks who make *Borden's Fine Cheeses* all decided to take a day off now and then. Our men at the front, and the people backing them at home, would not get this important, body-building food as often as they should have it. And that's not good! For cheese is one food that fighters and workers need—it's *concentrated* nourishment!"

"Oh-ho!" triumphed Elmer, sitting bolt upright,

"I begin to catch on. All this talk about a crisis is a come-on for a lecture on Borden's. Let me tell you, Mrs. Beat-around-the-bush, there'll be a *real* crisis in this house if you don't change your tune, and let me get a little sleep!"

"The very nicest tune I can think of," teased Elsie,

"is a little baby's gurgle over his formula made with *Borden's Evaporated Milk*. Loads of doctors approve it; it's pure, wholesome, *sterilized!* And it's fortified with Vitamin D."

"Oh, woman," said Elmer wearily, "go hire a telephone booth! I'm going to get my forty winks if it kills me. The boys are doing pretty good without me."

Tune in BORDEN'S New RADIO SHOW Mondays, 9 P.M., E.W.T. Blue Network

— if it's Borden's it's *got* to be good

© The Borden Company

FIGURE 6

FIGURE 7. Reprinted by permission of Oneida Ltd.

returned serviceman-husband at the moment of his homecoming" (13). Published only in *Life* and *Ladies' Home Journal*, the series began in September 1943, at which time the ad copy spoke of such reunions as to-be-wished-for future events. By late 1944, actuality gradually replaced wishing, and such copy became possible as "Stop the clocks, blow the whistles, catch-your-throat, hold-your-heart—it's true, dear God, it's true, he's home for keeps. [. . .] all the life for two you've ached for will be yours to have and to hold" (*Life* 13 Nov. 1944: 45; see fig. 7). The series continued through December 1945, months after the war was over but while GIs were still coming home. Not just servicemen's wives, but, according to *Life*, high school and college girls, and even GIs "who have wearied of the anatomical pin-up" swamped Oneida with requests for the artwork "without advertising," which the company gladly sent them in numbers well into the millions. While the ads never stated it, a clearly intended effect of the sentiment in the "Back Home for Keeps" series was to help sustain the morale of wives and girls back home during the last two years of the war.

★ ★ ★ A graphic representation of the number and frequency of war ads in national magazines from January 1942 through December 1945 would look like a slightly skewed bell curve, falling off earlier and more rapidly on the right than it rises on the left. War ads were slow to appear in the early months of 1942, which is understandable considering the amount of time it took for companies and their ad agencies to plan war-related ad campaigns, design the art, write the copy, and meet the magazines' advertising deadlines. Even *Life* ran just one or two per weekly issue in January and February of 1942, although it ultimately published about 2,530 war ads, the most in any national magazine. *Time* and *Newsweek*, published on the same day of the week, were first off the block with a combined total of eleven war ads on January 5, 1942, but this relatively large number so early in the war is not as impressive as it appears. Nine of the eleven ads were of the informational sort addressed to business and manufacturing interests that advertisers were producing well before Pearl Harbor. Nothing in these ads indicates the copy was written after the United States was in the war; more likely, they had been in the pipeline for eventual publication in *Time* or *Newsweek* whether the country was at war or not.

It didn't take many months before the number of war ads in magazines began to escalate, slowly at first, then more rapidly. By March *Life* averaged six or seven per week, by the summer of 1942 between twelve and nineteen, the number increasing until the issue for November 16, 1942, in which war ads in *Life* peaked at thirty-five. After that the magazine continued to run between eighteen and twenty-eight war ads a week until the spring of 1944. The relative figures are similar for most of the other weekly and monthly magazines, considering their overall totals of war ads were much smaller than *Life*'s. Not counting duplications of ads that appeared in *Life*, in the largest-circulation magazines "new" war ads for the duration of the war came to roughly 597 in the *Saturday Evening Post*, 470 in *Collier's*, 440 in *Time*, 328 in *Ladies' Home Journal*, and 278 in *Newsweek*. The most war ads appeared in 1943, with 1942 second, followed by 1944 and 1945 bringing up the rear.

That is about the only sweeping generalization about war ads in magazines that can be made with complete confidence as to its accuracy. Otherwise, for example, there are no consistent, logical, or meaningful patterns of what kinds of war ads appeared in different magazines, what advertisers most regularly placed their ads in which magazines, or even how frequently a given advertiser placed such ads at all. What are available, however, are a few generalizations about advertising during the war that reveal the success of war advertising against the backdrop of "business as usual" ads in print media that merely sold a product. As early as the summer of 1942, the Department of Commerce conducted an "analysis of newspaper, magazine, trade and industrial paper, poster, and car copy submitted by 107 agencies" that resulted in a table showing the kinds of appeals being used in ads and "their relative popularity among advertisers" (*Business Week* 12 Sept. 1942: 94). Based on 1,037 ads, for so early in the war the table rather astonishingly reveals that war ads of all varieties were more than holding their own compared to ads "not themed to war." Just to highlight some of the ten categories in the table, there were 313 ads promoting increased war production, or 30% of the total; 172 ads selling War Bonds, or 16.6%; 149 ads dealing with conservation of critical materials and food, or 14.4%; 97 ads advocating improving national health, or 9.4%; and 34 ads promoting salvage drives, or 3.3% (94). The table also listed 132 "miscellaneous wartime ads," though it's hard to imagine what those might have been. Compared to all these and a few smaller categories of war ads in the table, the entry for only eighty-eight ads "not themed to war" seems slight indeed. This data should have put to rest the fears of the advertising industry and national advertisers that having nothing or next to nothing to sell during the war would cause advertising to suffer greatly in terms of both its influence and its revenue.

Fears of financial loss should have decreased even more in 1944 and again in 1945 when *Business Week* published detailed revenue breakdowns of magazine advertising alone for the preceding year. The text and a table in each article demonstrated the tremendous gains in magazine advertising revenue over the previous year, the figures based on the "advertising sales in 90-odd magazines listed by Publisher's Information Bureau" (*Business Week* 5 Feb. 1944: 86). In 1943 all previous records for magazine advertising were broken with a figure of $232,071,971, an increase of more than $54 million or 31% over 1942 (86). Then 1944 broke the 1943 all-time record with a total of $274,931,873, an 18% gain (*Business Week* 20 Jan. 1945: 84). Both articles also remarked that the actual demand for advertising space in both years could never be known since the wartime paper shortage forced many magazines to turn down much revenue-producing advertising copy. What neither article points out, however, is that the record-breaking advertising sales during both years ran concurrent with the large number of war ads in virtually all magazines, many of those ads not selling anything at all. Whether the increased advertising sales occurred because of or in spite of so much war-associated advertising is impossible to say. All that can be said for sure is that the war ads didn't hurt. Also, according to both articles, five magazines that led in increased advertising revenue both years also published large numbers of war ads: *Life* and the *Post* in first and second place among general-interest weeklies; *Time* first among news magazines; *Ladies' Home Journal* frontrunner among women's magazines; and *Farm Journal* second among national farm magazines. (*Country Gentleman* was first, but for this study it had a less representative rural readership than *Farm Journal*; the two magazines, incidentally, merged not long after the war.) Despite the doubting Thomases, these magazines clearly demonstrated that running war ads was not incompatible with high advertising revenue.

★ ★ ★ While the two *Business Week* articles spell out with crystal clarity the robust health of magazines' advertising revenues during the war, what is much murkier is how advertisers chose where to place their war ads and invest their advertising budget. Somewhere in the formula must have been the input of each advertiser's marketing director and/or someone comparable at the ad agency hired by the firm who could be counted on to hazard at least an educated guess as to where a war ad would be most effective and the advertiser's money best spent. Beyond that, the random placement of some war ads suggests that the remainder of the process lay somewhere between arbitrary and whimsical. International Sterling and Gorham, two of America's premier makers of sterling silver tableware, each placed a considerable number of war ads between 1942 and 1945 — Gorham exclusively in *Ladies' Home Journal*, International only in *Life*. It's hard to imagine that marketing research showed the readers of one magazine heavily preferred one company's silver patterns over the other, yet no other explanation for this odd exclusivity of war ad placement comes readily to mind. Similarly, to thumb through the pages of *Life* one would think that Hormel's legendary canned meat product Spam never existed. *Life* was full of war ads sponsored by two similar items, Wilson & Company's Mor, and Swift & Company's Prem, both long gone, yet Spam lives on. While invisible in *Life*, war ads by Spam appeared regularly in *Ladies' Home Journal* and even in the businessmen's-oriented *Time*. What prompted three major meat packers to place war ads for their canned meat in this seemingly arbitrary fashion remains a mystery. In the sphere of industrial advertising, United States Steel's war ads were everywhere, while Bethlehem Steel's were only in *Newsweek*, and Black & Decker's war ads focusing on tools for defense industries, not for the home handyman, appeared only in the *Saturday Evening Post*.

The seemingly inexplicable placement of some war ads reaches an apotheosis of absurdity with a single ad in *Esquire*, the self-proclaimed "Magazine for Men" that had a targeted audience and, in fact, an actual readership primarily of affluent urban males. Although each issue of *Esquire* was packed with ads for high-end jewelry, liquor, and men's furnishings, the magazine published only sixty-two genuine war ads throughout the war. One of *Esquire*'s advertisers that created responsible war ads was the upscale men's clothing manufacturer Hart Schaffner & Marx, which also placed such ads in the *Post*, *Collier's*, *Life*, and *Look*, on topics such as shortages, conservation, War Bonds, and scrap drives. But given *Esquire*'s readership, the Hart Schaffner & Marx ad on page 29 of the October 1944 issue is a complete and utter anomaly. An elegant illustration of a man and woman standing next to an automobile (see fig. 8) is captioned "Picture of you in Navy Blue . . . **Join the Waves,**" for

Picture of you in Navy Blue...

Join the Waves

Does your job seem heigh-ho and
humdrum when a whole world's at
war? Then get off the sidelines and
into the uniform of the WAVES.
In this uniform you have the chance
to serve your country as women
have never served before ... in
the biggest, most exciting, most
important job a woman was ever
offered. To serve, to work and win
where America needs you most ...
shoulder to shoulder with the
gallant men of our Navy.
Join the WAVES ... today!

What is the "Hart Schaffner & Marx touch"
... subtle tailoring ... sensible design?
Whatever it is, it's made
Hart Schaffner & Marx the best-known
clothing name in the world.

HART SCHAFFNER & MARX

The Trumpeter Label .. a small thing to look for .. a big thing to find

FIGURE 8. Original advertisement featured in Esquire magazine
October 1944 issue (p. 29). Copyright 1944 by Hart Schaffner & Marx.
Reprinted with permission.

indeed the woman in the illustration wears a WAVE uniform. How many women could have seen, let alone responded to, a WAVE recruiting ad buried in a magazine read almost entirely by men?

Overall, the patterns of war ad placement by the biggest advertisers are much easier to see and comprehend. As a general rule those advertisers that were most prolific in terms of the number of war ads they produced were also the most nearly ubiquitous with respect to the number of magazines in which they placed them. Of the eight leaders in the creation and placement of war ads, only General Electric placed war ads in all ten magazines I examined, and it did so with a total of 78 different ads. The Bell Telephone System (better known later as AT&T) led in the number of war ads by one advertiser with 105, and placed those ads in nine of the ten magazines. Three giant companies, United States Rubber, United States Steel, and Westinghouse, placed a combined total of 137 war ads in eight magazines apiece. Some figures surprise a bit, but none in an earthshaking way. Camel Cigarettes created 94 war ads but placed them in only seven of the ten magazines, and Philco, one of the most consistent of the industrial war-advertisers, placed 84 war ads in just six. Coca-Cola, which seems to be everywhere, in actuality produced only 64 different war ads, placing them in just six of the magazines.

An even more telling figure suggests how savvy these advertisers were about placing their war ads where they would do the most good: Of the total of 562 war ads created by just these eight advertisers, 284 or 50.5% of them were published in *Life* even though the sponsoring companies could pick and choose among a wide range of magazines in which to place their ads. And of course they did place ads in those other places as well, just not as many of them. Because *Life* was the most-read popular magazine, with a weekly readership of about 21,900,000, the war ads it published were simply the most visible, and not just to home front civilians. A survey of weekly magazine audiences reproduced in an advertisement for *Life* found that 63% of servicemen in all the branches read it, whereas only 28% read *Collier's* and 25% the *Post* (*Time* 21 Sept. 1943: 91). This helps explain why so many advertisers chose *Life* as the place to put their ads that focused on building GI morale.

★ ★ ★ As the number of war ads in other magazines rose proportionately with those in *Life*, so too did they proportionately fall. In the spring of 1944, around the time of D-Day (June 6) there began a disheartening tailing off of the number of war ads in national magazines (disheartening not just to me but to many concerned observers of the decline as it was happening). It began slowly but accelerated rapidly throughout the rest of 1944 and all of 1945. Even each weekly *Life* seldom ran war ads in double digits any more; by the early months of 1945 there were only between three and eight.

The magazines of course were not the cause of this drop-off in war ads; the advertisers were. The sharp decline in war ads, especially by major manufacturers, shows that while some companies and their ads continued to go all-out, too many others seemed all in and tuckered out. The reason for their lethargy was that the Allies were winning in Europe. Ever since Pearl Harbor the American people had recognized Emperor Hirohito's Japan as a formidable enemy, but in the popular imagination only Adolph Hitler was viewed as the devil incarnate, making his Nazi Germany the Axis power to beat. (Mussolini was seen as a pompous buffoon, and at any rate by July of 1943 he had been overthrown and his Fascist Italy was all but out of the war.) The Allies' decisive conclusion of the North African campaign on June 13 and their successful if prolonged invasions of Sicily and Italy, starting in July and playing out over the summer and autumn of 1943 and well into 1944, were, if you will, prologue to the main events—the massed Allied D-Day invasion on the coast of Normandy on June 6, 1944, the liberation of Paris on August 25, and the formal surrender of Germany on May 7, 1945. While nothing ever broke apart Americans' national unity in support of the war, the successes of the Allied and, especially, American forces starting in the summer of 1943 set off waves of complacency and overconfidence among some home front civilians, primarily those within corporate and industrial America. This overoptimistic attitude led to slowdowns in the production of necessary war materiel, and long before the war was over the ads of many companies began to emphasize plans for postwar production of consumer goods, letting slip somewhat the present business of helping to fight the war.

But other manufacturing firms still working all-out for the war became whistle-blowers about complacency and slacking off war production, blowing their whistles in very conspicuous places—ads in national magazines with a large readership of business and industry executives. York Air Conditioning and Refrigeration produced one such ad that appeared both on page 80 of *Time* on September 13, and page 4 of *Business*

Week on September 18, 1943, just days after the Allies landed at Salerno, Italy. Nominally the ad was part of the Treasury Department's Third War Loan campaign to help sell more War Bonds, but only the final sentence did just that. The rest of the ad was a large, eye-catching illustration of a U.S. Infantryman in full battle gear barging into a company boardroom. The accompanying copy was the soldier's tirade to the startled executives, urging them to relegate postwar planning to someplace well behind the continued production of equipment and supplies American forces still needed to fight and win the war (see fig. 9). Though few in number, other ads by industrial firms conveying similar sentiments appeared with some regularity well into 1945. To cite just two, in 1944, courtesy of the Wickwire Spencer Steel Company, an ad appeared in *Time* on October 9, featuring a grotesque drawing by noted illustrator Boris Artzybasheff captioned "The Spirit of Over-Optimism." The copy that followed contained such cautionary statements as "Allied victories are becoming more impressive and there are those who feel it's time for celebration—that we can coast from here on. But, think again. The tragedy and horror of war is still with us—*all* of us. There is [. . .] still need for those in war industries to stay on the job" (57; see fig. 10). Then in 1945, on page 54 of *Business Week* on March 31 and page 65 of *Newsweek* on April 9, the Gaylord Container Corporation ad was short on words but long on power. The entire copy consisted of "We <u>must</u> speed up production and delivery of war supplies to the fighting fronts," followed by a brief one-sentence pitch for buying War Bonds.

Yet none of these ads addressed the shrinking number of war ads in magazines. It took an advertising agency, Young & Rubicam, to confront that problem directly, and without the motive of attracting new clients for itself, as is evident from the number of other agencies' war ads Young & Rubicam displayed in its own ads as examples of effective war advertising. Four such ads by Young & Rubicam appeared in *Newsweek* over the course of a year, from March 6, 1944, to March 5, 1945. Its first ad about war ads focused on dispelling one putative reason for their declining numbers—that the public was losing interest in them and no longer read them as it once did: "Readership studies, however, show that interest in the war *as a subject* is increasing, not decreasing. In general, ads devoted to the war effort are being read more today than a year ago, particularly by women" (81). After remarking on four outstanding war ads reproduced in the ad (only one by Young & Rubicam itself), the copy

WAIT A MINUTE—BUD!

"POSTWAR PLANNING IS OKAY . . . it's got to be
done if we are to have jobs when we get back. But
remember one thing. 'Postwar' starts with a 'V'.
Until we win, we've got nothing but hopes.

"I don't have to tell you that we fighting men can
take it . . . whatever is in the book. But maybe I
ought to remind you that we can't dish it out any
faster than you at home provide the stuff. You
pass the ammunition, *and keep it coming!* We'll put
it where it will do the most good.

"And here's something everybody can paste in
his hat . . . buying more War Bonds *now* is the best
postwar planning any one can do."

FIGURE 9

Enlarged reproduction free on request

The Spirit of Over-Optimism

Allied victories are becoming more impressive and there are those who feel it's time for celebration—that we can coast from here on.

But, think again. The tragedy and horror of war is still with us—*all* of us.

There is still plenty of fighting ahead —still need for those in war industries to stay on the job—still need to save fats, scrap and paper; to give blood and to buy bonds—to do everything possible to hasten the day when *all* of us will really have something to celebrate—the day of ultimate and final victory.

We of Wickwire Spencer are working for the day when our wire and wire products will be helping to rebuild a war-torn world. But until then we will continue to help provide the steel sinews for weapons of war.

WICKWIRE SPENCER
STEEL COMPANY
500 FIFTH AVE., NEW YORK (18), N.Y.... AND KEY CITIES

FAMOUS FOR QUALITY IN STEEL, TUNGSTEN AND MOLYBDENUM WIRE; TUNGSTEN CARBIDE DIES AND TOOLS; WIRE ROPE; SPRINGS; CHAIN LINK FENCE; METAL CONVEYOR BELTS; WIRE CLOTH; PERFORATED METALS; CARD CLOTHING; POULTRY NETTING; HARDWARE CLOTH; INSECT SCREEN CLOTH; ELECTRICALLY WELDED FABRIC

FIGURE 10

concluded with, "This information about the reading of war advertisements may encourage additional advertisers to run messages promoting the country's war effort. We hope that it will. It may also serve to prevent a 'letting up' on the part of those now engaged in advertising of this kind. We hope that it will do that, too." Regrettably, the ad seems to have done neither. Young & Rubicam's effort on April 3, 1944, also reproduced some war ads and began with the headline, "Are ads like these still necessary?" (43). After considerable copy enumerating some wartime problems still to be solved, from meeting the increasing demand for food to getting more women into the workforce, the ad concludes that "the quickening tempo of the war is intensifying many of these problems. And the need is for *more* advertising—not less." On February 5, 1945, in an ad with no art headed "What's the quickest way to end the war?" Young and Rubicam's answer was, "Don't get tired of the war. But worry plenty about other people getting tired of it. Then remember that, to hold people steadfast, to build resolution, one of the great forces in America is advertising" (9). And finally, on March 5, 1945, the ad agency pulled no punches in describing how industrial America—smug, complacent, making plans for postwar production and publishing ads about them—was totally caught off guard on December 16 by the news of the Battle of the Bulge and American troops in retreat, leading to the ad's conclusion, "Let us continue to devote part of our advertising to the most important job in the world." Yet even though Young & Rubicam was correct about the need for continued advertising on behalf of the war effort, the agency's ads largely fell on the deaf ears of industrial America. Of national advertisers that used war ads to encourage home front support, only a few stalwarts like Bell Telephone and Borden's stayed in for the duration, while in the latter half of 1944 and all of 1945, many more, like old soldiers, just faded away.

The War Advertising Council
The United States had been at war barely two months when the War Advertising Council was hatched out of ideas incubated at a joint meeting of the American Association of Advertising Agencies (A.A.A.A.) and the Association of National Advertisers (A.N.A.) at Hot Springs, Arkansas, in November 1941. Thereafter the Council became a significant presence in wartime advertising whose importance cannot be overestimated (*Business Week* 7 Feb. 1942: 58; Fox 49). Yet its precise role vis-à-vis ad agen-

cies, advertisers, the media, and the federal government has been often muddled or misunderstood. Even its name is a bit misleading. "War Advertising Council" suggests it comprised solely admen and ad agencies, as Don Wharton implied in his description of it in the trade journal *Advertising & Selling* in June 1944. Wharton inaccurately characterized the Council as "a purely voluntary outfit set up by the nation's top advertising men" (49), when in fact it equally included representatives from advertisers (the companies that bought advertising space or time), and from print media and radio. The initial membership of the Council's board of directors reflects its diversity: Chester J. La Roche (chairman of the board of Young & Rubicam), chairman; Paul B. West (A.N.A. president), secretary; Frederic R. Gamble (A.A.A.A. managing director), assistant to the chairman; William C. Chandler (member of the Scripps-Howard executive committee), newspaper representative; Albert E. Winger (Crowell-Collier executive vice-president), magazine representative; and Paul W. Kesten (Columbia Broadcasting System vice-president and director), radio representative (*Business Week* 7 Feb. 1942: 58). Later in February, the Council hired Dr. Miller McClintock, an authority on advertising and marketing who had taught at Harvard and Yale, as the Council's managing director (*Business Week* 21 Feb. 1942: 48).

From its inception, the Council's stated aim was to serve as the liaison between the advertising industry, advertisers, and the media on the one hand, and Washington on the other, in order to "lend greater continuity, effectiveness, and better timing to government campaigns" (*Business Week* 7 Feb. 1942: 59). Or, as the Council itself defined it, its purpose was to "help the government to utilize, for the purposes of inspiring and instructing the public concerning the various phases of the war effort, the talents, techniques, and channels of advertising, which in normal times have proved they can help shape the thinking and action of the public" (qtd. in *Business Week* 21 Feb. 1942: 49). In a word, the Council existed to help Washington make the most effective use of advertising in order to promote to the home front such government initiatives as its seven War Loan drives for War Bonds during the war and an eighth for Victory Bonds after the war was over. This is a far cry from Frank W. Fox stating in his 1975 monograph *Madison Avenue Goes to War* that the Council's raison d'être was to "coordinate the internal war effort of the entire [advertising] industry" (49). To the contrary, the Council never aimed to involve, let alone benefit, the totality of the advertising industry, but rather to help *Washington* by enlisting the aid of the right ad agencies, advertisers, and media to produce and promulgate war ads for each government-sponsored program, drive, or informational campaign.

The process by which the War Advertising Council functioned as a liaison was simple enough for Fox to condense it into two perfectly straightforward sentences: "A government agency would set the process in motion by contacting the council and describing its problem. The council would then summon its best strategists, boil the general problem down into an advertising exercise, and then find an agency willing to undertake the necessary copy and layout work" (50–51). The nuances and details of the process are best understood by looking at a specific example of the Council's work, as did *Business Week* on July 3, 1943. First, it was usually the Office of War Information (OWI) with which the Ad Council worked as liaison between the federal government and the advertising industry. Hence, whatever government agency wanted something publicized, it would take its request to the OWI. The OWI in turn contacted the Council about it, as when the "War Manpower Commission decided that we need to mobilize 2,000,000 additional women workers for our war industries by 1944" (82). The Council then turned the matter of advertising to recruit women war workers over to one of its more than a dozen "coordinators" who specialized in specific aspects of the war effort, in this case A. O. Buckingham, the Council's coordinator on manpower problems. Buckingham in turn selected from the Council's list of 446 advertising agencies the one he considered "best qualified to do the initial research," assigning the groundwork for the "womanpower" campaign to J. Walter Thompson (womanpower being the wartime term for the female equivalent of manpower, nothing more). The ad agency that did the initial research wasn't always the same one that finally prepared the copy and layout for the actual ads, since the latter agency was often the one employed by whatever advertiser agreed to sponsor a particular campaign. For some of the enormous campaigns such as the successive War Bonds drives, numerous sponsoring advertisers and advertising agencies were assigned to the same task.

As lucid as the *Business Week* article is on the workings of the War Advertising Council, it errs once when it remarks that "the organization writes no copy," restricting its role to its liaison and advisory capacities. But in fact, for certain government drives, notably those for which the Council seemingly could not find the right ad agencies to prepare ads or private sector advertisers to sponsor the campaign, the Council itself did create ads. One such campaign was the anti-inflation ads mostly in 1944 and 1945, but occasionally in 1943 as well. Although the ten magazines examined here contain only eleven different anti-inflation ads sponsored by seven different companies, in that same time frame at least sixteen such ads proclaiming "Prepared by the War Advertising Council, approved by the Office of War Information," were published not only in these magazines but also in *Vogue*, *The New Yorker*, *Redbook*, and the trade publications *Telephony* and *Buildings & Building Management* ("Ad Access/World War II"). So, indeed, when necessary the War Advertising Council got into the business of writing war ads as well as organizing and managing war ad campaigns.

The Council coordinated and facilitated numerous government advertising campaigns—thirty-seven in 1943 alone. Its chairman Chester J. La Roche received *Advertising & Selling*'s Gold Medal as advertising's man of the year for 1942 for "his role in making the industry an instrument of national defense" (Wharton 49; *Business Week* 6 Feb.1943: 72). Yet there was one vast category of war ads over which the Council had no oversight whatever, even though these ads accounted for the majority that reached out specifically to Mr. and Mrs. Home Front (as opposed to industry) and included many of the most effective ads of the war. These were the war ads that are the subject of this book—ads prepared by admen for commercial advertisers and placed in magazines independently of coordinated government campaigns. They were of two basic kinds, eclectic ads on random and miscellaneous topics, and runs of ads on one topic of special concern to an advertiser who placed numerous ads on that subject over several months in one or more magazines. While unified, these ads were not coordinated with government campaigns (nor were they necessarily serial ads of the kind earlier discussed).

In addition to Borden, mentioned earlier, whose ads covered themes from the shortage of ice cream to bolstering GI morale more efficiently by using V-Mail, there were other eclectic advertisers. Budweiser's ads urged carpooling for conservation, paid tribute to women on the home front, and encouraged voluntary rationing. Chiefly through humorous cartoons in *Esquire*, Calvert Distillers' ads treated such matters as conserving heating fuel, rumor control, and saving kitchen fats.

The single-topic runs of ads are particularly notable because each dealt with a subject that, while important to home front morale or support of the war, never was the objective of a government-backed drive. These mini-campaigns were mounted entirely at the initiative of the advertiser sponsoring them and its ad agency. Several such series are especially striking. The Eureka Vacuum Cleaner Company ran eleven ads in the *Post* and *Collier's* between January 1943 and April 1944, each ad paying tribute to women in war work, at home on the home front, and/or in the armed forces. In about twenty ads between February 1942 and December 1943, in five different magazines, Exide Batteries promoted what was called "thoughtful buying"—buying only what one needed at a cost below government-imposed ceiling prices, and buying goods of the best possible quality that would last for the duration and thus foster conservation. Imperial Whiskey ran a long series of ads from August 1943 through November 1944 in *Life, Time,* and *Newsweek* featuring wonderful drawings of birds and animals that illustrated copy explaining the concept of rationing as sharing. And one series qualifies as literally unique, Hammond Organ's throughout much of 1944 in *Newsweek,* in which each ad honored the heroics of a different army, navy, or marine chaplain. All these series are fully discussed in later chapters.

One useful thing the War Advertising Council did beyond implementing government-initiated war ad campaigns was to create a hierarchy of war ad types produced by commercial advertisers, each label reflecting an advertiser's degree of commitment to getting out a war message. From the top down, in the "ALL OUT" ad the whole ad promotes some aspect of citizen involvement in the war by an advertiser "who is shooting the works in his sponsorship of a war theme" (Wharton 78). Next is the "DOUBLE-BARRELLED [sic] JOB" that "supports a war theme and sells merchandise to boot," which the Council deemed "just as effective as the 'All-Out'" (78, 146). Third is the "SNEAK PUNCH" war message an advertiser gets in "by working it deftly into his product copy," and next to the bottom is "'A PLUG IN A SLUG' (such as a note at the bottom of an ad, 'Buy War Bonds,' etc.)," which the Council considered "nearly worthless" (78, 146). Last and definitely least are the "BUSINESS AS USUAL" ad and advertiser who go on their merry way selling their wares with no mention of the war. It's primarily the All-Out and Double-Barrelled ads that figure large in this study of wartime advertising.

Even if the War Advertising Council had wanted to have oversight over the vast field of independently produced eclectic and thematic series of war ads (and there is no evidence that it wanted to), it would have been a more than Herculean task to ride herd over all the advertisers and ad agencies producing such ads without the Council significantly increasing its manpower and budget.

The Intention and Objective of War Ads

Institutional advertising aside, the myriad messages aimed at the home front in war ads had one intention in common—the same intention advertising has always had—to encourage the reader to do something. Also, the advertising industry had an objective it hoped to achieve by implementing that intention. To understand what that objective was it will help to eliminate a few things that it wasn't.

The purpose of some advertising parading as war ads was, at its worst, little more than product promotion or the self-aggrandizement of various manufacturing firms. This sort of pseudo-war ad had its critics, none more notable or vocal than the chairman of the War Advertising Council, Chester J. La Roche, who flatly stated that advertising is not war advertising if all it does is proclaim how a manufacturer's products are helping the war: "It certainly is not, if it doesn't help get action by the people. In the midst of a struggle for survival, while American boys are dying by the thousands, blatant brag advertising is in questionable taste" (qtd. in Clark 205–06). There is *some* difference between a factually informational ad in which an automotive company describes how it is now making tanks and an ad in which a similar company boasts how the landing craft it built were single-handedly responsible for the successful invasion of the Solomon Islands. Both types could be construed as brag ads whose primary aim was keeping a company's name or products before the public and future clients until the firm was again in peacetime production. That aim may be sound economics in the worlds of business and industry, but for La Roche it was not the stuff of true war ads (for more on this, see Chapter 3).

Yet there were others during the war who believed in this purely economic rationale not just for war ads but for the war itself, none more extreme and blunt about it than Arthur H. Deute, owner of the now defunct National Brewing Company of Baltimore, in an address to the Baltimore Advertising Club in December 1941: "The big 'it' of our American way of life is brand strength built on brand demand," and the very reason the United States is at war at all is "to assure ourselves good futures for these brands of ours" (qtd. in Fox 46). Clearly for Deute the war was strictly a war to preserve private enterprise, supply-and-demand capitalism, and the survival of the fittest among product brands.

Not quite as extreme but similar in its reasoning, Frank W. Fox's *Madison Avenue Goes To War*, written close to thirty years after World War II, is more a book about the ad industry than about advertising or war ads per se. It is therefore understandable that when Fox refers to the objectives of war ads he is referring to those that will benefit the ad industry itself, not the war effort universally. Accordingly, Fox's study is a parochial and inward-turning account of how the ad industry turned the war to its own advantage. His central thesis is that admen used the war to help return to the advertising profession the dignity and public confidence that had been lost over the previous two decades thanks to the "Truth-in-Advertising" movement and the Consumers' Union challenging the credibility of advertising. The ad industry did this in great part, according to Fox, by writing ad copy extolling American virtues, American values, and, most of all "The American Way of Life." To that end Fox handpicked for discussion a narrow range of ads that appeared mostly in such magazines as *Fortune* and *Business Week* and the trade journals *Printers' Ink* and *Advertising & Selling*, ads that interpret "The American Way" strictly as free enterprise and the corporate world's desire for minimal governmental regulation of business, banking, and industry. Fox demonstrates, credibly, that advertising is an integral part of free enterprise and so has a stake in promoting such a vision, but he fails when trying to maintain that this narrow interpretation of "The American Way" was an essential theme throughout war advertising. To the contrary, of the 5,143 war ads in my database only 72 or 1.4% touch on "The American Way" strictly as free enterprise (see Chapter 2). Clearly the intention and objective of war ads overall cannot be found in a view so narrow and promoted in so few ads.

If this view was too constricted to define a genuine intention and objective in war ads, another put forth later is simply too broad. In her 1992 article "Madison Avenue Goes to War: Patriotism in Advertising During World War II," Sue Hart wrote, "Whatever their wares—beauty aids, car parts, or kitchen appliances—World War II era advertisers were selling patriotism and promise first; their products second" (125). Promise, yes, in the relatively few ads that told Americans what they could buy after the war. But patriotism? Definitely not. First, it's extremely hard to "sell" an abstraction like patriotism, and second, as already discussed in the section on national unity, the American people were already as patriotic as could be. What they needed to be sold on, or at least informed about, was how they could express that patriotism through tangible and specific ways of participating in the war effort. Enter advertising. Grounded on the patriotism already in place, admen were able to create war ads that appealed to home front civilians. This, then, in large part was the ad industry's wartime intention: to use Americans' patriotism to energize them and sell them on proactive ways they could help win the war.

This intention of war advertising—to get Americans actively involved in the war effort—was articulated by a number of influential people central to the stateside running of the war and advertising's role in it. Publisher Willard Chevalier devoted almost his entire column in *Business Week* for November 21, 1942, to excerpts from a talk by Donald Nelson, director of the War Production Board, at the New York meeting of the Association of National Advertisers. Among other things, Nelson said, "We make a mistake when we try to distinguish between the military and the civilian sides of our war effort. It is all one effort. . . . Extremely valuable work has been done by the national advertisers, the great advertising agencies, and the various advertising media in supporting such things as the salvage drive," which was, of course, largely citizen driven (127). Concurring with Nelson was A.N.A. president Paul West, who listed what he perceived to be the functions of advertising in a war economy. One was "to help the war effort by informing the public and arousing action in such a way that the public, the industry, and the war effort all benefit" (127). And again, War Advertising Council chairman Chester J. La Roche had something to say on the subject: *"By war advertising we mean advertising which induces people, through information, to take certain actions necessary to the speedy winning of the war"* (qtd. in Clark 206). So there was considerable consensus among people who mattered that the fundamental intention of war ads was to induce the home front to participate in whatever would help the war effort, whether by giving blood, buying War Bonds, saving scrap paper, or in dozens of other ways.

The larger objective of war ads and of citizen participation in the war effort was rarely articulated as cogently and concisely as was their intention. Still, a statement of that objective and how it is inextricably linked to the intention of war ads is appropriate and necessary here. Usually the expression of this objective occurred in ads themselves, often as an underlying theme rather than directly. To take an early example, in *Time* on January 5, 1942, an ad for Dixie Cups observed that contagion "for centuries, has been the plague of troops" and then described how Dixie Cups were used to prevent contagion on naval vessels and "at canteens and refreshment spots near military posts." The copy then moved from the military to the civilian, noting that "because sickness is such a threat to our defense production, industry too is . . . installing Dixie Cups, that are used but once and thrown away" (45). Yes, there's no arguing that the ad was selling Dixie Cups, but it was doing something else extremely vital—expressing a concern about illness in defense plants that could lead to absenteeism, which could lead to slowdowns in production. What the ad was addressing without stating it is *efficiency*, and thousands more war ads would go on to do the same. That home front efficiency was the primary objective of war ads can be seen just in the number of those types of ads that addressed the issue directly or by implication in the leading popular magazines: women in war work—230; War Bonds—407; home front efficiency generally and home front morale (necessary for efficiency)—644; home front support of GI morale—385; and conservation of food and vital materials—338; over 2,000 in all.

One of the most eloquent expressions of the role of war ads came not from a Washington bureaucrat or an advertising executive, but, instead, from a magazine advertisement, and not one for an ad agency. The ad was placed by the Kimberly-Clark Corporation in *Newsweek* for January 18, 1943, and it said in part, "Keeping the home front alert to the need for cooperation and personal sacrifice is a most important part of the war effort and provides an outlet for the high talents and tremendous influence of America's advertisers [. . . in] campaigns which are designed to inform civilians on the help the Country needs from its every man, woman, and child." As I read the final phrases and mentally compare them with the five thousand-plus ads I examined, I'm convinced they are absolutely literal. Linking the intention with the objective of war ads, the overarching reason for them thus becomes: to enlist the active participation of all Americans—men, women, and children—in order for the home front to reach a state of *efficiency* that would thoroughly support the military both materially and spiritually.

"THIS IS WORTH FIGHTING FOR" MOTIVATIONAL WAR ADS

The best of the wartime admen were smart, as first-rate admen always have to be—smart, savvy, and canny mass psychologists, if only by instinct or intuition. As already discussed in Chapter 1, from Pearl Harbor to the Japanese surrender, home front America didn't need to be sold on patriotism even in its literal dictionary sense of simply "love for one's country." Knowing this, the advertising industry broke down large philosophical abstractions like "patriotism," "liberty," and "democracy" into their smaller components, some still quite lofty, others more tangible and even mundane, so that the average American could more easily relate to them not just intellectually but emotionally. To that end ads were crafted to appeal to emotions ranging from sentiment and nostalgia to fear and even selfish self-interest. The admen then used the various segments of these abstractions and ideals as the basis for ads whose aim was not so much a call for specific actions as it was a reminder to the home front of why we were at war, why we had to win, and what we'd stand to lose if we lost the war.

That admen broke down the large abstractions into more easily digested parts is obvious in the copy and art of such motivational war advertising. One striking ad fairly early in the war makes it explicit that this was how such ads were conceptualized and crafted. Starting in early October 1942, the United States Rubber Company placed in such magazines as *Time, Newsweek,* and the *Post* a brief series of ads with the unvarying heading "*WHAT ARE WE FIGHTING FOR?*" In the *Post* on October 24, that question was answered with, " . . . THE HOMELY FRAGMENTS OF DAILY LIFE . . . words like *freedom* or *liberty* draw close to us only when we break them down into the <u>homely fragments of daily life</u>" (49). The ad continued with concrete examples like "the strollers on Main Street who gossip to their hearts' content, unaware of such a thing as a concentration camp." Sometimes motivational copy appeared in ads asking for the public's support in the war effort, or even in ads selling a product, but there were also strictly motivational ads whose sole purpose was to help readers grasp the reasons that America was at war without asking for their direct participation. These ads are featured in this chapter.

"The Blessings of Liberty" and "The Pursuit of Happiness"

Motivational war ads all have to do with some aspect or aspects of "The American Way of Life," or what I prefer to call American values, since there is little unanimity as to just what *the* American way of life is. Everyone who has ever discoursed on the concept has stopped short of offering any concise definition of "The American Way." The closest they come is in maintaining that "The American Way of Life" has its roots in the Declaration of Independence's "life, liberty, and the pursuit of happiness," to which some people also attach the word "democracy" and Americans' privileges and liberties as established by the Bill of Rights. Other frequently mentioned components of "The American Way of Life" have been freedom, individual responsibility, individualism, freedom of choice, and even a high standard of living. Free enterprise gets into "The American Way" by a loose, fuzzy reading of "the pursuit of happiness" that embraces not just individual opportunity but also private businesses operating in a competitive, generally unregulated environment.

Even "American values" doesn't entirely describe what the United States was fighting for unless "values" as expressed in motivational ads is expanded beyond its usual meaning of a society's accepted principles or standards. The "values" in many such ads embraced more tangible, down-to-earth traditions, social and cultural norms, and pastimes that Americans *value*—a Fourth of July parade and picnic, owning one's home, Sunday dinner with the folks, baseball games, ice cream sodas, and those other qualities of life that make America, in today's parlance, a "comfort zone" for its people. Yet motivational war ads didn't wholly ignore the loftier ideals of American society, some ads even reaching back to both facts and myths about the Constitution and Declaration of Independence for their messages.

Although numerous war ads cited the Constitution—mostly parts of the Bill of Rights—only a purely motivational ad placed by the Chesapeake and Ohio Lines in *Business Week* on November 27, 1943, invoked the Declaration of Independence alone. Predictably enough, the phrase from the Declaration that launched the ad's lengthy copy was "the pursuit of Happiness," describing it thus: "The right every man was to enjoy in this new country was the right to *pursue* happiness. To roll up his sleeves and go after it and struggle and win it with his own two hands and his wits" (3). While the Declaration's phrase implied in "happiness" things like choosing where to live, whom to marry, where (or if) to pursue an education, and other "pursuits," this ad's reading of "pursuit of Happiness" implies something like the groundwork of free enterprise. In some people's minds, free enterprise was equivalent to "The American Way of Life" to the exclusion of all else the expression embodies (see the following section). But the C&O ad more generously embraced preserving the larger ideas of individualism and liberty implied in "pursuit of Happiness" as reasons why we had to defeat the Axis.

Many more ads invoked one or more of the Rights in the Bill of Rights as motivational reasons for fighting the war. "I'm fighting for my right to boo the Dodgers!" hollers a civilian loaded down with combat paraphernalia in the Texaco ad in the *Post* on October 17, 1942, vividly underscoring right from the top that this ad's concern was protecting the freedom of speech guaranteed in Amendment I of the Bill of Rights. The fairly brief copy restates the concept of free speech in ways anyone could comprehend, as the man laden with battle gear goes on, "I'm glad I live in a country where a guy can sound off. Don't get me wrong. I think the Dodgers are tops in baseball. But that isn't the point. What I ask for is the right to squawk when I think things could be run better. That's the American way. It's worth fighting for" (38). Key is the ad's definition of "the American way" that had absolutely nothing to do with free enterprise, but with one of the personal liberties guaranteed by the Constitution.

An ad by the National Steel Corporation in *Newsweek* on August 2, 1943, gave readers several motivations for winning the war, most but not all harking back to the Declaration of Independence and the Constitution: "Of all the blessings that are ours as Americans, the most precious by far is Liberty—the right to work, and to enjoy the fruits of our labor; the right to vote; the right to worship as we please; the right to seek happiness in our own way for ourselves and for our children" (10). "Liberty," of course, immediately precedes "the pursuit of Happiness" in the Declaration of Independence. Similarly, "the right to worship as we please" appears in the "free exercise" of religion clause in the First Amendment, but "the right to work" and "the right to vote" occur nowhere in either writing. The Constitution is full of "phrases, clauses, and amendments detailing ways people cannot be denied the right to vote," but nowhere does it ensure Americans the *right* itself (see "Things"), or even "our right to vote secretly and without fear of reprisal," as a Republic Steel ad suggested it did in the *Post* on May 22, 1943 (47). But it mattered little to wartime admen if such cherished American values were guaranteed constitutionally or if they became established through legislation, case law, or mere tradition, custom, or common practice. Whatever their origins, these ideas made for potent motivational copy.

It's one thing to pack into a single ad six different American rights and privileges, as National Steel did, and it's quite another to prepare a series of twelve different ads published over as many months, each ad zeroing in on one specific Right in the Bill of Rights and why the United States must win the war to preserve it. This serial approach to motivating readers by letting them focus on just one right or privilege at a time is how the advertising firm of Geare-Marston, Inc. and its client SKF Ball and Roller Bearings determined that their Bill of Rights series would be most effective, and, indeed, as a series it is. The copy and art in each ad are rarely brilliant but some are powerful and all at least adequate to the task. SKF's Bill of Rights ads ran from late January through late December 1942 in *Business Week*, one ad per month except for none in July and two in October, and also during the same months in *Newsweek*, except for the ones about "cruel and unusual punishments" and the "right to petition the Government," which appear nowhere in that magazine. Why SKF and its ad agency decided to place the Bill of Rights series in only *Newsweek* and *Business Week* is difficult to imagine since during the war advertising in these magazines normally ran to the institutional, informational type, and the Bill of Rights ads focus squarely on the rights and privileges of individual American citizens, not on business or industry.

The layout of the first SKF ad started the series off with a bang. On religious freedom, the ad in *Business Week* on January 24 (*Newsweek* Jan. 26) featured an illustration of an idyllic small American town whose capstone is a typical white-steepled church. Writ large across the picture is "*Hands off, Mr. Dictator!*" The brief copy notes that the right of religious freedom is "only one of the many that are Constitution-clad and greatly loved," alerting readers that more "Constitution-clad" rights would follow in later ads. The blunt, allusive reference to the war "Whoever threatens them, beware!" closes the ad.

On February 21 in *Business Week* (*Newsweek* Feb. 9) was freedom of speech, which like religious freedom is contained in the First Amendment. But on March 9 in *Newsweek* (*Business Week* March 21), the third SKF ad drew on the Fourth Amendment for its content. This ad brings a Constitutionally guaranteed right down to a very human level; in the art a young mother says to her daughter playing with a doll on the floor, "Go see who's at the door, Mary." The following copy elaborates: "We live in a land where a knock on the door may mean a neighbor, maybe a salesman. It *never* means a Storm Trooper or a brute from the Gestapo," illustrating the Constitutional tenet that Americans, unlike Europeans under the Nazis, were secure "against unreasonable searches and seizures."

In the ad on April 6 in *Newsweek* (*Business Week* April 18) the drawing of a man in his bathrobe stooping to bring in the milk and morning paper is captioned "He gets his news 'un-Goebbeled.'" The slightly amusing reference, of course, was to Herr Doktor Joseph Goebbels, the Nazi Minister of Propaganda who freely censored and distorted public information to the advantage of the Nazi regime, a far cry from the First Amendment's freedom "of the press." But then the May ad (May 6 in *Newsweek*, the 18th in *Business Week*) suggests that someone at Geare-Marston either didn't do his homework or decided his copy would say what he *wanted* the Sixth Amendment to say. This ad perpetuates the myth that Americans have the *Constitutional* guarantee of a trial by a jury of our peers, "*guaranteed*, right there in our square-shooting Bill of Rights." But the fact is that "of our peers" turns up nowhere in the Constitution, least of all in the Sixth Amendment guaranteeing "the right to a speedy and public trial, by an impartial jury of the state and district wherein the crime shall have been committed" (see "Things"). Still, the "of our peers" myth was put to good use since the ad contrasts places where anyone could be sentenced to a concentration camp "at the whim of a dictator or his stooge tribunal" with the United States where "twelve everyday folks, just like ourselves, will hear our case and decide our fate."

The First Amendment's "right of the people peaceably to assemble" was the subject of a rather uninspired SKF ad in *Newsweek* on June 1 and *Business Week* on June 13. On August 8 in *Business Week* only, SKF took the circuitous route of comparing police in the United States as a "symbol of security" with those in Axis countries as "the servants of tyranny," to get to the Eighth Amendment's protection against "cruel and unusual punishments." At best the copy in these ads and the remaining five is rather verbose and flabby compared to the crisp, vivid ads earlier in the series. Accordingly, a simple listing of the remaining ads with little or no commentary will illustrate what other rights in the Bill of Rights the SKF ads hoped would educate and motivate their audience.

"Nor shall private property be taken for public use" is the theme of the ad for September 5 in *Business Week* and September 21 in *Newsweek* celebrating the Fifth Amendment's guarantee against the government's seizure of citizens' property "without just compensation." Slightly redundantly, the ad in *Business Week* on October 3 and *Newsweek* on October 19 picks up on the previous phrase in the Fifth Amendment stating that no one will "be deprived of life, liberty, or property, without due process of law," this ad placing the emphasis on due process as the previous one had on compensation. An ad that wasn't published in *Newsweek* at all was the second SKF ad in *Business Week* in October. This one, on the 31st, returned to the First Amendment for Americans' right "to petition the government for a redress of grievances." November's ad, on the 16th in *Newsweek* and the 28th in *Business Week*, addressed "the sanctity of the home" in America, something the ad asserts Nazis never heard of, or at least never respected. Accordingly, that section of the Fourth Amendment was invoked that forbade search warrants without "probable cause" and the warrant "describing the place to be searched, and the persons or things to be seized." Finally, on December 14 in *Newsweek* and December 26 in *Business Week* the last ad in the series took up the Eighth Amendment's opening clause that "excessive bail shall not be required" for persons awaiting trial. There is no way to measure the effectiveness of the SKF Bill of Rights ads, but it's at least certain they gave those who read them a good understanding, in comparatively few words, of a dozen of Americans' Constitutionally guaranteed rights, rights that could well be lost were the Allies to lose the war. And that's what motivational advertising was all about.

Free Enterprise and "The American Way"

On November 27, 1943, about a year after its Bill of Rights series ended, SKF Ball and Roller Bearings launched a series in *Business Week* extolling the virtues of free enterprise. These ads, however, were not war ads since none of them related free enterprise to the war or linked it to "The American Way of Life" the United States was fighting to preserve. But between 1943 and the end of the war some other advertisers made free enterprise virtually synonymous with "The American Way" even though no two definitions of "free enterprise" agree on its precise meaning. According to bits and pieces from several definitions, about all they agree upon is that free enterprise is the "freedom of private business to operate competitively, for profit," "free and independent from state control" "beyond regulation necessary to protect public interest and keep the national economy in balance." Various definitions also equate free enterprise with laissez-faire economics, a free-market economy, or with just plain capitalism.

None of these definitions of free enterprise includes the idea of individual *opportunity* whereby anyone can rise from slag shoveler to company CEO by dint of hard work and brains. And yet, it is this virtual "right" of individual opportunity that becomes the centerpiece of free enterprise in all but a very few wartime ads that discuss it. Indeed, the art of the first ad in the SKF free enterprise series depicts a man addressing a business meeting at an industrial plant captioned "Fifth Freedom." The brief copy explains: "This man, not long ago, worked with his hands in a steel mill. He's a top executive today, thanks to free enterprise. In America a man is free to choose his work, free to develop his talents, free to advance to the limit of his ability [a phrase repeated frequently in such ads]. It is *opportunity*, incentive to individual effort that has made America strong" (*Business Week* 27 Nov. 1943: 2).

The second SKF free enterprise ad contains a much more orthodox definition of free enterprise when it maintains that there is "a reason why America has the highest standard of living the world has ever known. It's a natural product of *free enterprise*. Under the American competitive system, a producer must give his customers quality merchandise *at a fair price* . . . and keep improving his product . . . if he is to remain in business" (*Business Week* 19 Feb. 1944: 2). But the Geare-Marston copywriter couldn't leave well enough alone with that rendition of the economic workings of free enterprise. No, he had to tack on "Furthermore, *free enterprise* gives the individual the opportunity to advance to the limit of his ability." So many other ads that were genuine war ads kept making individual opportunity the focal point of free enterprise, it is almost as if wartime advertisers and admen were deliberately forging a new meaning, almost a new myth, for what free enterprise really was.

More importantly, prior to the war ad campaigns of some large companies "The American Way" never exclusively *equaled* free enterprise to the exclusion of all else. Most advertisers appear to have genuinely believed in this equation of free enterprise with "The American Way" and used it as a motivational force for the readers of their ads, but one large company's ads were almost entirely self-serving. One of the genuine companies was Warner & Swasey, a manufacturer of turret lathes used in machining all manner of war materiel. From one end of the war to the other in *Time*, *Newsweek*, and *Business Week*, Warner & Swasey ran variously themed war ads notable for their virtual absence of artwork and for copy that was always blunt, tough-talking, and direct, occasionally even running to negative copy, hard sells, and scare tactics (see the following section). Ten months before the first SKF free enterprise ad, in *Newsweek* on January 4, 1943, a Warner & Swasey ad looked at and lauded free enterprise from an unusual angle, as is apparent from the headline "Without free enterprise this war would have been lost months ago." The rest of the ad takes the tack that free enterprise is more efficient than the planned industrial economies of dictatorships; it took Germany nine years "to build enough plants and equipment to fight a war," Japan twenty-five years, and even our ally "splendid Russia" twenty, but "American industry under free enterprise has done it in 2 years . . . built and tooled the plants to turn out *1000 times* the war materials we could make before the war" (13). The ad goes on to describe free enterprise as the "intelligent cooperation of labor-management-government," a very reasonable position compared to some others. Here, in the straight-shooting Warner & Swasey manner, the contribution of free enterprise to the war is laid out in clear, specific terms.

The meat-packing firm of Armour and Company was one of several businesses that occasionally placed in popular magazines ads that either assumed "The American Way" and free enterprise were one and the same or used some pretty flimsy rhetoric to make it appear that they were. Armour published a number of columns signed and ostensibly written by the company president, George A. Eastwood. These appeared as sidebars to what were otherwise thoroughly business-as-usual full-page ads selling Armour's products. Two of Eastwood's columns in *Life* about five months apart demonstrate how Armour insinuated to the home front the supposed synonymity between the American Way and free enterprise, thereby seeming to offer a motivational message about why the U.S. must win the war.

Eastwood's column on September 11, 1944, titled "Spiritual Dividends," opens with the sentence "The American Way is prolific in providing spiritual as well as material dividends" (10). Then throughout thirteen paragraphs in very small print it enumerates what some of those "spiritual dividends" are, focusing on what Eastwood calls "freedom of choice," including everything from the housewife's "invaluable privilege of selecting goods and services of her own choosing" to the right of "producers to engage in congenial work of their own choice." About two-thirds of the way through, the column sums this up by saying, "In simple terms, the American Way is opposed to pushing around the individual citizen, however humble," and "no corporate or governmental dictator is permitted in law or in morals to substitute his judgment and taste for that of the individual citizen." Eastwood then wraps up his presentation by stating, "Thus, the American private enterprise system involves much more than the special privilege of business owners," quietly substituting this equivalent of "free enterprise" for "The American Way." Via this questionable rhetorical gimmick the American Way *is* free enterprise—period.

The Armour ad on February 2, 1945, gets to the same conclusion by a different route. Eastwood's column begins, "The American Way provides a magic fusion of individual effort along cooperative lines" (8). He then points to the synergism of management, stockholders, and industrial employees that enables the American worker "to turn out more units per year than the worker in any other land." Soon after he reveals that *his* "American Way" is in fact "the typical fruits of capitalism—of the competitive society," or, again, free enterprise. These two ads make it clear that Eastwood was trying to *defend* free enterprise as "much more than the special privilege of business owners." Still, Eastwood's equations of free enterprise with the American Way were benign compared to the rhetoric in the frequent, often strident war ads by another company patently and blatantly trying to defend itself.

Between January 1943 and October 1944, Republic Steel placed twelve full-page war ads dealing with free enterprise and the American Way only in the *Saturday Evening Post* except for variations of three of them that appeared in *Farm Journal* along with one wholly original one eight months later in June 1945. Most likely, Republic chose these magazines because both the *Post* and *Farm Journal* were fairly conservative, with readerships to match. Each ad had a different "dramatic context"—a country doctor giving the "boys" at the general store an earful, a father imparting last minute wisdom to a son going overseas, two workingmen chatting at a lunch counter, and so on — but the substance was virtually identical from ad to ad. The only major difference is that the ads' fear of regimentation and government regulation approaches paranoia in the later ads. All the Republic ads stress three salient features of the free enterprise/American Way equation that can be illustrated with just a few excerpts.

First, the equation itself was spelled out most fully and unequivocally in the earliest ad of the series on January 30, 1943 (inside front cover; all dates refer to the *Post* unless *Farm Journal* is specified). Comparing what he's seen in Europe to America, one GI says to another, "I like the way we've always run things back home — you know — the American way of life." The copy elaborates, "Call it what you will — free enterprise, private enterprise, our commercial competitive system, the American brand of freedom, or any of a dozen other labels, they all help explain the American way of life." Later, the equation was succinctly summarized in an ad about a newsboy on October 7, 1944: "We're all capitalists in America. [. . .] That's free enterprise. That's *AMERICA*" (73).

Second, eight of the ads mention individuals' opportunity to succeed and/or rewards for personal initiative, both of which are arguably a part of "The American Way of Life." But by equating the American Way with free enterprise the ads make opportunity central to that as well, even though there is no historical basis for including individual opportunity in the concept of free enterprise. Typical of these remarks are the words of the country doctor on April 22, 1944: "It [free enterprise] offers *opportunity* to anyone who really wants it. It rewards thrift, hard work and ingenuity" (88). A comment about the newsboy's chances of rising in the world proclaims, "Each of us is free to take his own future in his own hands — and pull himself up by his bootstraps." What is telling about the newsboy ad, and implicit in the others, is the description of "each of us": "We carry life insurance, or have savings accounts, or hold war bonds, or own farms, garages, fruit stands, drug stores, or other businesses — large or small." Conspicuously absent from this list are the millions of Americans who didn't own any of those things but who comprised the labor force in industry and agriculture — skilled, semi-skilled, or unskilled, unionized or not. Where was the "opportunity" for them?

The third recurrent theme in these ads displays Republic's narrow self-serving motive for them. On February 12, 1944, the departing GI's father tells him, "You're fighting to protect your own right to live your own life in your own way without being pushed around by some bright young bureaucrat who wants to do all the planning for you" (66). On August 12, 1944, one man at a lunch counter says to another, "Tom, it sure worries me when I hear all this talk about *keeping wartime restrictions on business after the war*. . . . It's a cinch that business has got to have freedom from a lot of this unnecessary meddling if it's going to get anywhere" (73). And in the last ad in the series in the June 1945 *Farm Journal*, a farmer says to his son back from active duty, "Every bit of needless regimentation that comes along to interfere with our right to manage our affairs in our own way is . . . a weed. And that's true whether we're running a farm, a store in town, a manufacturing plant, or just trying to get along as private citizens" (14). Wartime readers should have seen that these weren't words fearful of Nazi or Japanese regimentation and planned economy if the Axis won the war. No, they were referring to just one thing—Washington. And those readers for whom the events of 1937 were still in living memory would have immediately grasped why Republic Steel ads contained those words.

On March 1, 1937, without even a strike, John L. Lewis and the CIO unionized Big Steel, which was, effectively, United States Steel. But during that spring Little Steel, a group of steel mills headed by Republic Steel and its president Tom M. Girdler, turned a deaf ear to all overtures toward unionization. This was not surprising, since, according to Benjamin Stolberg in *The Nation*, "Little Steel . . . is corrupting the authorities, is heavily subsidizing vigilantism, has turned its plants into arsenals, and has literally hired the organized underworld in its fight against organized labor" (31 July 1937: 119). In his open defiance of labor and the Wagner Act, Girdler in his steel domain was as much a totalitarian as any Axis dictator or emperor, or, as Stolberg neatly put it, "Girdler is an open fascist, to whom Roosevelt, Miss [Frances] Perkins, John Lewis are 'Communists.'" Things came to a bloody, deadly head on Memorial Day at the Republic plant in South Chicago when about two hundred police and Girdler's own goons confronted workers peacefully picketing for unionization. The police wounded ninety and killed ten strikers, most of them unarmed; of those killed, seven were shot in the back while trying to flee. Aside from the most anti-union segments of the population (the *Chicago Tribune* labeled the strikers "Communists"), the public's feeling was outrage at the police, Republic Steel, and Tom Girdler. Senator Robert Lafollette's investigatory committee concurred that the police were wholly in the wrong for their handling of the strike and solely to blame for the mayhem in what quickly became known as The Massacre at Republic Steel (see Allen 291–93; Stolberg *passim*; Bork). Yet in spite of the Massacre, violence and carnage continued "outside Republic Steel plants and involved strikers and local law enforcement agencies" (Bork), with six more strikers losing their lives on a picket line in Ohio.

Despite the supposed inclusiveness of the Republic ads, Tom Girdler's rigid anti-union stance makes it transparent that in fact he did all he could to deny working-class men and women a place in the ads' ideal of the American Way and free enterprise. After the Massacre Girdler continued to resist organized labor getting a foothold in Republic until he could simply resist no longer. In 1942, compelled by the War Labor Board, the companies comprising Little Steel had no choice but to sign contracts with the United Steel Workers of America (see Bork). But to hear Girdler tell it in his usually unrepentant, arrogant autobiography *Boot Straps* published in 1943, he sounds like the soul of humility when he writes of the settlement: "My associates and I are law-abiding citizens, so when the Supreme Court finally decided that labor union agreements must be written contracts, we obeyed. [. . .] Ever since we have done our conscientious best to make the relationship work to the mutual advantage of our employees and the company" (374). Yet in the next breath Girdler shows his true colors: "But this does not mean that my opinions have changed. In our private conversations my associates and I find ourselves unreconciled." Girdler's anti-union voice shouts off the page in Republic's free enterprise ads so stridently that I wouldn't be surprised if he either wrote the copy himself or at least had tight personal control over it. Put simply, the source virtually discredits the ads' alleged message.

Scare Tactics, Hard-Sells, and Plain Bad Taste

In nearly all motivational war ads the copy was uplifting and positive, genuinely intended to exhilarate and inspire readers of the ads. But—uncommon though not altogether unknown—there were also some negative ads whose scare tactics were frankly designed to frighten the daylights out of readers. This class of ads is so small it's only worth mentioning because one series of them won an ad industry award for "advertising as a social force" even though the ad-reading public didn't seem to agree.

About three months before the award-winning scare series began, in *Time* on August 24, 1942, Warner & Swasey's usual tough talking turned to out-and-out scare copy, something the turret lathe manufacturer never did again, although it slipped some pretty chilling rhetoric into the frank copy of its many other war ads. Here, however, the scare tactics began up front with the headline *"It is later (and worse) than you think!"* The rest of the ad debunked Americans' habit of overoptimistically "kidding ourselves" through eight statements and their rebuttals, such as:

"This country has never been beaten in all its 166 years."
Japan has never been beaten in its 2000 years.

"They can't get at us, 3000 miles away."
Japan got to Burma 3600 miles away — and conquered it.

Our allies will hold until we get there."
Singapore, Philippines, Pearl Harbor, Burma — and now Libya.

There's no letup to this litany of American wishful thinking right to the end of the ad, including the reply to the final question, "Anyway, what can one man do?" Answer: "What if all the other 130,000,000 Americans felt the same? [. . .] Nobody else is going to win this war for you. YOU win it — or YOU lose it. And if you lose it, you and your family will pay for it in agony and starvation the rest of your lives. Ask the Poles, the Czechs, the French" (41). Addressed especially to war industries, as were almost all Warner & Swasey ads for the duration, the ultimate message was "And this war is nearer to being lost than you think. *Work* by *you* can save it. But — *there isn't much time to get busy.*"

Like nearly all Warner & Swasey ads, this one was devoid of art save for a tiny photo at the bottom showing a man at work in a machine shop. But in the American Locomotive Company's award-winning series of ads based on "scare appeal" (Fox 35), the more than half-page color illustrations were just as scary as the copy, if not more so. With an empty hangman's noose in the foreground, five people in silhouette hang from a communal gallows in the distance (*Life* 30 Nov. 1942: 136). In shadow, a man looks up at a grim-visaged uniformed judge in a Nazi tribunal (*Life* 4 Jan. 1943: 32). A starving man scavenges for food in a garbage can while seen through a window behind him overstuffed Nazi officers gorge themselves at dinner (*Post* 30 Jan. 1943: 85). Against a background of the United States Capitol flying their empire's flag, a five-man Japanese firing squad levels its rifles point blank at the reader (*Post* 3 April 1943: 65) — and yet more, each wordless illustration wailing like a prophet of doom, "It *can* happen here." Equally grisly is the copy in each ad, and the combination of art and copy was enough to sir up most of the home front's worst nightmares. This is no better seen than in the ad on page 55 of *Collier's* on February 13, 1943, and page 14 of *Life* two days later. At first glance, a reader might have found the art alone ambiguous or unclear— three attractive young women in drab gray dresses stand against a wall as if in a police lineup; some uniformed Nazis scrutinize them while outside the door a soldier stands guard and a swastika flag is partly visible (see fig. 11). But the picture's caption, "A HIGH HONOR FOR YOUR DAUGHTER," and the copy instantly and frighteningly clarify everything; "For they're great believers in eugenics, these Nazis. They're strong for selective breeding. [. . .] Your daughter . . . well, if she's young and healthy and strong, a Gauleiter with an eye for beauty may decide she is a perfect specimen for one of their experimental camps. [. . .] Two, three, four, five years from now they may ship American girls to some far corner of the earth . . . may select your daughter . . . if *you* relax, if *you* fail to do your part now. If you say, hopefully, 'It can't happen here. We can't lose.'" But would such copy motivate people to do their part or simply paralyze them with fright? If not fully answered, that question has at least been addressed.

The mastermind behind the American Locomotive ads was Walter Weir, chief copywriter at the Kenyon & Eckhardt agency. Weir is said to have "pioneered the movement for emotionalism in war copy," but he dismissed nostalgic or romantic emotion as "gooey, soggy, sentimental nonsense," in favor of his own brand of scare tactics (Fox 35; Weir in *Printers' Ink* 7 Jan. 1944: 104). When the trade magazine *Advertising & Selling* gave out its 1942 Annual Advertising Awards, the Medal Award for Advertising as a Social Force went to the advertiser and ad agency (as it did in all categories) American Locomotive and Kenyon & Eckhardt, not to Weir as creator of the ads' concept and, presumably, writer of their copy. As a sidebar, Weir himself served on the nineteen-person judging panel (*Advertising & Selling* Feb. 1943: 4); one just hopes he was "out of the room," so to speak, when the panel voted to give his ads the Social Force Medal. Part of the judges' rationale for awarding the Medal to these ads was that "by blasting apathy [they would] dispose readers to all war action in other advertising or public appeals and put them in a frame of mind to accept in good spirit any necessary sacrifice" (8).

Although the awards panel felt these ads would have a positive effect

A HIGH HONOR FOR YOUR DAUGHTER

THE NAZIS look upon us as a degenerate nation. But they have a great respect for our accomplishments. And, if they win, they may decide that we have something in our blood which they can use in building their master race.

For they're great believers in eugenics, these Nazis. They're strong for selective breeding.

You they may cast aside and put to some ignominious task, such as scrubbing the sidewalks or sweeping the streets. But your daughter...well, if she's young and healthy and strong, a Gauleiter with an eye for beauty may decide she is a perfect specimen for one of their experimental camps.

A high honor for your daughter...

Does this seem a story spun in the realm of fantasy? It isn't. It is now happening, all through

Europe. The latest experiment of the victorious Nazis has been to ship Austrian and Hungarian girls to the Northern countries. The result of these unions...unblessed, of course, by matrimony...will not be known for some time. But the Nazis, you must admit, are not above innovation.

Two, three, four, five years from now they may ship American girls to some far corner of the earth ...may select your daughter...if *you* relax, if *you* fail to do your part now. If you say, hopefully, "It can't happen here. We can't lose."

No, we can't lose. We can't afford to. We must not. Else all the terrors, all the degradation, all the misery and suffering that have been loosed upon Europe will be loosed upon us. We of all people will not escape it. We shall be the chosen...we

shall be the elect...in the Nazi scheme of things.

We who have only just begun to win. We who risk the danger of resting on our new-won laurels and considering the job done.

This is no time to relax. This is the time...the opportune time...to do all we can to get this war over sooner.

We *must* measure up to the job!

AMERICAN LOCOMOTIVE

30 CHURCH ST., NEW YORK, N. Y. • MANUFACTURERS
OF TANKS • GUN CARRIAGES • ARMY AND NAVY
ORDNANCE • STEAM AND DIESEL LOCOMOTIVES

FIGURE II

on readers, the copy in every one of them contains a fatal flaw in the most critical place of all, the very end. All the ads include some variation of the thought put forth in the earliest in the series, the hangman ad, that we can lose the war, "Unless we do not wait to be *told* what to do, but to go out and *find out for ourselves* what to do, and *do* it." There are two problems here. In the first place, few readers would have known that early in the war just where to go on their own in order to help the war effort. And, more tellingly, such a remark effectively abrogates advertising's historical role of getting people to act in some concrete way (usually by buying a product) as well as its wartime charge of informing the public where to go and how to become involved by vividly providing information, reasons, and above all, motivation for getting involved. In effect, then, the ending of each ad renders its supposed call for action ineffectual.

The history of the American Locomotive ads and the magazines may shed some light on whether Weir's scare copy and art were effective or a case of overkill, though, granted, some of what follows is necessarily conjectural in the absence of concrete information. According to the awards citation, a "concentrated 18-week campaign [. . .] to appear in three national weeklies was decided upon" (*Advertising & Selling* Feb. 1943: 8). This did not mean eighteen different ads; advertisers rarely placed ads in national magazines more than once, occasionally twice a month. I turned up just six different ads, or one roughly every three weeks, over eighteen weeks, from the first in *Life* on November 30, 1942, to the last in the *Post* on April 3, 1943. The "three national weeklies" presumably referred to *Life, Collier's* and the *Post*, although only *Life* ran the complete series; just random ads from the group were scattered in the other two magazines. The first ad also appeared simultaneously with *Life* in *Time*, but *Time* published no more after that. The implications, again purely conjecturally, are several. Most simply, perhaps Kenyon & Eckhardt and American Locomotive originally bought space in *Time* for the ad, thought better of it, and dropped plans for the rest of the series to appear there. Or, perhaps the readership or publisher of *Time* found the tone and tenor of the ad so off-putting that pressure was brought to bear on the advertiser not to run the rest of the series in that magazine. And, perhaps, something similar may have accounted for the appearance of only selected ads from the series showing up in the *Post* and *Collier's* for fear of offending the magazines' readers, especially their subscribers. Whatever the case, the magazine-reading public apparently did not find the American Locomotive series as compelling or desirable an approach to wartime advertising as did the ad industry itself.

Frank W. Fox tries to make the case that Weir's scare tactic "contribution was significant," concluding that "By war's end Walter Weir and his talented copywriters could look back and claim [. . .] the distinction—and with considerable justification—of having altered the entire course of advertising development" (58). But Fox's words ring hollow since he provides no documentation and cites no examples of Weir's influence in other war ad copy. The reason for this is simple: Weir's approach in fact had no appreciable effect on the copywriters of ads in major magazines. Not just in motivational advertising but in every class of war ads, the "gooey, soggy sentimental type," the humorous type, and the reasoned, rational type predominated. So although Fox fills two pages with hosannas to Walter Weir as the patron saint of scare tactic advertising, Weir's legacy in fact had no legitimate heirs.

This is not to say that there were no brutally frank, tough-talking ads within the motivational group as elsewhere, but their approach was to motivate through guilt rather than through fear. Some of these ads had tremendous power, while others descended into the depths of bad taste. Within the space of five weeks in 1943, for example, the Magazine Publishers of America placed one ad of each type in *Collier's*. The ad on February 13, 1943, featured a half-page, thoroughly realistic drawing of a dead American soldier lying face down, one hand clawing the ground, the other arm draped lifelessly over his machine gun, followed by the caption "What did *you* do today . . . for Freedom?" (71). The copy would have been strong and effective enough had it stopped right there, but it spent a few more words elaborating on this message: "Today, at the front, he died . . . Today, what did *you* do? Next time you see a list of dead and wounded, ask yourself: 'What have *I* done today for freedom? What can I do tomorrow that will *save* the lives of men like this and help them win the war?" In small type at the bottom, the ad urges people to join the Citizens Service Corps, a branch of Civilian Defense Councils. There's no arguing with the fact that this ad contained a powerful message powerfully delivered.

But five weeks later, on March 20, the Magazine Publishers of America couldn't leave well enough alone. At the top of the ad is another pitch for citizen involvement, but the eye immediately runs to the color illustration filling the space just beneath it (see fig. 12). Lying face up this time

It is not pleasant to have your peaceful life upset by wartime needs and restrictions and activities. . . . It is not pleasant to die, either. . . . Between you who live at home and the men who die at the front there is a direct connection. . . . By your actions, definitely, a certain number of these men will die or they will come through alive. If you do everything you can to hasten victory and do every bit of it as fast as you can . . . then, sure as fate you will save the lives of some men who will otherwise die because you let the war last too long. . . . Think it over. Till the war is won you cannot, in fairness to them, complain or waste or shirk. Instead, you will apply every last ounce of your effort to getting this thing done. . . . In the name of God and your fellow man, that is your job.

BY HIS DEEDS . . .
MEASURE YOURS

The civilian war organization needs your help. The Government has formed Citizens Service Corps as part of local Defense Councils. If such a group is at work in your community, cooperate with it to the limit of your ability. If none exists, help to organize one. A free booklet telling you what to do and how to do it will be sent to you at no charge if you will write to this magazine. This is your war. Help win it. Choose what you will do — now!

EVERY CIVILIAN A FIGHTER

CONTRIBUTED BY THE MAGAZINE PUBLISHERS OF AMERICA

FIGURE 12

is another dead GI, unshaven, bare chest and arms exposed, rifle lying across his body, his arms outstretched, bloody palms up, with barbed wire encircling his head; in the background, as if this weren't enough, is a broken cross also entangled in barbed wire; the caption, superimposed on the picture itself, reads, "BY HIS DEEDS . . . MEASURE YOURS" (78). Without meaning to belittle the ultimate sacrifice made by so many American servicemen, still, for an ad to equate the death of each individual GI with the Messianic sacrifice of Jesus Christ is at the very least tasteless and, for some, blasphemous.

The American Values Americans Valued

"I saw a little old cabin and the river that flowed by the door / And I heard a voice within me whisper / THIS IS WORTH FIGHTING FOR." This is the second stanza of "This Is Worth Fighting For," a song with lyrics by Edgar De Lange and music by Sam H. Stept that in the late summer months of 1942 had strong sheet music sales and successful recordings by both Kate Smith and Jimmy Dorsey's orchestra with Bob Eberly's vocal. Like the most effective motivational war ads touching on American values, the song "brings the lofty abstractions of democracy, freedom, liberty, [and] 'the American way of life' down to a very immediate level in the tangible manifestations of what a man and his family had worked hard to achieve for themselves" (Jones 121). Evidently, both America's songwriters and copywriters were attuned to what personally touched average home front Americans as the most meaningful reasons for fighting and winning the war. As early as April 10, 1942, one of the pundits at the advertising trade journal *Printers' Ink* understood that this was the route for admen to take: "This is not a job that will be accomplished by flag-waving so much as by simple, little things" (36). Over the course of the war the volume of motivational ads stressing the small but precious aspects of life that Americans most valued proved the pundit right, as did the even larger body of ads designed to keep up home front morale (see Chapter 6). The content of all ads focusing on what Americans most valued is extremely similar, but the ads divide into two groups according to their points of view. The first group presents what we were fighting for through the eyes of a serviceman in combat. The second defines and describes the little but durable things that make America American from the perspective of the home front. There was also a small number of "seasonal" ads whose special character concludes this chapter.

Central to motivational ads featuring GIs overseas or away from home stateside are their thoughts and feelings about what they hope to find when, God willing, they return after an Allied victory. In the imaginations of copywriters and very likely in reality, these servicemen's ruminations almost universally run to sentiment and nostalgia. These emotions aren't portrayed as weak or unseemly, but as perfectly understandable in fighting men longing for what they miss and value most about their lives prior to the war: "It wasn't just a meal . . . that Sunday dinner back home, clear across the continent from here. It was more of a tradition. It stood for the family and the way we felt about one another . . . for all the feelings we didn't talk about" (Fred Harvey Restaurants, *Life* 11 Sept. 1944: 52). "Tell us how bright the dresses swirl when the girls go into Putnam's in the afternoon for a coke. . . . Tell us they're still beautiful, still true as they were two years . . . one hundred and four weeks . . . seven hundred and thirty days . . . seventeen thousand five hundred and twenty hours ago" (Nash, *Collier's* 14 Oct. 1944: 9). "If you mentioned home-made apple pie, or the nine o'clock show at the Colonial with his girl friend, or the gang harmonizing down on the corner, he'd grin — and understand. That's what he's fighting for. That's what he wants to come back to" (Acushnet Process Company, *Post* 25 March 1944: 84). An ad by Sergeant's Dog Medicines featured a nearly full-page illustration of a mother dog and her six puppies, the copy a letter from a GI to his mother saying that "what all of us are fighting to get back to [is] that world back home where a fellow can give the sort of welcome he ought to give to a litter of setter pups in the spring" (*Life* 29 May 1944: 11). Although rarely mentioned by name, what was most highly prized, deeply valued that these GIs were fighting for was *home*.

Home is also implied in a small number of ads from the fighting man's point of view not as the object of nostalgia but as a place where aspirations can be attained and a better future achieved, both equally worth fighting for: "I see new cities rising up . . . new farms . . . new roads, new homes, new schools . . . new factories that will plan and build for peace the way they planned and built for war. I see a place for me, and for the kids I'll have some day . . . a place for every man . . . a future to look forward to" (Nash-Kelvinator, *Collier's* 19 Aug. 1944: 8). A submariner knows he's fighting for "the right to stand up in the world with my bride by my side and her hand on my arm. [. . .] For the right every night to run up the steps of my house back home and pick up and hold a son of my own" (Nash-Kelvinator, *Time* 23 Aug. 1943: inside front cover). Behind such thoughts are the larger American values of freedom, liberty, and, in some of the ads, even a bit of borderline free enterprise, but because they were more vivid these concrete images were far more inspiring than a litany of the abstractions that define America.

Curiously, Frank W. Fox attempts to make a case from the nostalgia-based ads that American GIs were fighting, in essence, for stasis—for keeping everything about the America they loved absolutely unchanged (see 77–79). Yet less than ten pages later he discusses briefly those ads just mentioned focusing on a dynamic vision of progress and a better future for the United States, apparently seeing no inherent contradiction (see 86–87). And, of course, there really isn't one. Traditions, the familiar, and the comfortable in no way imply stasis or stagnation but a nurturing, warm environment within which the returning servicemen— and the country as a whole—could move forward to yet bigger and better things. That the two visions in fact complement rather than contradict each other was made patently clear in a Nash-Kelvinator ad in *Collier's* on June 26, 1943, when a fighter pilot thinks out loud, "Home to my town, to the house where I was born. And there I want to find everything the way it always was. *Everything!* I don't want anyone to take even a pennant from the wall in my old room . . . or change a single picture from where it's always hung! [. . .] Most of all, we want an America where we can look forward, as we always have, to better things. The same America we've always known . . . where you and I can plan and work and build our futures. . . . That's the America we're fighting for!" (9).

In the ads from the point of view of the home front, the most valued things are similar but given a somewhat different emphasis. For instance, traditions, both national and personal, figure large: an ad from the Miller Brewing Company in *Collier's* on the Fourth of July 1942 lists the "concert in the park—voices lifted in song and speech-making— gay basket picnics—friendliness and good fellowship" (53); and in *Life* on April 16, 1945, the United States Brewers Foundation extols "the friendly rivalry of an Iowa corn husking bee . . . the excitement of a Saturday afternoon yacht race . . . the love of home and the dreams we have of one day building our own" (45). The idea of the continuity of families through children resounds in a number of uncommonly striking ads. The copy accompanying a picture of a GI away stooping to admire a baby in a carriage says, "they're fighting so babies like these may have a safe world to grow up in" (Vanta Garments, *Ladies' Home Journal* Apr. 1943: 169). The illustration of a tousle-headed infant asleep in its crib captioned "ALL THE REASON WE NEED" is followed by "the main idea of this war is to give your Mary, and our Harry, the right, for always and always, to go to sleep unafraid" (Alcoa Aluminum, *Ladies' Home Journal* Dec. 1942: 63). And in a virtual classic of advertising art as inspiration (see fig. 13), the nearly full-page photo of two irresistible toddlers slurping milkshakes at a soda fountain says all it needs say along with its caption "THIS IS AMERICA * * * HELP PRESERVE IT" (Kendall Refining Company, *Post* 26 June 1943: 79).

As with servicemen away, home was for stateside Americans the most valued treasure and the strongest reason for fighting and winning the war. Copy written from the home front's perspective used the word "home" much more often than the ads written from servicemen's point of view. To a woman war worker boarding a bus to work, "home, you know, isn't just a place and a roof. It's love, and security, and freedom from fear and want and drudgery, and freedom itself!" (General Electric, *Post* 17 Apr. 1943: 45). "Home is where you hang your heart. Home with its trials and triumphs . . . its pride and humility . . . its secrets and its hopes . . . and the unshakeable loyalty of people who stick together. Today, it's home we're fighting for" (Canada Dry, *Ladies' Home Journal* Apr. 1943: 134). In an ad that combined a picture of the comfort and security of home with a vision of the future, a wife writes to her husband overseas, "A bright, sunny house that's a blend of old and new, with a white-shuttered door and a picket fence around a world all our own . . . A garden where you can dig while sunshine warms you through and through . . . and you're alive right down to your fingertips [. . .] when our days are filled with the peace of being together in our very own home . . . forever and ever" (Kelvinator, *Life* 16 Apr. 1945: 57). Sentimental? Of course, but for families separated by a global war this kind of honest sentiment and inspiration resonated deeply throughout the home front.

'Tis the Season

As in peacetime, for most Americans during the war the Christmas season was the most sentimental and inspirational (not to mention commercial). Wartime admen were cognizant of this; Christmas played a major role in the art and copy of 110 war ads in the leading national mag-

FIGURE 13

azines. Most of the Christmas messages were tied to a call for action such as giving War Bonds as gifts or giving blood. Other ads kept readers mindful of the war by suggesting the perfect gift for a special marine, a favorite WAC, or a cherished war worker, male or female. But there were also some single-mindedly inspirational Christmas war ads very much in a class by themselves.

Two Christmas ads one year apart each featured the Star of Bethlehem. The copy of both was half prayer, half Christmas greeting to servicemen everywhere: "On this Christmas . . . when so much of the world is still smothered 'neath the black robe of slavery . . . let the Lamp of Liberty burn brightly . . . to warm the hearts of all mankind . . . while we pray . . . that Christmas may be *Christmas* soon again!" (Rolex, *Esquire* Jan. 1944: 3); "Let's keep our eyes on that star with its promise of peace—another year and another Yuletide when again we will hear your familiar voice shouting 'Merry Christmas!'" (Studebaker, *Life* 20 Dec. 1943). In its minimalist simplicity, one ad that was an extraordinarily potent prayer let the art do most of the talking (see fig. 14). Stromberg-Carlson's Christmas ad on page 10 of *Collier's* for December 9, 1944, and on page 65 of the *Post* on December 16 was a large drawing of the head of a pigtailed little girl in front of a blue Service Star hanging in the window of her home, her hands pressed together in prayer. Above her in quotation marks indicating her own prayer was "GOD BLESS DADDY," and below without quotation marks, universalizing the thought, GOD BLESS THEM ALL!

Children have always been a big part of Christmas, and as in other ads expressing what Americans valued, children and the continuity of families had their place in Christmas war ads. The copy following a drawing of three small siblings in their nightclothes holding hands before a roaring fireplace includes the words "Christmas lives forever in the hearts of small children [. . .] because 'grown-up' men and women have sacrificed their lives and their fortunes that it may continue to live in the hearts of small children . . . forever" (Ball-Band Footwear, *Collier's* 23 Dec. 1944: 67). Beneath an illustration of a soldier lifting his infant son high in the air, the copy explains, "Christmas furlough, 1943 . . . a little fellow he's never seen [. . .] Ask this man, *any* man what he's fighting for. [. . .] It's families and homes" (North American Aviation, *Newsweek* 20 Dec. 1943: 45). There's that word again—home—the focal point of Christmas war ads even well after the war was won. In one a

.."GOD BLESS DADDY."...

GOD BLESS THEM ALL!...

STROMBERG-CARLSON

FIGURE 14

wife describes her feelings, and those of her returned GI husband: "This time, instead of a foxhole, there's a house hung with mistletoe. Instead of cordite, the fragrance of bayberry and balsam. Instead of a GI Santa, there's me in a red house coat [. . .] Because I know Bill as I know my heart, I can feel the magic of this Christmas Eve touching him as it touches me. Perhaps, in those other years we'd never have dared show we were sentimental" (International Sterling, *Life* 3 Dec. 1945: 62). This and many other Christmas war ads published after Victory make it plain that admen felt the idea of home and all it stood for continued to inspire Americans as the most precious and valued gift for which the war was fought and won.

But purely motivational ads aside, magazine advertising revealed its true power in the thousands of ads enlisting the home front's full and active participation in specific endeavors to support the fighting of the war—the kinds of ads that, by and large, fill all the remaining chapters.

"THE ARMS BEHIND THE ARMY" INDUSTRIAL SUPPORT OF THE WAR

Those Americans who worked in manufacturing and agriculture most materially supported the country's fighting forces, so it stands to reason that the dominant category of war ads in magazines—a category not in the War Advertising Council's five classes of ads (see Chapter 1)—was informational and institutional advertising placed for the most part by large manufacturing firms. To embellish a bit the definition in Chapter 1, institutional advertising "has the primary purpose of promoting the name, image, personnel, or reputation of a company, organization, or industry" and promotes "an institution or organization, rather than a product or service, in order to create public support and goodwill" ("Marketing Terms Dictionary"; "Texas Advertising"). Unlike war ads urging home front civilians to participate in the war effort, these ads mostly just described manufacturers' war work. Institutional ads outnumbered all other kinds dealing with industrial support of the war but barely touched the home front public at all. Still, they were war ads of a sort, but ones addressed by business to business, rather than to civilians at large. Such institutional ads are taken up here along with ads suggesting how companies, workers, and the public could help increase industrial productivity and efficiency. Only the many ads concerning women in war work are postponed to a later chapter of their own, and deservedly so.

Industry Speaks (About Itself)

Chester J. La Roche's damning of institutional war ads as "blatant brag advertising" (see Chapter 1) was especially courageous since this sort of copy mostly appeared in the ads of manufacturers engaged in war work, the single biggest category of war ads between 1942 and 1945, and, accordingly, one of the largest sources of advertising revenue. *Business Week* noted twice in three years that among war ads "industrial advertising predominates" and that "Institutional copy [. . .] constituted the most characteristic advertising in 1944 as it did in 1943" (12 Sept. 1942: 94; 20 Jan. 1945: 86). Of more than 5,000 war ads in ten leading national magazines, 1,525 or 31% were of the institutional kind.

Other voices within the ad industry also criticized the legitimacy of institutional ads. In an article titled "Opportunity!" in *Printers' Ink* on April 10, 1942, Walter Weir, then copy director at Lord & Thomas and prior to becoming the guru of scare copy, came down hard on institutional advertising when he wrote that "in all too many instances, advertising has become a skilled worker out of a job. Oh, certain jobs have been created for him, jobs to help keep himself fed, to give him something to do. They're called 'institutional' jobs" (13). Later in the war, in *Advertising & Selling*, Don Wharton quoted an unnamed adman on the matter of brag ads: "Why should industry arrogate credit to itself for doing its share in the war? Sure, the public wants to know of the inspiring war performance of industry, but can't we tell them the facts without a lot of back-slapping and self-congratulation?" (June 1944: 78). In fairness, overt brag ads were in the minority of wartime institutional advertising, but institutional ads of all stripes continued to pay a large part of Madison Avenue's bills and put bread on the tables of the admen (and very occasional women) who staffed the agencies.

A key reason for wartime institutional advertising was keeping brand consciousness alive both in the business community and among the public even though few consumer products were being made or sold. So too, public support and goodwill were acceptable functions of institutional war ads since these ads reinforced people's awareness of industry's role in fighting the war. Accordingly, at least as many institutional ads appeared in such popular weeklies as *Life, Collier's,* the *Post,* and *Look* (actually a biweekly) as in magazines with a larger proportion of readers from the business community—*Newsweek, Time,* and *Business Week.* Strategically, dominant among institutional ads in the popular magazines were those of companies that had a broad consumer market in peacetime—Westinghouse, General Electric, Philco, and other appliance manufacturers; Chevrolet, Studebaker, Packard, Dodge, and all the other major makes of automobiles; Texaco and Shell among the oil and gasoline refineries, and so forth.

Yet the Ford Motor Company was virtually absent from institutional advertising during the war. There are several possible reasons for this, all but Ford's own flimsy explanation equally plausible. Ford's *first* advertisement of any kind in *Life* after Pearl Harbor appeared only on May 29, 1944. It featured a charming illustration of an early Ford chugging along a snowy street in 1900 with awed spectators (and a horse) marveling at the contraption. Like the art, the ad's copy was historical except for the sentence "Much of the present news of Ford is 'restricted' for it has to do with the mass production of giant aircraft and other tools of victory" (9). This statement might have explained the absence of Ford institutional ads from *Life* since America entered the war—an absence that continued until the Allied victory—were it not that legions of institutional ads about the "restricted" war work of General Motors, the Chrysler Corporation, Studebaker, and other automobile manufacturers regularly ran in *Life* and the other major magazines. The ingenuousness of Ford's explanation renders it suspect. While they were only six, Ford did run institutional two-page spreads in the *Post*, *Look*, *Collier's*, and *Newsweek* describing, with lavish illustrations, the war work the company was engaged in.

Then too, the Ford Motor Company may not have wished to advertise its war work in the largest-circulating weekly because its mass production of B-24 bombers at the giant Willow Run plant near Ypsilanti, Michigan, wasn't going as well as popularly believed. After touring the plant as a consultant, Charles A. Lindbergh (a great admirer of Henry Ford) admitted, "I had to say bluntly that we were *not* making schedule and that the workmanship on the first bombers that went through Willow Run was the worst I had ever seen" (qtd. in Wallace 311–12). That, in fairness, was in 1942, before Willow Run bomber production had gotten up to speed, averaging about one plane per hour.

The most compelling reason for the absence of Ford informational ads from *Life* for the duration was Henry Ford himself. In the words of latter-day automobile magnate Lee Iacocca, Ford's antisemitism is "now a matter of historical record" to the extent that Ford spent the prewar years and beyond "canonizing Adolf Hitler" (Iacocca 9). As early as 1922, the *New York Times* reported that Ford "was financing Adolph Hitler's nationalist and anti-Semitic movements in Munich." In 1938, after Hitler came to power, Ford "became the first American recipient of the Grand Cross of the Supreme Order of the German Eagle, created by Adolf Hitler a year earlier as the highest honor Germany could give a distinguished foreigner" (Sutton 90, 92; Wallace 145). Furthermore, while it remains unclear how much of this was known and by whom while the war was on, it has since been verified that at the very time Ford plants in the United States were manufacturing tanks, jeeps, and B-24s for the American military, a number of Ford's holdings in Europe—some still with a strong if clandestine American interest—were turning out trucks and cars for the German army, with the effect that "the Ford Motor Company worked on both sides in World War II" (Sutton 97).

How all this helps to explain the absence of Ford informational ads from *Life* is, admittedly, conjectural, but all the possibilities are plausible. First, given Henry Ford's own ambivalence about the two sides fighting the war, he may not have wanted to have splashed across the pages of the largest and most liberal popular weekly magazine ads proclaiming his extensive support of the American armed forces. Then too, *Life*, being privy to Ford's antisemitism and mutual admiration relationship with Hitler, may have declined to accept institutional advertising from the Ford Motor Company since Ford's views were hardly in keeping with the magazine's own. Finally, another possible reason for the Ford vacuum in *Life* has nothing whatever to do with Henry Ford's politics and biases. With its enormous volume of automobile sales before the war and the Ford name indelibly engraved on the American consciousness, the company may have simply decided that keeping its name before the public during the war was unnecessary. Whatever the actual reason for it, the absence of Ford Motor Company informational ads from *Life* remains the single greatest mystery about wartime institutional advertising.

But there was nothing mysterious about the character and appeal of the best institutional ads placed by makers of consumer products in magazines with a largely consumer audience. Eye-catching art and comparatively brief, crisp copy were the order of the day, as typified by a Chrysler ad in *Life* on December 6, 1943. The content of the ad was serious, explaining how the Chrysler Division of the Chrysler Corporation found a solution to unreliable tank engines, but the presentation bordered on the whimsical: six cartoon-like drawings were accompanied by short sentences in large type in the manner of a "Dick and Jane" primer, starting with "This is a Tank" (14; see fig. 15). Other institutional ads by automobile manufacturers took a more wholly serious approach in both the copy and art, as in Cadillac's ad on page 50 of *Life* on May 1, 1944, explaining in layman's language the company's role in making parts for the Allison engines that powered the Army Air Force fighter planes in the illustration.

This is a Tank.

Without an Engine
it's not much good...

Last year we
needed hundreds

of very high
powered Engines
for Tanks

But there was
none ready

and it would take
months to develop
new Engines!

This is the
amazing Engine

that came to
the Rescue...

It is made of
5 Engines.

The very same
Engines
you get in a
Chrysler car...

It works perfectly.
Even when

2 Engines are
knocked out—
the Tank keeps
rolling along!

This Engine
was developed
and built by
Chrysler Division

WAR PRODUCTS OF CHRYSLER DIVISION
Industrial Engines • Marine Engines
Marine Tractors • Navy Pontoons
Harbor Tugs • Anti-Aircraft Cannon
Parts•Tank EngineAssemblies•Tank
Parts • Airplane Wing Panels • Fire-
Fighting Equipment • Air Raid Sirens
Gun Boxes • Searchlight Reflectors.

CHRYSLER

DIVISION OF CHRYSLER CORPORATION

The nation-wide Chrysler Dealer
Organization offers owners
service facilities to meet their
wartime transportation needs.

|BACK THE ATTACK WITH WAR BONDS!

FIGURE 15. Reprinted by permission of Chrysler LLC.

Of makers of consumer products other than automobiles, the Philco Corporation deserves a prize for the sheer entertainment value of its institutional ads. The copy was invariably a longish straightforward account of the ways in which Philco was producing for the war, but each full-page black and white ad featured a large Axis-bashing cartoon by a leading editorial cartoonist, including such eminent names as Arthur Szyk and Rube Goldberg. The tone of the cartoons ran from the macabre to the patriotic to the outright hilarious, as each one took its own tack on how American industrial (and, occasionally, agricultural) production was fighting the Axis. Full-sized reproductions of each were available from Philco for the asking. Typical of the more than sixty such ads illustrated by over twenty different cartoonists is the one in *Life* on May 18, 1942. The drawing by Rollin Kirby depicts Hitler spouting from a soapbox, "Democracies can't organize for war," with Tojo sniveling on his right, and, on his left, Mussolini shining Der Fuehrer's shoes. A huge bomb labeled "All-Out American Production" is heading toward them from the rear (3; see fig. 16). How many on the home front actually read the fairly dense Philco copy will never be known, but the cartoons became wartime collectibles.

It wasn't manufacturers of consumer goods alone that placed institutional ads in popular magazines during the war, but also other major companies whose names the public would have recognized even though Mr. or Mrs. Home Front would never have been likely to buy an airplane from Boeing, Lockheed, or Martin Aircraft, a steam engine from American Locomotive, airplane parts from Thompson Products, or naval craft from Electric Boat. And even though more and more people had telephones in their homes, they didn't buy them as they would in future decades but, in effect, leased them from the Bell Telephone System (AT&T) when they signed up for phone service. Still, Western Electric, the manufacturing arm of Bell, went all-out in placing some of the war's most graphically exciting institutional ads, such as that in *Collier's* on August 5, 1944, to which U.S. Navy Combat Artist Dwight Shepler contributed his painting "Air Defense—South Pacific" dramatically depicting a naval engagement of an American battleship and fighter planes (7; see fig. 17).

These kinds of industries sometimes also ran ads in popular magazines urging citizen support for the war effort, as will be seen in later chapters. But one major manufacturer, and one alone, was remarkably

"Don't look now boys, but…"

THIS impression by Rollin Kirby is the first of a series that is being posted before the workers of the Philco factories who are helping to produce the weapons of victory . . . a reminder of the glorious purpose of their labors . . . an expression of the spirit that spurs them on. *"More . . . Better . . . Sooner"* is their goal!

* * *

Today, Philco's soldiers of industry are devoted to the production of communications equipment, radios for tanks and airplanes, artillery fuzes and shells for the service of our armed forces . . . doing their part to give our men at the front not only the vast superiority in equipment that America's mass production experts can produce, but also *new* weapons of victory, yet unknown to the world, that America's industrial scientists can devise.

Out of this inspired and unrelenting effort comes an abiding faith in victory and the survival of the American way of life. And with it . . . *new hope for the future!* For some good comes out of all this excess of human effort devoted to the evil ways of war. Scientific progress moves on at breakneck speed. Some of our greatest scientific achievements for the enjoyment of peace . . . radio as we know it today, the modern airplane . . . have emerged from the stress of war.

Today, in the closely guarded walls of the Philco laboratories, engineers have already worked out problems of

tremendous importance to the ways of peace. Others are in the making that will cause the evil of these stormy days to live only in the history books of future generations and the good survive in the abundant joys of their daily lives.

This is Philco's hope, faith . . . and *pride* for the future!

Free Limited Offer . . . While available, a full size reproduction of the original drawing by Rollin Kirby will be furnished gladly upon request. Simply address Philco Corporation, Philadelphia, Penna., and ask for Cartoon Number 2D.

PHILCO CORPORATION

Through its national service organizations, Philco offers to its millions of owners throughout the land, at uniform and reasonable charges, the means of conserving and prolonging the use and enjoyment of Philco Products.

**RADIOS, PHONOGRAPHS, REFRIGERATORS
AIR CONDITIONERS, RADIO TUBES, PARTS**

INDUSTRIAL STORAGE BATTERIES FOR MOTIVE POWER,
SIGNAL SYSTEMS, CONTROL AND AUXILIARY POWER

FIGURE 16

"Air Defense—South Pacific," by Dwight Shepler, U. S. Navy Combat Artist

Nerve Systems for Battle Wagons

When a U. S. warship goes into action, officers must make split-second decisions—men must receive their orders instantly. Throughout the battle, orders and reports—coordinating all activities—are flashed by telephone.

The huge battleship *"Wisconsin"* has as many telephones as a city of 10,000 inhabitants. Two separate systems were supplied by Western Electric.

1. *The sound powered telephone system*, with 2200 instruments connecting all battle stations. These battle phones operate on cur-

rent *generated by the speaker's voice*, so damage to the ship's electrical system cannot interrupt communications.

2. *The battle announcing system*, with 20 transmitter stations and over 300 loudspeakers to broadcast orders in a giant voice.

All this for just *one* battleship! Carriers, cruisers, destroyers, submarines, merchant ships, too, must have telephone equipment.

Skill acquired in years of experience as manufacturer of all kinds of equipment for the Bell Telephone System has been turned to making

vast quantities of telephone, radio, radar and other specialized apparatus for use on land, at sea and in the air. Western Electric is today the nation's largest producer of electronic and communications equipment for war.

To speed Victory, buy War Bonds regularly!

Western Electric
IN PEACE...SOURCE OF SUPPLY FOR THE BELL SYSTEM
IN WAR...ARSENAL OF COMMUNICATIONS EQUIPMENT.

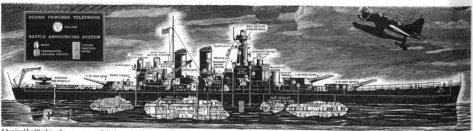

A typical battleship, showing some of the important battle telephone stations and units of the battle announcing system. We cannot show all—there are more than 2,500!

FIGURE 17. Reprinted with permission of Lucent Technologies Inc./Bell Labs.

consistent in its devotion to strictly informational advertising. Boeing, maker of such aircraft as the B-17 Flying Fortress, and, later, the B-29 Superfortress, placed forty-three institutional ads in magazines, almost all of them in *Life*, between June 1942 and August 1945. Two-thirds of each ad was taken up with a vivid black-and-white illustration or photograph of Boeing's products or their manufacture, the rest very cogent copy about how Boeing solved problems and created precisely the kinds of aircraft the military needed. Typical of the impressive artwork was the picture of a fleet of B-29s flying past Japan's Mount Fujiyama in an ad that prophetically just happened to appear in *Life* on August 6, 1945, the very day that the Enola Gay, the most famous B-29 of all, dropped the first atomic bomb on Hiroshima (12; see fig. 18). In one detail this ad, like many other institutional ones including some just mentioned, was not strictly speaking just informational. Each contained, usually in tiny type, a one-sentence Plug in a Plug for some kind of home front support, usually War Bonds. But, again, "according to advertising men, these plugs [were] nearly worthless" (Wharton 146). Under the picture of the B-29s in the Boeing ad appeared "Finish the Fight—with War Bonds," the Cadillac ad urged at the bottom "LET'S ALL BACK THE ATTACK," the Chrysler ad, "BACK THE ATTACK WITH WAR BONDS," and the Western Electric ad, *"To speed Victory, buy War Bonds regularly!"* But since such urgings in small type were easy to miss, all such ads remained first and foremost institutional advertising.

One other species of informational advertising appeared almost exclusively in magazines with a wide business and industry readership. These were ads placed not by companies generally familiar to the public, but by manufacturers of machine tools, other equipment, and parts that went into the making of war materiel by the better-known companies. The firms that placed such ads were hardly household words to the home front public: Worthington Pump & Machinery Corporation, Rheem Manufacturing Company, Marmon-Herrington, Bundy Tubing, Boots Aircraft Nut Corporation, and many others. Their ads filled the pages of *Time*, *Newsweek*, *Business Week*, and *Fortune* alongside ads from the kinds of manufacturers just discussed. With their illustrations or photographs of arcane parts, weapons of war, or manufacturing processes, these ads look pretty much like those by more familiar companies. The difference is in the copy—often more voluminous and certainly more technical. Although such ads were of an institutional character, it could be argued

Finish the Fight—with War Bonds

Peacemakers

Peace in the Pacific can be achieved in only one way – by the unconditional surrender of Japan's military masters.

To shorten the road to victory, our leaders foresaw that we must do more than reconquer territory island by island. *We must knock out the enemy's ability to make war.* And to carry out that strategy they chose the Boeing B-29 as our major weapon.

Built, tested and flown into combat under the terrific pressure of global war, the Superfortresses are doing all that was expected of them and more.

They have enabled us to reduce American casualties and save precious months in striking enemy war production, because they are the only aircraft in the world that can cover the vast distances from bases in the Marianas.

In early operations before present island bases were secured, they transported their own supplies over the "Hump" from India into China. They have not only reduced the output of Japan's war industries by the steadily mounting tempo of their bombing but have taken a huge toll of the fighter

planes sent against them. And they have tightened the blockade on enemy ports by sowing mines.

The versatile efficiency of the B-29 reflects Boeing's unparalleled experience in designing and building four-engine aircraft, and it forecasts the same qualities in the great Boeing planes of the future.

• • •

The performance of the B-29 stems directly from Boeing principles of research, design, engineering, manufacture. In peace, as today, you can count on any airplane "Built by Boeing" to lead the way.

DESIGNERS OF THE B-29 SUPERFORTRESS · THE FLYING FORTRESS · THE NEW STRATOCRUISER
THE KAYDET TRAINER · THE STRATOLINER · PAN AMERICAN CLIPPERS **BOEING**

FIGURE 18

that, however indirectly, they were also selling their products to the manufacturers of guns, planes, tanks, and the rest, if only via government contracts.

Justifiable Pride

A little flag that appeared in numerous industrial advertisements had great meaning for thousands of companies engaged in war work. This banner was the visible symbol of the Army–Navy E Award that the two branches of the armed forces began granting for excellence (the "E") in war production in July 1942. By the third anniversary of the program in August 1945 "the award had been granted to 4,044 plants. Of these, 2,782 were nominated by the Army, and 1,262 by the Navy," with another 134 awards belatedly given after the termination of the program on September 7, 1945 (*Business Week* 18 Aug. 1945: 51; 15 Sept. 1945: 56). These numbers reveal that war production truly was the business of the nation for the duration, since recipients of the flags represented only about 4½% of all companies engaged in war work. In addition to flying their flags above factories, refineries, and shipyards, some companies made the Army–Navy E the centerpiece of magazine advertisements, while others found at least a small space for it in their ads. But all to little avail. *Business Week* reported on June 5, 1943, that a survey "found 257 Army–Navy E advertisements appearing in national weekly magazines to be definitely below average observation compared with all war-effort advertising. In most cases, these ads were lower in interest and observation than other advertisements placed by the same companies" (96). Yet this assessment apparently meant next to nothing to the recipients of E Awards, since such ads continued to proliferate as more and more companies received an award right to the end of the war.

But another sort of "pride ad," for want of a better term, had the capacity to touch the home front more closely and deeply than those just flaunting firms' bragging rights for production awards. These were ads by companies that publicly acknowledged their pride in their employees, those still in the workplace and those in the military. These ads were inherently more human and humanizing for the average magazine reader and also much more varied in their art and copy than E Award ads. Among ads honoring workers in the service, for example, was a brief all-text piece by General American Transportation that actually downplayed its right to boast about its war production, headed

"YES, WE'RE DOING WAR WORK, BUT WHAT OF IT?" and continuing "We don't pat ourselves on the back for doing something expected of us. But we do take pride in our 2017 employees in service, and we honor the memory of 31 who have given their lives. No matter how much war work *we* do, it is nothing to what *they* have done" (*Time* 11 June 1945: 83). Similarly, Bell Telephone depicted its little "telephone man"—a product icon as familiar then as the Campbell Soup Kids or, later, the Pillsbury Doughboy—saluting a Service Flag bearing the numbers of Bell employees in the military (46,200) and the casualties among them (64) (*Farm Journal* June 1943: 57). And Weirton Steel in a single ad paid tribute to both its men still in the mills and those in the service by saying, "Twelve thousand Weirton Steel employees have kept faith with their 34 fellow-workers who have made the supreme sacrifice in dying for victory. Weirton people are determined to continue keeping the faith with the 3802 Weirton Steel men and all Americans who today are in the armed forces" (*Newsweek* 24 July 1944: 47).

Other companies expressed their pride in the work being done by their employees on the home front alone. "The Jeep Calls Them Daddy" proclaimed the headline of an ad by Willys-Overland paying specific and special tribute to the company's automotive engineers (*Look* 2 June 1942: 3), and Studebaker began its tribute to plant employees with "SALUTE the arms behind the army" for "Still giving more than we promise" (*Look* 10 Feb. 1942: 5). As for giving more than promised, the Package Machinery Company of Springfield, Massachusetts, singled out one stand-out employee, Ray Wood, for logging 120 production hours in a single week, holding him up as an exemplar to workers everywhere (*Newsweek* 11 Jan. 1943: 10). Even companies not directly engaged in war manufacture took out advertising space to acknowledge the special contributions of their employees in wartime. Beneath a large drawing of an operator wearing her headset and the caption "HER BIGGEST JOB IS WAR," Bell Telephone simply described her and her compatriots: "Calm in emergencies, capable and courteous, the telephone operators are earning a nation's thanks for a job well done" (*Life* 27 March 1944: 3). Waitresses too came in for their share of public recognition and praise. Fred Harvey restaurants and dining cars daily served "tens of thousands of meals" to GIs traveling by rail across the country, so on page 19 of *Life* on May 15, 1944, the restaurant chain saluted the thousands of "Harvey Girls" who cheerfully and efficiently shouldered this extra burden of service while continuing to serve the public.

But easily the most distinctive of the employee tributes was the six-ad series by Revere Copper and Brass, each ad saluting an actual immigrant worker or one from a racial minority—one British, one Hungarian, one Italian, two Polish (one of them a woman), and, in the last of the series, an African American, each of whom had worked at Revere for two decades or more. Richly illustrated with photographs of these men and woman's family life as well as their work for Revere, and naming their names, the ads featured a long quotation from each about what Revere had given him or her materially and spiritually in getting a leg up in the United States. In a sense, then, the ads were a tribute to the company as well as to the singled-out employees. The final ad, in *Life* on September 27, 1943, presented William Hayes, a black who, among other things, was able to buy a house and small farm from his earnings at Revere. It is especially notable for being not just one of the rare war ads to include an African American at all, but also for doing so without humor, condescension, or racial stereotyping.

Helping Industry Help the War

According to numerous articles in the national press, the single biggest cause of slowdowns (or "bottlenecks") and inefficiency in war plants was worker absenteeism. War ads did what they could to help combat it in various ways. Such articles, especially in *Business Week*, began early in the war and showed that while expected absences from work due to illness normally ran to about 2.5%, in any given month of 1942 and 1943 the absentee rate in various war industries ranged between 5.4% and 10%. Translated into man-hours of work, these seemingly low percentages showed that absenteeism accounted for a tremendous loss of production time and productivity. Aside from illness and accidents—legitimate and excused reasons for absenteeism—the biggest cause was what today we would call unexcused "personal days" taken by employees without company permission. Among men these included recovering from a hangover after a weekend or the day after payday, and among women, taking "a day off now and then to go to the beauty shop or buy a new dress" (*Business Week* 21 Nov. 1942: 42). While much of the advertising industry's time and creativity went into addressing absenteeism in company house organs, posters, and employee newsletters, admen also expended some of their effort on magazine ads to make the general public aware of this critical situation and ways of coping with it.

Most ads addressing absenteeism were by advertisers still with something to sell, whether to industry or to the home front at large, and offering their products to help cope with the problem. Only one ad was a purely cautionary warning against absenteeism. On May 22, 1943, the Carrier air conditioning and refrigeration company placed an ad in the *Post* in which the large helmeted head of a soldier peers over the edge of his foxhole to say, "Having trouble, Civilian? So am I! . . . But we're not doing much talking about it. And yet, I'd like to say to all America—LOST HOURS in the plant may mean LAST HOURS for us!" (64). The product ads themselves never appeared specious or far-fetched merely in an effort to sell the advertisers' goods. All were in the field of health and hygiene, and all made a perfectly plausible case for the products helping to reduce absenteeism because of illness. A small ad for Kleenex in *Look* on April 23, 1942, began "DON'T BE A PUBLIC ENEMY—Be patriotic and smother sneezes with Kleenex to help keep colds from spreading to defense workers. America needs every man—*full time*!" (4). A Listerine Antiseptic ad in *Look* on April 3, 1945, not only proclaimed the benefit of its product but also listed several ways for war workers to prevent catching cold (3), while Dixie Cups harkened back to the killer influenza of 1918, saying, "It happened then . . . it could happen NOW!" and discussed how to prevent the spread of disease in war plants (*Life* 7 Dec. 1942: 53). In yet more detail, Kotex placed a frank ad addressed to women war workers headed "I was an absentee 3 days each month" in the *Ladies' Home Journal* for November 1943. The copy not only provided a few guidelines for relieving the discomfort of their menstrual period, but also invited women to write for a more extensive free booklet called "That Day Is Here Again" containing information on such things as proper diet, exercise, and sleep for coping with "problem days" and avoiding absenteeism (59). This ad, incidentally, included virtually no direct selling of Kotex. Typical of product ads addressed to industry was a long, irregular series from the Scott Paper Company for its ScotTissue [sic] Towels headed "THE MISSING MAN." Each ad included a photo of men at work in a war plant, but with a white "hole" in the picture outlining where an absent worker should be. These ads cited some scary statistics, as on March 2, 1942, in *Time*: "HIS ILLNESS ads up a daily loss equal to 10,000 MACHINE GUNS!" and "Absences were cut 29.7% in companies which established health programs." Only later did Scott suggest how its paper towels could help prevent the spread of disease and, hence, absenteeism (60).

Even scarier were statistics about industrial accidents. Historian Geof-frey Perrett observed that by the end of the war nearly 300,000 workers died in industrial accidents, more than a million were permanently dis-abled, and three million others "nursed lesser wounds" (399). While the war was still on, Madison Avenue of course didn't have these staggering figures in the aggregate, but those that admen had they put to good use in some grimly effective copy: "IN TWELVE MONTHS, industrial ac-cidents cost America a billion and a half man-hours—enough work-ing time to build 45 battleships or 195,000 light tanks or 15,000 heavy bombers!" (Hartford Insurance, *Collier's* 31 Jan. 1942: 37). "Yes, 11,600 workers killed or injured in accidents— *every day!* Hard to believe, isn't it? But the figures are there—a total of 23,500 dead and 2,000,000 in-jured in the first six months of this year!" (International Nickel Com-pany, *Time* 19 Oct. 1942: 93). Ads reeling off this grisly string of figures sold no products. Instead they warned industry about the problem, sug-gested safety education programs for workers, or recommended means of combating industrial accidents like installing "safety guards wherever needed," having "proper lighting and ventilation," and keeping "prem-ises free of rubbish" (from the Hartford ad).

Throughout the war a major concern of the federal government was proper nutrition, not just for the armed forces but equally for the home front in general and war workers in particular. While eating healthy could only indirectly help prevent industrial accidents and somewhat more directly aid in reducing absenteeism caused by illness, a proper diet went a long way toward maximizing workers' energy, strength, effi-ciency, and, above all, productivity. But, by and large, the America of the 1940s was not an especially healthy-eating America. To get the home front with its millions of war workers to change eating habits was just the job for the marshaled forces of the ad industry, with the War Adver-tising Council leading the charge. As it has continued to do ever since, the government divided what the home front and military should eat into essential food groups, although by today's standards some of the wartime groupings and the absence of recommended daily portions look naive at best. Unlike today's food pyramid, when the Department of Agriculture's National Nutrition Program redefined the groups late in 1942, it designed their visual presentation as items in a circle surround-ing the Program's logo and its watchword "U.S. NEEDS US STRONG— EAT THE BASIC 7 EVERY DAY" without any indication of how much to eat from each group. Clockwise from the top, the groups were (1) green and yellow vegetables, (2) oranges, tomatoes, grapefruit, (3) potatoes and other vegetables and fruits, (4) milk and milk products, (5) meat, poultry, fish, and eggs, (6) bread, flour, and cereals, and (7) butter and fortified spreads (i.e., margarine—included for the first time because of the butter shortage and rationing). Below the circle, "as a tipoff to what the realists in drive headquarters hope to accomplish," were the words "In addition to the basic 7 . . . eat any other foods you want" (*Business Week* 3 Apr. 1943: 58).

Needless to say, the makers of food products of actual or dubious nutritional value had a field day touting their wares' role in proper nutrition, only the rare advertiser simply promoting the program. One of those rare few, in a richly humorous and informative ad in *Collier's* on December 19, 1942, was Borden. Again Elsie, the intrepid Borden spokescow, rose to the occasion of lucidly explaining a seemingly difficult matter as she, her grouchy husband Elmer, and her chirpily inquisitive calf Beulah went grocery shopping. In less than two columns of copy and six wonderfully funny pictures, Elsie managed to lay out all the elements of the nutrition program in a way anyone on the home front could understand. And as a display of wartime advertising as goodwill, the final line is noteworthy: "Elsie says: *'We at the Borden Company are so enthusiastic about the National Nutrition Program that we're using this space to tell you about it, instead of talking about our products'*" (20; see fig. 19).

The appliance manufacturer Westinghouse went above and beyond by not only promoting the government's nutrition program in ads but also through its Health for Victory Clubs, a hands-on face-to-face nutrition education program for war workers, their wives, and others. The primary goals of the Clubs were "improving the diet of war workers" and stressing "the importance of careful food preparation as well as careful food selection" through monthly meal-planning guides and meetings of the wives with home economists from local utility companies—and "Westinghouse appliances [were] not mentioned anywhere" in the literature or at the meetings (*Business Week* 4 July 1942: 28). To publicize its war worker nutrition program, Westinghouse mounted a saturation ad campaign between July 1942 and January 1944, with ads appearing regularly in *Collier's, Ladies' Home Journal, Life, Look,* and the *Post,* most of them two-page spreads splashed with black-and-white photos of women at the meetings, at the grocery store, serving meals to their families,

least one helping of green or yellow vegetables—some raw, some cooked."

"Green vegetables!" bellowed Elmer, "I say it's spinach and to . . ."

"And to this," interrupted Elsie hastily, "should be added potatoes, other vegetables, or fruits in season."

"Bread and butter, too?" Beulah wanted to know.

"Certainly," said Elsie. "Both bread and cereal are

excellent foods. They should be either whole grain products or enriched white bread and flour, or cereals restored to their whole grain nutritive value. Butter, vitamin-rich fats, peanut butter, and similar spreads are fine, too."

"They won't get away with it," said Elmer positively. "Men want meat."

"Everybody *needs* meat," Elsie told him, "or fish, or poultry . . . every day. Then, folks occasionally ought to have dried beans, peas, or nuts."

"Daddy, daddy," screamed little Beulah, "the packages on top are falling off!"

"Oops, I've got 'em," panted Elmer. "O-w-w, the bottom came out of that bag. I hope you didn't buy any eggs."

"Of course, I bought eggs," said Elsie. "Everyone needs at least 3 or 4 eggs a week. We're lucky that we can cook them anyway we choose, because, from the looks of these packages, we're going to have an omelet!"

"Trouble, nothing but trouble," groaned Elmer. "What'll I do?"

"Stop grumbling and tote home these packages," prompted Elsie. "It will build up your muscles. That's the whole idea—the big reason for the National Nutrition Program: '*U. S. needs US strong!*'"

Elsie says: "*We at the Borden Company are so enthusiastic about the National Nutrition Program that we're using this space to tell you about it, instead of talking about our own products.*"

"Stop grumbling, Elmer, I'm just balancing your diet!" laughed Elsie

"Humpf!" grunted Elmer, the bull. "Every newfangled idea you get seems to wind up as a lot of work for me. There's not a word in the National Nutrition Program about my having to lug all these bundles."

"What's nutrition, mummy?" interrupted little Beulah, who doesn't know too many long words. "Is it something you catch—like the measles?"

"Mercy, no," laughed Elsie, the Borden Cow. "In times like these, particularly, good nutrition is just good eating sense. It's eating the right amounts of the right kind of foods—foods that make us strong and healthy so we can do our part to help America win the war."

"I guess valuable foods like that must be pretty scarce and expensive," sighed little Beulah.

"Not at all," said Elsie. "They're the appetizing,

everyday foods all Americans know and love. Take milk products, for instance. Everyone needs at least a pint of milk a day, and children need a quart. Or there's cheese, and evaporated or dried milk—and ice cream, which are practically the same as milk."

"I might have known milk would be *your* idea of good nutrition," snorted Elmer sarcastically.

"It isn't mine, it's Uncle Sam's," smiled Elsie. "Milk, of course, is only one part of good nutrition. Among other things, everyone ought to eat oranges, tomatoes, grapefruit, raw cabbage, or salad greens every day."

"How can one person eat all that at the same time?" asked Beulah, rubbing her small stomach anxiously.

"*One* of each a day is enough," explained Elsie. "Because, in addition, every day a person ought to have at

© The Borden Company

FIGURE 19

workers enjoying box lunches prepared along the program's guidelines, and the like. The Health for Victory Clubs and the ads for them were a success; from an initial meeting of "350 wives, mothers, and landladies of war workers" at Westinghouse's own Mansfield, Ohio, plant on March 10, 1942, the program grew by the end of 1943 to 1700 clubs sponsored by war plants and other organizations, with the Meal Planning Guide distributed monthly to "500,000 other homemakers from New England to Hawaii" (*Post* 11 July 1942: 46; 1 Jan. 44: 37). And from beginning to end it was an entirely noncommercial venture on the part of Westinghouse.

While public-spirited at least in part, most advertisements for food products were not so purely altruistic. Virtually all these ads were Double-Barrelled, devoting as much as half the copy (but often much less) to the nature and importance of the National Nutrition Program and the rest to advertising a product as satisfying the nutritional value of one or more of the food groups. In the vanguard of such advertising were the makers of breakfast cereals. Numerous and frequent ads for "restored" (i.e., fortified) cereals like Kellogg's Rice Krispies, General Foods' Grape-Nuts Flakes, and General Mills' crunchy little Os then called "Cheerioats" sang the praises of their vitamin and grain content for war workers whether behind a drill press or an office desk. All these ads pointed to the cereal as part of a well-balanced breakfast with the addition of fruit and milk. Most likely because of sugar rationing, no ads mentioned putting sugar on one's cereal. Margarine, which had a difficult time gaining acceptance among Americans, used the war and the butter shortage to proclaim its nutritional value: "NUCOA furnishes as much food-energy as the most expensive spread . . . and its VITAMIN A value is *more dependable*" (*Look* 15 Dec. 1942: 40). Producers of canned fruits and vegetables like Libby's, Stokely's, and Del Monte had a built-in argument for the nutritional value of their products, but the ads for some "foods" can only raise a smile today. "America has a big job to do—a big job that requires every ounce of energy of men and women anywhere," declared one ad picturing a war worker on lunch break, noting that its product contained more calories than the 178 in a lamb chop, 92 in a potato, 70 in an egg, and 20 in a tomato (*Time* 9 March 1942: 57). That product? Pepsi-Cola!

The Great Imponderable—War Worker Morale
While it was easy enough to quantify employee absenteeism, excused and unexcused, as well as the efficiency and productivity of workers on

the job, never during the war (or before or since) was a satisfactory means developed to measure the role of that ineffable thing called morale in war work. One would have even been hard put to describe precisely what constituted morale for war workers (a rather different thing from the morale of the home front generally—see Chapter 6). But there was general agreement that good worker morale involved contentment with one's job and pride in it, an understanding of how that job fit into the manufacture of a larger product (say, a submarine), and the function of that larger product in the war itself (see *Printers' Ink* 10 Apr. 1942: 70, 72–73). To help morale, some employers found ways to make employees' work easier, more comfortable, safer, and more efficient, and to ensure periods for rest and relaxation during the workers' shifts. Many large plants also provided on-site food services to cut down on employees' time away from the job and aid their proper nutrition. Print advertising dealing with these matters appeared only in industrial posters and publications, not in popular magazines, and yet some commercial advertisers of products for both industry and individual workers suggested ways of raising war workers' morale and offering products for sale to do so.

Several articles and photo spreads in *Business Week* laid out the benefits of music for employee morale and plant productivity, though it's beyond me how anyone could hear piped-in tunes above the din of a riveting gun! Nevertheless, "in 75% of the factories studied by the Stevens Institute of Technology, total production was 4% to 11% greater with music than without it," and in England increases of 23% were reported (3 Apr. 1943: 64). The same article pointed out that "industrial psychologists value factory music chiefly as an emotional control, helpful to suiting a worker to his task." Later, a photo showed Coastguardsmen painting a troop ship "while the ship's band tootles swing and martial airs [to] speed the sailors' monotonous tasks of housekeeping" (*Business Week* 16 Dec. 1944: 88). At least five providers of electronic music, great and small, got on the bandwagon to sell their services to industry—four advertising in *Business Week*, with only Muzak seemingly not advertising in any national magazines. But the others—RCA, Stromberg-Carlson, Rauland, and Operadio—all devoted space in their ads to the benefit of music for employee morale, efficiency, and productivity.

Recognizing the need for rest and refreshment for war workers, a company unfamiliar to most people called Pfaudler ran a thoroughly delightful ad in *Business Week* on June 26, 1943, featuring a cartoon-like drawing of a woman war worker eating lunch on the grass outside a factory and captioned "ADOLPH . . . THIS IS LULU." The copy began, "LULU works in a war plant, Adolph. She helps make little gilhickies that control the fuses on bombs. Just now she's starting her lunch with a sparkly *soft* drink. People can get along without soft drinks. In fact, as you know, Adolph, people can exist without almost everything that makes life pleasant and worth living. But that drink happens to make Lulu feel peppier, and after lunch she'll turn out calamity for you a lot faster than your workers can operate on a diet of ersatz victuals and forlorn hope" (94). Pfaudler didn't make any brand of soda; it manufactured "mixing and storage tanks [that] are standard equipment in an overwhelming proportion of beverage plants," including those for wine and beer — a small photo in the ad showing an array of such tanks at a Pepsi-Cola plant. While Pfaudler did not sell morale-lifting products to either industries or war workers, its ad stressed the value of employee morale very effectively.

Morale ads aimed specifically at war workers (rather than the home front at large) were all by makers of "life's little necessities" during the war — candy, chewing gum, cigarettes, and soft drinks — and the ads invariably sold the advertisers' products. Featuring photos of a male factory worker and a marine in dress uniform, in *Look* on February 9, 1943, Milky Way proclaimed "GOOD CHEER ON BOTH FRONTS! On the home front . . . on the war front . . . it's a precious moment when you bite into a Milky Way bar! [. . .] Back on the job you feel refreshed" (37) Following the picture of a man bending over a piece of machinery, the copy of an ad for Wrigley's Spearmint Chewing Gum began "a delicious trifle always . . . Today A Blessed Trifle Bringing Blessed Relief to Nerve-Strained War Producers" (*Collier's* 11 July 1942: 79). It would have been illegal even as long ago as World War II for the tobacco industry to claim that cigarettes calm nerves, so Camel Cigarettes in an ad that began "When Bombers are your Business — YOU WANT STEADY NERVES" could only state that "The smoke of slow-burning Camels contains LESS NICOTINE than that of the 4 other largest selling brands tested." Apparently the idea was that workers in bomber plants as well as bomber pilots who smoked Camels could enjoy their inevitable cigarette breaks with less chance of getting the jitters from smoking (*Life* 27 July 1942: back cover). In this Camels ad, incidentally, as in nearly all

FIGURE 20. Reprinted by permission of The Coca-Cola Company.

Camels ads featuring both a war worker and a GI (real ones, with their names), the war worker (and Camel smoker) was a woman.

Worker-morale related or not, magazine ads for Pepsi-Cola and Coca-Cola during the war are a study in contrasts. Aside from a number of the "calories = energy" ads of the type described earlier, Pepsi confined itself, almost entirely in *Life*, to less than full-page wordless or nearly wordless comics by cartoonist O. Soglow, creator of the long-running comic strip "The Little King." While amusing, these black-and-white promotions for Pepsi were rarely war related. Only beginning in mid-1943, and almost exclusively in *Time* and *Newsweek*, did Pepsi switch to war-themed ads, still in cartoon form but switching cartoonists to Robert Day. Until late in the war when the topic turned to GI morale, these cartoons almost always touted the morale-building properties of Pepsi for war workers. Typical is one in *Time* on December 20, 1943, in which a company's employees stage a grand welcome complete with brass band and huge floral "good luck" horseshoe for a new Pepsi-selling snack bar outside the plant's main gate, one company executive saying to another, "I've never seen Ajax morale so high" (31). By contrast, Coca-Cola ads were full-page masterpieces of brief copy and handsome art in glorious color. The industry giant clearly poured considerable money into the creation of these ads and into buying space for them in *Life*, *Collier's*, *Ladies' Home Journal*, *Newsweek*, *Time*, the *Post*, and undoubtedly other magazines beyond the ten examined here. While most Coke ads centered on GI morale, a few focused squarely on war workers, such as the classic study in minimalism on the back cover of *Collier's* for January 3, 1942—simply two hands, one grasping a wrench, the other a bottle of Coke, and the words "Pause . . . Work refreshed" (see fig. 20). Vivid, crisp, sparkling—the apotheosis of morale in a bottle!

THE FARM FRONT
AGRICULTURAL SUPPORT
OF THE WAR

There's no clear sense of who coined "farm front" or when it first came into use in the media and advertising, but whatever its origin it was an apt term to describe the role that America's truck farms, orchards, dairy farms, ranches, citrus groves, vineyards, and "amber waves of grain" played in fighting World War II. That "farm front" was in use very early in the war is evident from its appearance in a Camel ad in *Farm Journal* for March 1942. Factoring in the magazine's deadline for advertising copy, the term had to have been around at least by early February. In the photo, a GI in dress uniform is offering a farmer a Camel, the farmer saying, "You bet I'll have a **CAMEL**. They're first on the farm front, too!" (9). The copy describes agricultural America as just as much of a "front" as was the home front generally in the sense of a "line of battle": "His weapon may be a plough, a milk pail, an axe — but every farmer is in the front line of America's defense today." Describing food as vital ammunition for fighting the war continued for the duration. By May 1, 1944, things were well enough in hand at least in Europe that it might have seemed farmers and Victory Gardeners needn't keep going all-out in food production as they had done earlier in the war. But the Young & Rubicam ad agency knew otherwise, and its ad in *Newsweek* for that date, an ad selling nothing, proclaimed, "Food is still critical . . . is still our greatest single potential weapon of war" (43). Descriptions of agricultural production, praise for the men and women who worked the farms, and finding ways to help them through the vicissitudes of everything from the shortage of farm help to disastrous weather for crops were continuing themes in magazine advertising from one end of the war to the other. Just as pervasive were ads of a rather different stamp stressing the importance of the largely urban Victory Gardens, encouraging their gardeners, and giving gardening advice to these "amateur agriculturalists."

While agriculture was on a par with industry in its importance for fighting the war, advertising about the farm front was, in the main, very different. Almost by definition, institutional ads are nowhere to be found, since farms, orchards, and the like didn't place strictly informational ads (or any ads at all, for that matter) about how they were helping fight the war, the only exception being some major canneries of fruits and vegetables. The ads of companies manufacturing such things as farm machinery or fertilizer often contained a sales component, or, if not that, at least advice on how to take care of one's tractor or cultivator when few new ones were being made. Overall, selling was more prevalent in agricultural than industrial war ads. To their credit, those advertisers selling products or services to the farm front or Victory Gardeners rarely did so gratuitously. In all but a few instances, the products being sold were of genuine value to crop production or canning, whether by professionals or amateurs. No ads trumped up or even exaggerated the importance of food production or the problems facing it in order to sell an advertiser's wares. The same kinds of information about the ups and downs of farm yields, crop goals, and farm labor problems that occurred in ads also appeared in more extensive detail in numerous articles on agriculture in *Business Week*. Apparently wartime admen did their homework well to make ads on agricultural support of the war as convincing as possible through a solid grounding in facts.

Calling a Spade a Spade—Or Selling One

While not informational in the same way industry's institutional advertising was informational, there was a class of agricultural war ads that might best be labeled descriptive. Always employing no-frills straight talk, these ads described—presumably for the enlightenment and appreciation of the city-dwelling and suburban home front—just what the farm front was doing for the war. In their frankness, such ads continued to call a spade a spade when they also laid out the difficulties America's farmers faced in their monumental task of feeding our armed forces, our Allies, and the home front. Descriptive ads were about evenly divided between those that were purely so and those that also sold products or services to aid the farm community; both kinds appeared across the entire spectrum of national magazines. Firms with some connection to agriculture placed most of the purely descriptive ads.

One purely descriptive ad illustrates the use of straight talk about the ups and downs of farming in a single ad. Placed by the Allis-Chalmers

Tractor Division in the *Post* on October 2, 1943, the copy refused to paint a rosy picture for the year's crop yields before all the returns were in: "The farmer serves his country well in these critical hours. [. . .] Bringing this year's crop through a season of unusual weather hazards, despite serious shortages of labor and equipment, has required extraordinary skill and effort. [. . .] With some crops still to ripen, it is too early to measure exactly in bushels and tons the amount of return this year's harvest will bring. Circumstances may cause it to be less than the bumper yields of previous years, yet we can be sure that the farmer has given everything he had to the task of trying to meet the constantly increasing needs for food" (89). Some ads, like the Pennsylvania Railroad's in *Life* on June 12, 1944, focused on a single problem farmers had to face throughout the war—insufficient farm labor: "Sure, a lot of fine husky farm lads have gone to fighting fronts, but their Dads are out there harvesting one of the largest crops ever to come to market" (24). While Dad doing Sonny's chores didn't come close to solving the farm help problem (see the third section of this chapter), the ad at least let readers know there *was* a shortage of farm hands and that something had to be done about it. Other descriptive ads focused only on the positive. Jenkins Valves, which made equipment for food processing plants, used statistics to show gains made by farming and food processing on July 7, 1944, in *Business Week*: "Since Pearl Harbor, our farmers have expanded crop lands more than 80 million acres. Between 1941 and 1943, our food processing industry boosted output 38 per cent—and 1944 will see all previous records shattered" (99). On page 83 of *Time* on April 30, 1945, an ad by the Bemis Bro. Bag Co., makers of burlap, cotton, and paper bags, featured a wry drawing of a helmeted gun crew plus a farmer in overalls together loading outlandishly huge ears of corn into an anti-aircraft gun. Not to be taken literally, of course, the art dramatized the copy's account of agriculture's non-food production for the fighting of the war, specifically the role of corn in making synthetic rubber, explosives, and penicillin.

The *Saturday Evening Post* ran the preponderance of farm front ads that both described some aspect of agriculture's role in the war and offered products or services for sale to farmers, suggesting that of all the large-circulation national weeklies, the venerable old *Post* had the biggest wartime rural readership. Advertisers began these kinds of ads very early. In the *Post* on February 28, 1942, the Barrett Division of the Allied

Chemical & Dye Corporation wrote of the generic American farmer and the need for increased crop production: "Uncle Sam needs a big crop and there are few hands to make it. One son is in the Army. Another will be called soon. The hired man has taken a better-paying job in a defense plant and help is hard to get. Faced with a labor shortage, the average farmer must produce more than his usual peacetime harvest of enough agricultural products to supply the needs of four American families. In addition to food, fodder, and fiber for 130,000,000 people, our 6,000,000 farms must yield extra food for our armed forces . . . and more food for our Allies" (79). All of which makes for a smooth segue into the sales portion of the ad: "This 'Food for Freedom' program would be impossible without the great basic crop-producing power of millions of tons of fertilizers." Like the Barrett ad, most other descriptive ads with a sales component focused on the advertiser's product or service helping the farm front do its part in the "Food Fights for Freedom" campaign. This government-sponsored drive for greater food production and food conservation had its slogan widely disseminated through the efforts of the War Advertising Council. The descriptive part of most such ads centered on either the urgency of high crop yields or the seemingly insurmountable obstacles farmers faced: "Never before in the history of our country did so much depend on agriculture . . . on the men who raise the wheat and corn and cattle . . . the fruits and vegetables . . . and on the women who as usual are patriotically pitching in to help." So began an ad by the Lee Rubber & Tire Corporation in the *Post* on July 3, 1943. It continued, "Getting food to market . . . carrying help to and from the farm . . . taking the family to church . . . calls for many miles of travel by truck and car. Farmers' driving is definitely essential. They are rightly numbered among those who have first call on the available supply of pre-war LEE DeLuxe tires" (81). The ad closed with detailed instructions for farmers and other priority drivers on how to apply for such tires, plus information on recapping, repairs, and general tire maintenance available at Lee tire dealers.

Studebaker began one of its ads with "No 'E' award flags fly above our nation's farms. Yet they've set a new food production record in 1943, for the seventh consecutive year" (*Time* 8 Nov. 1943: 47), and Chevrolet, similarly, with "Last year America's farmers produced the greatest volume of food *ever* produced in the entire history of the nation—to take care of the hungry millions here at home, to feed our fighting men and to supply lend-lease," appending a litany of the obstacles farmers fought, "inadequate farm labor—worn-out-equipment—long hours of back-breaking toil—and the unpredictable whims of nature herself" (*Post* 1 July 1944: 33). With not much to sell farmers or anyone else, these two automotive manufacturers took out ads offering the farm front ways in which they *could* aid in the fight for "food for freedom." Although Studebaker's manufacturing plants were engaged almost a hundred percent in war work, "Studebaker dealers in farming areas will gladly inspect and service any make of farm truck regularly at moderate cost." The ad also offered the free "48-page handbook 'Care and Maintenance of the Farm Truck in Wartime'" to farmers who were do-it-yourself auto mechanics, as indeed many were. Chevrolet, on the other hand, was still making a limited number of vehicles for farmers, as reflected in the ad's statement that the company was "supplying dependable, economical transportation for *more farmers* than does any other manufacturer of cars and trucks," but the ad's main thrust was that Chevrolet stood by farmers with older trucks and cars "by assisting them to keep their vital motor vehicles alive and running through the medium of Chevrolet dealer service." These two ads are typical of many by other manufacturers of trucks, tractors, and other farm machinery that switched their wartime advertising from selling to servicing their products, all with the aim of helping farmers conserve the trucks and equipment they already owned since few could be replaced for the duration.

"The Man Behind Our 3 Meals a Day"

This headline above a picture of a farmer on his tractor opened an ad by the Mutual Life Insurance Company of New York fairly shouting, "Three cheers for the American farmer—his wife and workers—as vital links in our country's total war effort!" (*Time* 14 Sept. 42: 72), just one of many advertising salutes to the men and women who worked the farm front during the war. The Mutual Life ad was unusual only in that it was one of a mere handful of agricultural tribute ads that also sold a product, in this case, obviously, life insurance. Some other tribute ads mentioned how the advertiser's products or services benefited the farm community, but direct selling was almost entirely absent from ads praising farmers and their families. And from ads that saluted a few other rural folks as well, like one placed by International Harvester paying tribute to farm equipment dealers (and not just IH's own) for keeping critically needed farm machinery up and running at a time when the war work of companies like John Deere, Caterpillar, Allis-Chalmers, and IH itself made it impossible for them to fulfill the demand for enough new agricultural equipment. Aimed directly at farmers in the July 1943 *Farm Journal*, the ad strikingly asked them to take a moment to personally thank their local equipment dealers for helping them sustain their livelihood as well as helping the farm front help win the war (3).

Most farm front tribute ads more conventionally applauded farmers themselves. In the July 1942 *Farm Journal*, Goodyear addressed the farmer both in its headline—"Chief Quartermaster to the United Nations . . that's YOU!"—and throughout the copy with lines like "America and her allies depend on *you* for both guns and butter" (23). Much later, in the *Post* on February 12, 1944, the Delco Appliance Division of General Motors headed a similar encomium "A SALUTE TO THE AMERICAN FARMER for distinguished service to the Nation" (32), and on May 20, 1944, less noisily but no less sincerely, a Kraft Cheese ad read in part, "You hear about the brilliant actions of our boys on the battle fronts, including the sons of our dairymen. None of us at home can match what they do for victory. But none of us here works more *days*, more *hours*, more *valiantly* than the people left on America's dairy farms. They're in the front line of the battle for food . . . and they know it" (42).

Farmwomen and children also figured large in advertising's accolades to American agriculture, sometimes sharing the spotlight with the men, other times taking center stage solo. General Motors' ad in *Farm Journal* for August 1944 embraced the entire farm family, saying, "because their farms are their business, their security, their very life, farm families always work together like no others. [. . .] The farm family symbolizes the spirit of American unity that has enabled us to carry the war to the enemy in such a short space of time" (19). The Easy Washing Machine Company praised farmer's daughters, wives, and other farm women for carrying on much of the burden of farming in the absence of men at war: "Thanks to the farmer's daughter, and the millions like her, our boys can count on a steady stream of the food and other supplies they need to win. Easy salutes the farmer's daughter, the farmer's wife, and all the other heroines fighting so valiantly on the home front" (*Collier's* 7 Aug. 1943: 55). Allis-Chalmers even singled out an *actual* little farm girl for special recognition: "All who hear the moving story of Dolores Costello, an 11-year-old Maryland farm girl, are awakened to the

grit and resourcefulness of farm youngsters. Single-handed, she culti-
vated the crops on a 167-acre farm when her father was called to war and
her uncle was killed last spring in an auto accident" (*Farm Journal*, January 1945: inside front cover). Of course Dolores was aided by the hydraulic lift on the family's Allis-Chalmers tractor, but the ad didn't sell
the machine, it merely described how Dolores used it to keep the corn
crop and 90,000 tobacco plants growing "until an uncle was released
from the army to help harvest."

The question may have crossed the reader's mind, just what was the
purpose of these tribute ads as well as the descriptive farm front ads previously discussed? They didn't function for advertisers as their industrial
counterparts the institutional ads and pride ads did in keeping product
and brand consciousness alive for the duration, nor did they ask for any
support of the war effort from their readers. Seemingly passive, they still
played an important role during the war, and a big one at that: helping
sustain the morale of the rural Americans the ads were written about,
making them feel good about their often frustrating fight to supply food
for freedom. At the same time, such ads benefited home front morale
generally by making people proud of the farm front and farm folks' contributions to the war—this going a long way toward helping urban
Americans better comprehend and appreciate the reasons for the rationing and food shortages they faced on a daily basis (see Chapter 7 for
more on this).

"Answer the Call to Farms!"
If farm front descriptive and tribute ads were relatively passive, those
dealing with the shortage of farm labor and cannery workers were anything but. Although far fewer in number than, say, ads for War Bonds or
conservation, ads soliciting volunteers—primarily paid volunteers—to
help bring in the harvest or can fruits and vegetables were no less aggressive or persuasive. Such ads ranged far and wide, from local newspapers to such major national weeklies and monthlies as the *Post, Ladies'
Home Journal, Collier's, Life, Look*, and even *Esquire*. While the government's own poster campaign for recruiting farm help was limited entirely to the summer of 1943 (see "WWII-Posters.com" *passim*), magazines ran ads calling for agricultural assistance from as early as June
1943 through the growing season in 1945. This fact alone suggests that
such ads were placed largely at the initiative of individual advertisers

rather than as parts of a concerted effort originating in Washington and spearheaded by the War Advertising Council; concerted campaigns always took place over just a concentrated period of a few weeks or months. It's possible that the cluster of magazine ads calling for farm help in the summer of 1944 was part of an organized Ad Council effort, but no available documentary evidence exists to support or refute this supposition. It may seem self-serving that the companies sponsoring calls for farm help were invariably involved in canning, milling, or other processing of agricultural products, including, not incidentally, the distillers of Calvert Reserve Blended Whiskey! Yet the odds that people answering the call in such ads wound up working the fields producing crops needed by a particular advertiser were fairly remote, so in truth their ads were placed to assist all American agricultural interests, not just their own.

The reasons additional farm help was needed, especially at harvest time, were three, only one of which was positive—the fact that the farm front was producing record-breaking quantities of fruits, vegetables, grains, and fiber plants (cotton and flax, mostly) to keep up with the increased wartime need. The other two reasons were the shortage of manpower and the often calamitous vagaries of the weather during the growing seasons in the middle years of the war. Farm boys and other rural young men enlisted or were drafted into the armed forces in record numbers, and, even more damaging for timely, efficient harvests, large numbers of the generally reliable migratory workers who followed the crops from harvest to harvest took higher-paying jobs in defense work, chiefly in the huge West Coast shipyards and airplane plants. Weather conditions from torrential rains to heat waves and parching droughts forced the harvesting of some crops before they rotted, of others before they shriveled up and died from the heat, with the effect that harvest hands had to be found earlier than usual to save them.

That the need for extra farm and cannery labor was a coast-to-coast concern can be seen from just the headlines and subheads of a few of *Business Week*'s many articles on the subject: "Victory Vacations: San Franciscans sponsor a plan for relief of farm labor shortage by recruiting city folk for duty in harvest fields" (25 Apr. 1942: 75); "Victory Picking: California citrus growers find part-time students helpful at harvest; but they still long for 'professional' pickers" (24 Apr. 1943: 106); "Nazis Hoe Cotton: In Texas camp, German prisoners work for their meals and seem glad to do it; farmers clamor for their help" (19 June 1943: 18); "A Crop

Is Saved: Swift action in recruiting labor saves hundreds of tons of toma-toes piled up on trucks at New Jersey canneries" (28 Aug. 1943: 20); "Big Cherry Crop: It was harvested with aid of vacationers, prisoners of war, and youths" (2 Sept. 1944: 42).

The ads began later than the articles, but they too stressed the urgency for help with a situation bordering on a crisis. The reason that the ads came later is simple enough. While articles in 1942 discussed the shortage of farm and cannery help and local volunteer efforts to cope with it, it was only in February 1943 that the U.S. Department of Agriculture instituted the paid-volunteer organization to be called the U.S. Crop Corps and its equivalents for young people and women, respectively, the Victory Farm Volunteers and the Women's Land Army. Only once those organizations were in place in the spring of 1943 could national advertisers begin to pro-vide information about them and where prospective volunteers could go to apply. The earliest farm aid ad, however, did neither. For months on end in *Esquire* and occasionally in other magazines, the Calvert Distil-leries Corporation ran small cartoon ads headed "Metropolitan Mo-ments," signed by a cartoonist calling himself "Wisdom." Each ad in the series featured a plutocratic Manhattanite looking for all the world like the little man in the Monopoly game, replete with white walrus-like moustache, cutaway coat, and top hat, together with his butler/valet, also appropriately dressed. Each ad was captioned with a two-line rhyme about a way to support the war effort, while the remaining copy just stated how Calvert's distilleries "are now converted 100% to war produc-tion," but ending with the reassurance that there were enough reserves of the company's whiskey that if *"Used in moderation . . .* **Calvert Re-serve** *. . . will last for the duration."* The firm's ad in the June 1943 *Es-quire* depicted the city gentleman and his trusty valet on a farm, still el-egantly dressed but barefoot and carrying suitcases, a rake, pitchfork, and milking pail, and captioned "Our Farmers Need Each Jack and Bill / Their Cows to Milk and Fields to Till," apparently taking no cognizance of "Jill" in the Women's Land Army, or, *Esquire* being a men's magazine, choosing to ignore her (169). More amusing than informative, this Calvert ad at least seemed to jump-start national advertising for farm volunteers, after which such ads began to appear regularly in all the major weeklies and monthlies.

The first such ad of any substance was by Dole (the pineapple people), just a month later in the July 1943 *Ladies' Home Journal*. Headed "Harvest waits for no man," the ad continued with useful and specific information: "America needs your help to turn ripe crops into fighting foods. Waste can't be tolerated. When your local call comes, sign up with your County Agricultural Agent or U. S. Employment Service office for service in the U. S. Crop Corps" (109). The appeal concluded with "Full or part-time work in field or cannery will give you extra money for U. S. War Bonds," getting in a plug for two wartime causes at once. Other food-processing companies such as Pillsbury, Kraft, and Del Monte followed suit, the major onslaught of such ads coming not in 1943 but in the spring and summer of 1944, presumably to revive any flagging interest in the volunteer program after the first season's initial enthusiasm. Some companies like Dole and Pillsbury ran multiple, and different, ads, placed strategically when the need for agricultural volunteers was the greatest. The most richly detailed ad was Pillsbury's in the *Post* for May 20, 1944, making it clear to readers that a few months, weeks, or even days spent on a farm or in a cannery during one's summer vacation could make a real difference. This was also the only ad that specifically mentioned the Victory Farm Volunteers for boys and girls and the Women's Land Army, concluding, "So, plan your vacation now. Work on a farm this summer—help grow and harvest the nation's vital war crops. When the call comes, answer 'Count me in'" (117). Inexplicably, only Dole's ad on page 131 of the August 1944 *Ladies' Home Journal* and page 16 of *Life* on September 11 let readers know they would receive "regular wages for full and part-time work."

None of these ads contained any selling, although some other advertisers did sell their wares as well as call for farm volunteers. In *Life* on October 23, 1944, Campbell's Soup's ad wasn't a call for help but a note of gratitude. Next to a large picture of a smiling boy in farm clothes holding a basket of tomatoes was the sidebar "Thanks, Boys and Girls—To the many high school students who pitched in to help pick and pack the 1944 food crop, all America joins in saying 'Thanks'" (35). The main copy sang the praises of tomato soup. That the need for farm help was critical all the way to the end of the war and beyond is seen in a Maxwell House Coffee ad on page 26 of *Collier's* on August 25, 1945, and in a slightly expanded version on page 37 of *Look* for September 4. Mostly the ad hyped the coffee that was "Good to the Last Drop!" but it also appended a much more vital message: "Answer the Call To Farms! Farmers and their families are working overtime getting in our country's crops . . .

but extra hands are needed. Four million emergency workers wanted, urgently—full time, part time, spare time! Experience is unnecessary. Be ready—and willing—to answer the call in *your* community." There's no good explanation for the first and only ad calling the critical shortage of farm help an "emergency" postdating the Japanese surrender by eleven days, since the word accurately describes what the farm front faced each year of the war and what national advertisers' calls for help assisted in alleviating.

"Lettuce Beet the Axis!"

Throughout the war advertisers placed far more ads promoting Victory Gardens than ads for farm help in the leading national magazines—under twenty farm aid ads, close to seventy for Victory gardens. Correspondingly, the number of Victory Gardeners nationwide significantly outstripped the number of farm volunteers. The reasons were primarily two: First, it was simply fun playing amateur "farmer" and providing one's family, friends, and neighbors with homegrown vegetables. (That Victory Gardens were clearly fun for admen too can be seen in the dreadful pun heading this section—it's the headline of a Victory Garden promotion placed by Seagram's 5 Crown Blended Whiskey in *Life* on September 20, 1943.) The second reason the home front so took to Victory Gardening is that people didn't have to range far afield to help support the war (and save on ration points) by feeding themselves. They could plant, cultivate, and harvest crops right in their own backyards, on the rooftops of big-city apartment buildings, or, as my father—an inveterate flower gardener even before the war—and many like him did, in a vacant lot across the street from one's suburban home. Career farmers also participated in Victory Gardens with their "farm gardens" or "kitchen gardens" for their own family's supply of vegetables beyond what they grew in their acreage devoted to commercial farming. Once Agriculture Secretary Claude Wickard announced the plan and the urgent need for it in the fall of 1942, Victory Gardens mushroomed into a wartime national pastime as big as baseball, possibly bigger.

The numbers quantifying the proliferation and productivity of Victory Gardens are nothing short of staggering. When the Department of Agriculture first conceived a Victory Garden plan along the lines of a similar scheme during World War I in the spring of 1942—months before Secretary Wickard sent out his call for home gardeners—the government explicitly did *not* want urban and suburban gardening enthusiasts to get involved for fear of a "waste of steel [in gardening implements] and a waste of vegetable seeds" by what it presumed would be incompetent amateurs. What Washington had in mind originally was limited to 5,760,000 "farm gardens, perhaps also a few community or school gardens where produce can be consumed within hailing distance, requiring no processing or transportation" (*Business Week* 6 June 1942: 68). How quickly the government changed its tune, once it realized its farm garden program would be hopelessly inadequate for alleviating the shortage of produce necessary for fighting the war. By the time Wickard made his announcement, the goal was set for eighteen million Victory Gardens, primarily by the home gardeners that Agriculture had tried to steer away from the project initially. But there were a few caveats, the most amusing of which was a warning against "the futile plowing up of front yards so prevalent in the last war. The clay-fill foundation of most lawns makes them an exceedingly poor risk for crop insurance" (*Business Week* 9 Jan. 1943: 17). In 1943, Wickard's goal was not only met but exceeded, with close to twenty million Victory Gardens up and growing, only about six million of those in the farm community. And that urban and suburban gardeners proved not at all incompetent was validated by their producing 7,949,000 tons of vegetables, which "represented 42% of the nation's vegetable production" (see *Business Week* 20 March 1943: 38; 27 Nov. 1943: 79). Arguably, with the single exception of War Bond sales, in the space of less than a year Victory Gardens became the single most successful home front effort in support of the war.

Did advertising play a significant role in this? Absolutely. In the spring of 1943, the Association of National Advertisers' survey of "Public Sentiment Toward Wartime Advertising" found 56% of those polled thought advertising "was instrumental in planning Victory gardens" (*Business Week* 19 June 1943: 96). The only categories of war ads receiving a higher effectiveness rating were those for selling War Bonds at 82% and those explaining how rationing works at 63%. The key word in the statement about Victory Garden ads is "planning." Many ads went beyond simply encouraging home gardening to include everything from a few helpful hints to meticulous step-by-step instructions for growing Victory Garden crops, and not only for growing them but for home canning and pickling produce as well. Unlike the ads recruiting farm volunteers, most of those just *promoting* Victory Gardens were not placed by food processing companies—Union Pacific Railroad, Dr. Pepper, Baldwin Locomotive Works, the *Los Angeles Times*, and Canada Dry, to name just a few. But most ads giving actual gardening advice came from titans of the processed produce industry like Birds Eye, Del Monte, and Green Giant. Very few of these ads did any selling, although more for home canning did, and legitimately so, as will be seen.

Curiously, several months after Secretary Wickard's appeal for Victory Gardens grown by the entire home front, the first national magazine ad encouraging them was addressed strictly to farmers in a magazine read almost exclusively by the country's rural population—*Farm Journal*. In the March 1943 issue, International Harvester reached out to farmers and their families to plant not just commercial crops but Victory Gardens for their own use. IH appealed both to farmers' patriotism in being able thereby to supply more crops for the military and our Allies, and also to their practicality, a trait that traditionally farmers have always had plenty of: "You will be thankful in summer to have fresh vegetables each day for the family table—and *doubly thankful* next winter to have abundant food when the markets are bare of canned goods" (33). The ad then offered a free eighty-four-page booklet designed specifically for the farm community called "Have a Victory Garden." One reason for an ad addressed solely to farmers well after Washington issued its general appeal for home front Victory Gardens may have been to encourage them to stay with the program and not think their own efforts weren't needed once the general public was involved. That farm families *did* stay with the program and were very much needed is illustrated by "Agriculture's estimate [in 1943] that 98% of all farm families will can an average of 243 jars of food per family; rural families (not farm) 184 jars each; and city families, 41 jars" (*Business Week* 17 Apr. 1943: 68). Still, factoring in their larger numbers, urban and suburban Victory Gardeners did more than their share.

And much of it thanks to national advertising, whether calling for more home gardeners or advising those already out there digging. Appeals for more people to get on the farm wagon, so to speak, were many: "All of us who can find a plot of ground . . . even if only twenty feet square . . . should do our bit to alleviate the food shortage. It's not only patriotic . . . it's sensible as well" (Dr. Pepper, *Post* 17 Apr. 1943: 67). A woman engulfed by burgeoning veggies says, "I planted *my* Victory Garden today and had fun doing it. Before long this is the way I'll look, picking my tomatoes, beans, lettuce and beets, right out of my own back yard. But what I'm *really doing* is sending some soldier-boy a dinner at one of the fighting fronts . . . because what *I* raise in my garden takes the place of what I'd have to buy" (Baldwin Locomotive Works, *Time* 19 Apr. 1943: 69). And another of Calvert Distilleries' cartoon ads proclaimed, "We've Turned Our Backs on Raising Flowers, / Now Peas and Beans Get Our Spare Hours—Producing for victory is a full-time job for all of us" (*Esquire* June 1943: 157).

Among ads giving gardening advice, it's a bit of a tossup whether Green Giant's or Birds Eye's are the most impressive, but I'd give my vote to Green Giant for two ads in *Life* in 1943, one about growing peas (March 8), the other corn (March 22). Focusing on the home gardener's efforts with just one vegetable, each ad could devote a whole page to detailed information on a single crop, from preparing the soil to harvesting the fruits of one's labors (see fig. 21 for the corn ad). Moreover, among wartime advertising of all kinds, the two Green Giant ads are arguably the best example of pure public outreach by a commercial advertiser, an unselfish outreach approaching actual altruism. Green Giant's government contracts called for about 50% of its pea and corn crops to go to our troops and those of our Allies, but the company still had sufficient quantities to pack reduced numbers of cans for the home front that were especially available during periods when rationing of canned goods was loosened (it kept loosening and tightening throughout the war). So, in effect, in these ads Green Giant was actually giving sound gardening advice to its amateur "competitors" to "grow their own." In addition to the advice in the ads, Green Giant offered readers a twenty-eight-page booklet filled with yet more information in exchange for their sending "three cents in stamps" to the company's address in Le Sueur, Minnesota.

By contrast, while Birds Eye gave a fair bit of gardening advice, the approach was entirely different, and the ads were anything but altruistic. Two in *Life*, on April 24 and August 28, 1944, both had rather Victorian-style graphics and were headed, in appropriately period type, "Birds Eye Almanac for Victory Gardeners," the first for May, the second for September of that year. Laid out like a page in an old-fashioned farmers' almanac, each ad contained snippets of random information like "Average Date of Last Killing Frost in . . . ," "The Bugs'll Get You . . . ," and "Winter Storage." Practical hints, no doubt, but not enough on any one subject to be entirely useful, and with no offer of a booklet contain-

How to grow your own Corn

FIGURE 21

ing fuller gardening tips. Moreover, each ad contained a large photo and accompanying copy selling a Birds Eye product: "Sweet Corn Takes About 80 Days, But—It's no use to wait all *that* time to enjoy country-fresh corn. *Not while your dealer has Birds Eye Golden Sweet Corn*—milky-sweet, tender, *delicious!*" (24 Apr. 1944: 40). The August ad stressed the year-round availability of Birds Eye frozen peas, and neither ad even acknowledged people's home canning their own for winter use.

Stranger yet among ads promoting Victory Gardens and home canning were two by Del Monte. Throughout the spring and summer of 1943, Del Monte ran ads in the *Post* enlisting Victory Gardeners and giving them practical advice, together with similar ads on the proper methods for canning fruit. But in the winter of 1943–44 the company ran two ads in *Look* that virtually subverted the efforts of home gardeners and canners. On December 14, 1943, a fictional Victory Gardener writes to Del Monte, "It beats me how you can grow vegetables that are all so good, every year" (inside front cover), and on February 8, 1944, a woman holding a jar of her canned peaches says, "I learned the hard way all right!—and believe me, since I put up fruit of my own I appreciate Del Monte quality more than ever!" (5). The rest of each ad touted the qualities of Del Monte's canned and jarred goods, giving no encouragement to people growing or canning their own. Whether there was an outcry against such ads undermining the efforts (and, undoubtedly, the morale) of home gardeners and canners or for some other reason, for the rest of the war, no Del Monte ads ever addressed Victory Gardens or home canning again.

Boris Artzybasheff's illustration for one home farming ad is so wacky (a favorite World War II adjective) that when I saw it, and even when I read some of the text, I thought the ad was a gag (see fig. 22). Rows of marching hens and eggs, the leader's shoulder insignia a pair of crossed drumsticks, preceded this off-the-wall copy: "Plenty of loyal and cooperative feathered Americans are waiting to volunteer as HAFFs (Hens Auxiliary Food Force). They're eager to enlist and augment America's food supply, in 'a hennery for every home'" (Wickwire Spencer Steel Company, *Newsweek* 26 Apr. 1943: 32). Silly as it sounds, the ad wasn't kidding, except about the group called HAFF. The copy promoted urban chicken coops to help alleviate the food shortage and gave helpful hints on how to get started, including buying Wickwire Spencer's brand of "poultry netting" (chicken wire to us) for building one's henhouse. After

Hens Auxiliary Food Force   *Enlarged reproduction free on request.*

Wanted...HAFF Recruiters

Food Shortage? There need not be for *your* home.

Plenty of loyal and cooperative feathered Americans are waiting to volunteer as HAFFs (Hens Auxiliary Food Force.) They're eager to enlist and augment America's food supply, in "a hennery for every home."

All you need do is decide *now* to put a HAFF Hatchery on one side of your garage, and a Victory Garden on the other.

Go to your neighborhood hardware merchant for advice and help. His stocks of famous Clinton Brand poultry netting and other supplies are low, but he'll help to his limit—and you'll find him resourceful. He knows it takes only a little poultry netting for a family-size hennery ... and the more families who recruit HAFF Hatcheries and plant Victory Gardens, the more food America can spare for our boys abroad, and for needy allies.

Visit your hardware dealer now!

Permission to reprint in whole or part gladly given on request.

DEALERS: If you haven't received your window posters and helpful suggestions, write us.

COPYRIGHT 1943

WICKWIRE SPENCER
STEEL COMPANY
500 FIFTH AVENUE   NEW YORK, N. Y.

STANDS FOR
FRIENDLINESS

FAMOUS FOR QUALITY IN POULTRY NETTING, HARDWARE CLOTH, INSECT SCREEN CLOTH, WIRE, WIRE ROPE, SPRINGS, METAL CONVEYOR BELTS, INDUSTRIAL WIRE CLOTH, ELECTRICALLY WELDED FABRIC FOR CONCRETE

FIGURE 22

recovering from my amazement and amusement, I recalled a rather eccentric semi-recluse living about a block away from my suburban home in Wilmette, Illinois, who had poultry clucking about his yard, although his birds (or their forebears) may have predated the war. My friend Sue in Minneapolis confirms the presence of suburban, if not urban, henneries; her grandmother kept a sizable brood of chickens at her suburban St. Louis home during and after the war. The oddest thing about all this is that poultry was never rationed, although there were periodic shortages of eggs.

Still, livestock of any sort was more a phenomenon of corporate Victory Gardens than of those tilled individually by Mr. and Mrs. Home Front. Corporate Victory Gardens were those maintained by large companies either to supply their own plant food services or, as the Union Pacific Railroad described in an ad on page 4 of *Esquire* for July 1944, to give its employees without land for gardening a place to grow their own vegetables. Other companies that embarked on such communal gardens on a grand scale were the American Bantam Car Company in Pennsylvania, which created a hundred-acre plot "to feed workers' families at bare production costs," and the Ilg Electric Ventilating Company in Chicago, which plowed up a nine-hole golf course to create Victory Garden plots for its workers (*Business Week* 10 Apr. 1943: 20). To return to the livestock, for its three-hundred-acre Victory Garden in Argo, Illinois, Corn Products Refining Company also bought a thousand chicks, 250 ducklings, and 100 goslings, not to mention some bunnies; "Eleven rabbits that were ordered (one buck, ten does) went all-out for victory, increasing to 38 before delivery." For all the fun and otherwise amusing aspects of Victory Gardens, there is no question that growing one's own "food for freedom" was serious business and took place on every scale, involving virtually every segment of the home front population.

As much can be said for the home canning, pickling, and preserving of fruits and vegetables, even though many urban and suburban women who took it up had no experience of it since watching their grandmothers "putting up" pickles, jams, and jellies decades earlier. And again national advertising did its part to revive and encourage the practice. Most of the ads that gave advice or encouragement to housewives who might never have put up their own produce sold a product as well. But the selling in these ads was very different from that in Victory Garden ads in which some companies promoted products that competed with what

Victory Gardeners grew. Rather, these ads sold products needed for home canning and the related arts of pickling or salting and drying vegetables. Morton Salt promoted its own salt products while at the same time offering a free booklet called "Salt Some Away" containing instructions for brining, pickling, and "drysalting," including how to make sauerkraut (*Life* 28 Aug. 1944: 12). H. J. Heinz ran several ads like the one in *Life* on August 23, 1943, which encouraged both home pickling and the use of the company's own Heinz White Vinegar, distilled vinegar being a necessary ingredient for the pickling of most vegetables. And along with offering for just ten cents the "Ball Blue Book" of "complete canning methods and recipes," the Ball Brothers Company sold its still-famous (among home canners at least) Ball Jars (*Ladies' Home Journal* July 1944: 126). This sort of selling was to assist home gardeners and their wives in putting up their own produce, not to compete with them. Prominent among the few home canning ads that did not sell a product was one by Westinghouse on page 98 of *Ladies' Home Journal* for August 1943, which offered for one thin dime a forty-eight page "Home Canning Guide," a gesture fully in keeping with the company's Health-for-Victory outreach.

While no ads encouraging volunteer farm aid, Victory Gardens, or home canning made a point of saying so, they worked toward advertising's goal of enlisting universal civilian participation in order to achieve the greatest possible home front efficiency for fighting the war. The more farm help, Victory Gardens, and home-canned produce, the more that was commercially grown could go to the military, and the less the home front would have to do without. Of the many other ways of effecting home front efficiency, some were big, others smaller and more scattered, but all equally vital, as detailed in the next chapter.

5

"USE IT UP, WEAR IT OUT, MAKE IT DO, OR DO WITHOUT"
CONSERVATION, SCRAP DRIVES, AND HOME FRONT EFFICIENCY

"Priority" and "priorities" were in the vocabulary of virtually every American on the home front and in the military during World War II. Simply put, they meant that the armed forces and war production came first, everyone else on the civilian home front came second. Yet home front civilians were asked to contribute heavily to providing necessary war material through conservation and scrap drives, and to expedite the tasks of the armed forces by helping the home front run as efficiently as possible. At the same time, these same people had to make do with less for themselves because of shortages, product unavailability, and rationing (see Chapter 6). Together with the government's own poster and ad campaigns, magazine ads by commercial advertisers played no small role in encouraging such support of the war. It's the nature of ads promoting conservation and home front efficiency that certain ones like those about carpooling could be classified as either conservation ads or home front efficiency ads, depending on their content or emphasis. In most cases I tried to group them with similar types of ads in order to achieve an internal logic among the many topics on home front support in this chapter.

Tough Talk—Making the Case for Conservation

Commercial advertisers in national magazines placed most of their ads promoting conservation during 1942. It was then that the majority of Americans needed most to be educated about how to protect and preserve what they owned in the face of shortages or the unavailability of products that would worsen as the war went on. After the lean Depression years, starting in 1939 the new affluence born of the buildup of defense industries led many people to take a fairly cavalier attitude toward making what they owned last, whether bed sheets or Buicks. Once the United States was in the war and industry almost exclusively in war production, these same Americans had to be made aware that they wouldn't have many of their necessities, let alone luxury goods, if they didn't learn to take care of them. The slogan in the chapter title—"Use It Up, Wear It Out, Make It Do, or Do Without"—was just one of several designed to make people wake up and smell the (rationed) coffee.

Most conservation ads, both in 1942 and for the rest of the war, told people how to maintain just one kind of product (car, refrigerator, clothing, etc.). Such ads were usually placed by the manufacturer of one brand of the product in question or by the manufacturer of a product, such as motor oil, useful for conserving another product, in this case an automobile, truck, or farm machinery. Most conservation ads provided useful tips on how to protect whatever product one owned, regardless of make, brand, or model, but some advertisers discussed conserving only their own product (such as Mimeograph duplicators). While this may seem self-serving, some justification for this kind of advertising was given by Willard Chevalier, publisher of *Business Week*, in his weekly column "The Trading Post" on November 21, 1942: "The manufacturer who is now selling his goods to the government instead of to the civilian may still have a very proper need for advertising. He can very usefully, for instance, tell his former customers how to use and conserve and service the goods which he has previously sold them. Those goods in service may very well constitute the country's sole remaining stock of such articles. It is certainly right for the manufacturer to use advertising to help make that stock last" (127).

Only a few advertisers, both in 1942 and beyond, took up the challenge of presenting the case for conservation generally, but they did so in uncommonly eloquent, tough-talking, and powerful language. The Stewart-Warner Corporation in peacetime manufactured everything from refrigerators and electric ranges to lubricating equipment and speedometers. Straight talk characterized almost all Stewart-Warner war ads, but nowhere more so than in their ad in the *Post* on May 9, 1942, the first ad to make the case for wartime conservation generally: "*Your* job—your *big* job—is the prompt elimination of all forms of waste. That job starts right where you are—in your own home. To ask *what* to save is to admit a total lack of understanding of the crisis we face. *Save everything! Waste nothing!* That is your answer. And start today. Every minute lost can postpone the day of victory" (40). The ad concludes with a five-point "pledge" for civilians to live by, ending with "I will recognize this war as my war—a war that will not be won without my help, and will consecrate myself and what I have to that job." More quietly but no less sincerely, in *Life* on April 19, 1943, the Hoover (vacuum cleaner) Company looked at both the big picture and many of its specific components in an ad headed "A quiet street but A FIGHTING STREET" over a picture of houses in a suburb or small American town. While the ad lists the many ways that each family, each house, can aid the cause of conservation, it does so within a larger context: "Inside those walls, the war is being fought as tenaciously as on any battle front. It is a war of saving and thrift, of conservation and salvage, of doing with what you have, of lending all you can to the government" (39). And also in *Life*, on June 7, 1943, Goodyear took out a two-page spread that is unapologetically emotional and sentimental in making its case for conservation. Page 52 is a full-page illustration of a mother holding a telegram and looking skyward, seemingly trying to hold back her tears; page 53 contains all the copy—a description of this woman's home before her son was killed in action, a list of things one might want to say to people whose sons died in the war, concluding with "No, you can't say these things and have them really mean anything," and then presenting its hard-hitting pitch for conservation: "You can't say anything—you can only do. [. . .] You can only try, a little harder than you thought you could, to make sure that no boy, yours or any other's, falls because of anything you do or leave undone. [. . .] You can only fall in line with friend and neighbor and, through scrap drives and conservation campaigns, play your part as fully as you can, as every good soldier on the home front should. You can only remember that every helpful act, no matter how small, not only hastens Victory but does its share to bring more boys back before their blue stars turn to gold." Barely a handful of such sweeping pleas for civilian conservation appeared in national magazines, perhaps because readers preferred reading practical advice about how to preserve the specific things they owned, a supposition borne out by the appearance of more than four hundred ads in these magazines giving tips on pragmatic conservation. Ads telling how to protect big-ticket, virtually irreplaceable items formed the bulk of ads offering practical conservation advice—with those about taking care of one's car leading the pack.

"If You're Careless Today, You May Be Car-less Tomorrow"

The conservation ads placed by most automobile and automotive products manufacturers look as if they had eagerly taken to heart the words of Willard Chevalier. Almost all attached conserving cars to selling their own products or services. Only the rare few offered car care advice strictly on its own merit, rather than making the life of one's auto seem dependent on using such and such a motor oil or having it serviced only by a particular car dealership or gas station mechanic. Such advertising worked as much to the profit of the advertisers as to promoting car conservation for the sake of people's prized possessions and helping the war effort. These product/service-oriented ads fall into the War Advertising Council's category of Double-Barrelled advertising that included a war message and sold something in the same ad.

The importance of the automobile in American culture is so obvious that it would be hardly worth mentioning were it not that wartime conditions magnified that importance yet more. Efficient and uninterrupted war production depended on most workers traveling to and from work in private cars. Basing its information on figures from the Office of Defense Transportation, an ad placed by Stewart-Warner's Alemite lubricants, lubricating equipment, and motor oil in *Collier's* on April 24, 1943, could say that "If all the streetcars and buses in America were packed to capacity every morning and night, they could carry just 1 out of every 5 workers to work and back. 4 out of 5 would have to get to work in private cars. Or walk! Or face the cold truth that the man who can't get to his job doesn't have a job!" (9). In *Life* on October 19, 1942, Chevrolet offered up the minutiae of eight separate statistics regarding the importance of both cars and trucks during the war, most based on reports from the Michigan State Highway Department. To cite just one of the most eye-opening ones, "2,314 U. S. cities, with a combined population of 12,524,000, depend on private cars for transportation; and 54,000 U. S. cities depend *entirely* on motor vehicles" (23; emphasis added). If all such vehicles were suddenly out of repair or out of commission entirely, American war production, indeed the entire American way of life as we know it, would grind to a halt. The moral: Keep your car in good repair or go without one.

That was the unambiguous message of the ads placed by numerous automobile dealers or manufacturers as well as by makers of tires, batteries, spark plugs, and antifreeze, not to mention the plethora of advertisements from producers of petroleum products. The message was the same whether the ad was selling a product or just offering sound advice on proper automobile maintenance. Most of these ads were so similar in their content and approach that a broad range of illustrative quotations would be simply redundant. By dividing the ads into those selling a product, those offering a service, and those suggesting car maintenance guidelines with no selling at all, just a few examples of each will illustrate the general character of automobile conservation ads.

The purveyors of lubricants and motor oil were uniformly the most aggressive salesmen. To an ad, each one devoted far fewer words to car conservation per se than to extolling the virtues of its products. From a Texaco ad in *Life* on June 29, 1942, we get: "Your car—like your Victory Garden—is a national asset these days. So care for it wisely! Spare it excessive wear with stem-to-stern Marfak chassis lubricant," the rest of the ad describing how Marfak lubricant is best for one's car (83). And from Mobil in *Life* on April 24, 1944: "Will your present car last until you can get a new one? Don't take chances—*do this now:* Get Summer Mobiloil, the world's largest-selling motor oil, for your engine" (9). While the message and emphasis were similar in a series of ads in *Life* from the Pennzoil Company, at least they were genuinely fun and funny, each featuring one of cartoonist Rube Goldberg's wacky machines, those in the ads supposedly designed to make a car run longer on less gas (see fig. 23a for a typical example). But after the fun at the top of the ad, it's back to the business of selling a car care product with only a nod to broader conservation: "With PennZoil [sic], you get the oil made especially to keep your engine clean and easy on the gas" (15 March 1943: 12). Ads for batteries (Delco, Exide), spark plugs (Champion, AC), and antifreeze (Prestone, Zerex) all recommended regular inspections of these products and replacing them, when necessary, with the brand the particular ad was promoting.

Ads offering a service were, in part at least, giving away something for nothing—the periodic inspection of one's car to keep it in top running order. It was only when an auto needed an oil change, grease job, or tuneup, or a part needed to be repaired or (God forbid, with the shortage of spare parts) replaced, that the car owner would incur an expense. Both dealerships and service stations used national advertising to promote such services, and, of course, tout their own as the best in the business. Most dealership ads were quite succinct, encouraging regular service without stating just what needed to be looked at. Late in the war, in *Life* on May 7, 1945, all that Packard had to say was "Go to your Packard dealer and have him check the *little* troubles before they grow into *big*

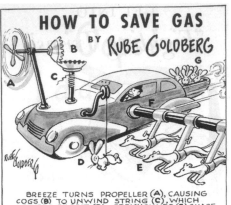

FIGURE 23A

FIGURE 23B

ones" (85). Chevrolet said of the Chevy service man, "Help him to help you and America by getting a skilled service check-up at regular intervals" (*Life*, 19 Oct. 1942: 23), and in the same magazine on May 18, 1942, Chevrolet offered a free "Car Conservation" booklet to anyone who stopped in at a dealership to get one or wrote for one (22). The Oldsmobile Dealers of America got down to a few more specifics in *Collier's* on March 13, 1943, when they explained that the Olds service man helps protect cars "against the ill effects of low speeds and limited driving— such as run-down battery, neglected tires, diluted lubricants, sticky valves" (35).

By and large, the ads placed by major chains of service stations provided drivers with far more information about what the stations' mechanics could do for their cars. One of the earliest of such ads, the Texaco ad headed "If you're careless today you may be car-less tomorrow," in *Life* on May 4, 1942, strung out quite a litany of what's in the regular "systematic servicing" of an automobile, including *"regular care* of tires, air-cleaner, battery, spark plugs, radiator, front wheel bearings, crankcase, transmission, differential, and body finish" (53). Similarly, in *Life* on both May 25 and August 10, 1942, Mobil included in its ad a ten-point checklist of what one's local Mobil dealer should check, inspect, or condition at various intervals of time or mileage. Sinclair dealers ran a series of seven half-page ads in *Life* between May 18 and October 5, 1942, that more briefly just recommended regular "Sinclair-ize service" for one's car. What makes these ads distinctive is that each is headed by a close-up photo of a particularly unpleasant looking person in a state of anger, dismay, or disbelief, saying such things as "Walk! Who Me?" "Walk? Don't kid me!" or "Walk! with my fallen arches?" at the prospect of not having a car if it's not properly serviced. One ad in the series is of special interest since the picture is that of a black man—actually looking more like a Caucasian in caricature blackface—saying "Walk! Is mah feet sad!" This is the only ad in the series *not* published in *Life*, but only on page 51 of *Collier's* for June 27, 1942, my best guess being that the generally liberal publishers of *Life* found the racist overtones of the ad not in keeping with the spirit of their magazine (see fig. 23b). Be that as it may, for all the good advice from dealerships and gas stations about having automobiles regularly checked and serviced, none of their ads addressed what car owners themselves could do to prolong the health and life of their vehicles. Such advice came only from ads that were selling absolutely nothing.

Advertisers offering such free car care advice included at least one company that had nothing to do with the automotive industry, and the ad gave advice on how to help conserve vehicles other than one's own. In a Black & White Scotch Whisky [sic] ad in *Time* on October 25, 1943, our ever-helpful, patriotic canine friends Blackie and Whitey are seen walking down a street, each with a neatly wrapped and tied package in his (her?) mouth. Blackie says, "That storekeeper was sure glad when we said we'd carry our own bundles, Whitey." To which Whitey replies, "He knows what it means to save trucks and tires—for Victory, Blackie." After this dialogue the copy explains that rather than having your purchases delivered (a common enough practice in the '40s), "Every package you carry saves trucks and tires for vital deliveries—to keep foodstuffs coming to the grocer and the dairy, to keep raw materials moving to factories. So don't go away empty-handed. Carry your own bundles—for Victory!" (61). All this with nary a word about buying the advertiser's brand of Scotch.

Taking vehicle conservation a giant step beyond passenger cars, a number of automotive and petroleum products companies gave advice to farmers on the proper care of their trucks and other equipment in ads published in *Farm Journal* and other agrarian magazines such as *Country Gentleman*. International Harvester and Studebaker were in the vanguard of such advertising, the former in the July 1942 *Farm Journal* admonishing farmers, "IN WARTIME, KEEP AN EYE ON EVERYTHING!"— following that general remark with a long paragraph of particulars such as "lubrication and greasing; periodic inspections and adjustments; repainting; . . . Care of sheet metal and wooden parts . . . Care of belts, chains, clutches, springs, bearings" and many more things to keep one's eye on in valuable and virtually irreplaceable farm machinery and trucks. IH then offered farmers the free booklet "Your Farm Equipment—Take Care of It and Make It Do," packed with more detail on how to maintain and repair seed drills, threshing machines, combines, and the like (12). Studebaker confined itself to the proper care of farm trucks in a series of five *Farm Journal* ads in 1944 and 1945. Each ad offered the free handbook, "Care and Maintenance of the Farm Truck in Wartime." Not to be outdone by the farm implement and automotive firms, in the March and April 1943 issues of *Farm Journal* Texaco gave away its own free book, "Harvest Gold—1943 War Edition: Texaco Farm Machinery Manual."

The most detailed conservation tips for passenger cars came from the Stewart-Warner Corporation, makers of Alemite lubricants and motor oil along with a host of things not related to cars. In a typical Stewart-Warner ad in the *Post* for April 25, 1942, a long list of practical advice appears, including in part: "Don't waste mileage! Limit your driving to essential transportation. Check tire pressure once a week—wheel alignment at regular intervals—to avoid needless tire wear. Drive at lower speeds—make tires, gas and oil go farther. [. . .] Watch brake and clutch adjustment—steering gear play—head and tail lamps" (55). Most striking about all the Stewart-Warner car maintenance ads is their generous, non-self-serving spirit when speaking of lubrication and oil changes: "Give your car ample lubrication. Whether you prefer Alemite lubricants or others—get them and get them regularly."

Also generous were the numerous car conservation ads placed by tire and rubber companies, notably General Tire and United States Rubber, as well as a leading manufacturer of tire repair materials and equipment, the Bowes "Seal Fast" Corporation. One reason such companies, with the possible exception of Bowes, could afford such magnanimity is that they literally had next to nothing to sell to home front civilians except the rare few, such as doctors, who had priority status for purchasing new tires when needed (doctors still routinely made house calls during the war years). Virtually all the ads by these rubber companies during the course of 1942 reiterated the same points about how to prolong tire wear. Typical is part of the list in the United States Rubber ad in *Life* on September 14: "Drive only when it is absolutely necessary. Keep under 40 miles per hour and well under. Take it easy. Start, stop and turn slowly. Keep away from curbs, ruts, holes, rocks, bumps. Have tires examined regularly for cuts and bruises. Keep wheels balanced and aligned and brakes adjusted" (55).

Yet for all the public-spirited helpfulness of advertisers giving car care advice, many home front civilians continued to neglect proper maintenance of their automobiles. According to a Mobil ad in *Life* on April 24, 1944, "At the present rate, over 600,000 U. S. cars will be junked between now and Fall—and many more will be nearing the end of the trail" (9). At that rate, some 4,800,000 cars wound up in the junkyards affectionately known as "automobile graveyards" over the four years of the war.

"I Will Take Good Care of the Things I Have"

So says a woman, her right hand raised as if taking a solemn oath, at the top of the Kalamazoo Stove & Furnace Company ad in *Life* on January 11, 1943. The copy then gives explicit and detailed instructions on the care of gas and electric stoves, heaters, and furnaces. The Kalamazoo ad is typical of numerous others that encouraged and gave pointers on the conservation of household appliances large and small throughout the entire course of the war, most such advertising sponsored by manufacturers of the kinds of products discussed in their ads. But occasionally such ads came from other sources. The Chesapeake & Ohio Lines in *Newsweek* on November 27, 1944, instructed homeowners on how to clean coal-burning furnaces, C&O's concern being conservation of the coal the railroad hauled in huge quantities from mines to steel mills and other war industries. Sometimes even totally disinterested parties chimed in, as when again those ever-vigilant doggies in the Black & White Scotch ads chatted in front of a blazing fireplace: "Blackie: 'See, Whitey—we can still be warm without wasting too much precious fuel.' Whitey: 'Yes, Blackie—but what should people do who have no fireplaces?'" (*Life* 7 Dec. 1942: 90). The rest of the ad answers that question: "You can save up to 50% of your fuel: 1. by checking your heating equipment to make sure it runs properly! 2. by making sure your home is *heat-tight*—to prevent leakage" and by getting fuel-saving suggestions from one's local heating expert.

But in the main advertisers gave advice on how to prolong the useful life of their own kinds of products, if not of just the brands that they themselves manufactured. The seemingly ubiquitous Stewart-Warner Corporation—in its capacity as maker of Dual-Temp Refrigerators—devoted an entire full-page ad in the *Post* on May 23, 1942, to the proper use (don't put hot food in the fridge), placement in a room, and care of refrigerators, as did the Frigidaire division of General Motors in *Life* on July 12, 1943. Similarly, General Electric ran an ad of practical do's and don't's headed "How to Make Your Radio Last Longer" in both *Life* on May 25, 1942, and in the July '42 issue of *Esquire*. Still other appliance conservation ads were brand specific: In several ads Hoover recommended steps to take for prolonging the life of its vacuum cleaners, and Toastmaster how to do the same for its toasters.

Not just big-ticket household fixtures and small appliances required special treatment to outlast the war. In its need for uniforms, fatigues, battle gear, sheets, blankets, parachutes, shoes, and boots, the military put a tremendous strain on the textiles and leather available for civilian consumption. The resultant shortages of household textiles such as sheets, blankets, and towels and of fabric for civilian clothing prompted

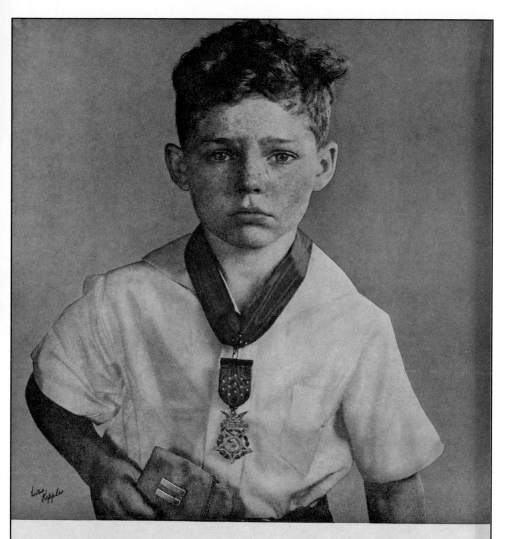

He knows why this Christmas
all of us should GIVE WAR BONDS

THE GENERAL TIRE & RUBBER COMPANY · AKRON, OHIO

See Figure 4 and the accompanying text

BACK HOME FOR KEEPS

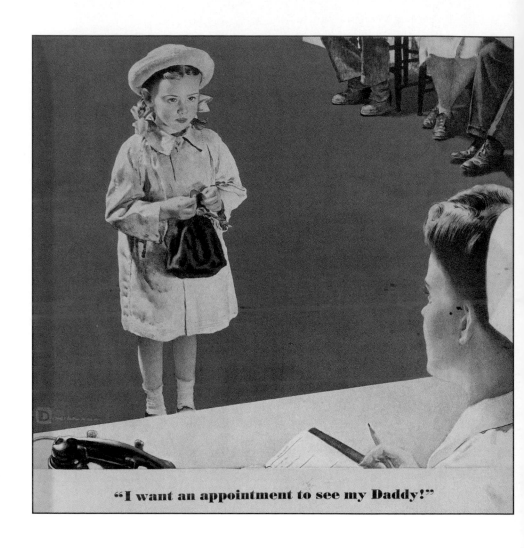

"I want an appointment to see my Daddy!"

The Less Said, the Less Dead

Keep it under your
STETSON

This is my Birthright!

This is what a man can tie to. No matter how black the casualty lists, or how long victory is in coming; no matter how truth is twisted to selfish ends; no matter how the effort of the nation seems to flounder: *here I will make my stand.*

No power on earth can shake my faith in this land which is my home. Its beauty and its bounty are part of me. I have breathed the free wind that blows across its mountains and prairies, woods and farms. *It has given me liberty to make a life in my own way. To work, to build a home and raise my children, to worship God as I see fit.*

I am sick of all wars, and who is not? I am worried about my fighter sons, and discouraged by long-drawn months of uncertainty. But there is an inner depth of my spirit that has never faltered.

I will keep on and I will do my best. My job, my gifts of blood to the Red Cross, the money I lend to my Government are small things by themselves. But I am not alone. There are millions of others like me—quiet, unimportant people, *willing to give all they have to keep their country free.*

I am protecting my future as an American with every War Bond I can buy.

Admiral Nimitz is Banking on You

American fighting men by the millions are expecting us at home to turn out war equipment and to buy War Bonds to the very limit. When you buy Bonds you help pulverize the enemy—yet make a sound investment and get your money back with interest. Buy an extra War Bond today.

Together Again!

MILLIONS of loved ones are now back home, taking up the pursuits of peaceful living. And the hope of all of us is that never again will they— or another generation—need to be separated from us by war. For the part that it was our privilege to play in speeding this reunion, we of the Chesapeake and Ohio are truly grateful.

Right now, as we welcome back our personnel who have been serving their country, we are going full steam ahead in a program to provide you with the finest of travel accommodations.

So that some day soon—after we have helped speed many more people in uniform on their way home—we can again suggest that you travel by the road on which you "sleep like a kitten."

The illustration above is from the new 1946 Chessie calendar. If you want one free of charge, better write and reserve yours now. We're printing only a limited number.

CHESAPEAKE AND OHIO RAILWAY

3312 Terminal Tower • Cleveland 1, Ohio

a large number of ads on how to make one's "soft goods" last until the Victory. (A few early ads dealt with shoe conservation, but since actual shoe rationing went into effect in February 1943, most shoe ads focused on coping with that. These are taken up Chapter 7.)

Most of the domestic textile conservation ads with different art and copy were those devoted to the proper care and feeding of bed sheets, not men's, women's, or children's clothing. All the major manufacturers came on board: Utica and Mohawk Mills, Pacific Mills, Pepperell, and, especially, Cannon, which led with twenty-eight sheet care ads between July 13, 1942, and November 5, 1945, plus another eight on towels, all of them in *Life*. What's remarkable about the Cannon ads is that while each reiterates certain basic ways to reduce wear on sheets by proper presoaking, washing, rinsing, and drying on a line outdoors, every ad manages to come up with yet more pointers for housewives on how to care for their precious store of bed linens (see fig. 24 for a typical Cannon ad on page 6 of *Life* for April 12, 1943). At the same time, Cannon ads encouraged replacing worn-out sheets with Cannon Percales, but they urged *buying* sheets as only a last-ditch maneuver during wartime. The other makers of bed linens were not so prolific in their conservation advertising, but they all gave at least basic advice on how to get the longest wear from one's sheets, as did Kenwood Mills and Chatham for blankets.

The promotion of clothing conservation was a more sporadic, catch-as-catch-can affair, inspiring no sustained campaigns like Cannon's for sheets, although a number of prominent clothing and stocking manufacturers put in an appearance for at least one or two conservation ads each. Arrow Shirts placed seven ads on "How to add months to the life of your shirts!"—all in *Life*—between September 27, 1943, and May 21, 1945. Each ad featured different cartoon-like drawings, but much of the copy was verbatim from one ad to the next, describing everything from proper washing of dress shirts to more difficult tasks like "turning" a frayed collar (reversing the seen and unseen sides of a shirt collar). Hart Schaffner & Marx, makers of fine men's suits, throughout the war published ads on numerous war-related concerns but only two on the conservation of clothes in the face of the impending wool shortage caused by military needs. In two different ads, one in the November 1942 issue of *Esquire*, the other in *Life* for November 16 of the same year, the clothing manufacturer presented eight practical ways to make men's suits last longer. Not to be outdone by the makers of shirts and suits, in *Life* on

"Look! There's a ███ man under my bed!"

"THAT'S BILL. He's my husband. I've put him to work fixing that loose bed spring that just tore one of my precious Cannon Percale Sheets. It won't happen again!

"Now that it's wartime, sheets just *have* to be Methuselahs! The government wants all of us to make *everything we have* last longer—so we won't need to buy more, unnecessarily. That's plain waste!

"And it's awfully easy to make sheets last and last. Why, a home-economics expert told me that if women took the best possible care of sheets, they'd probably last *twice as long*. The sheets would, I mean. So I've learned a whole bag of tricks that mean long life to a sheet!"

My common-sense sheet-savers.

"I make sure nothing about the beds can catch and tear my sheets. (Now that one sheet's been torn!) I lift sheets off gently instead of yanking them. And the minute I spot a rip or worn place, I scurry for my mending basket!"

My washday wiles.

"I'm a clock-watcher—15 minutes for soaking

sheets; 5 to 8 minutes of washing in the machine. Then plenty of rinses to get every smitch of soap out. And *then* I pray for sunshine—my favorite bleach!"

My hints for hanging.

"I fold my sheets hem to hem, and clothespin 'em with the fold hanging over about a foot. If it's windy, I hang them in a sheltered spot where they won't flap too much."

My ironing ideas.

"I don't use too hot an iron—that causes 'hidden scorch'—death on sheets! I never bear down directly on the folds. Before I put my sheets away, I make sure they're bone-dry so they won't mildew. And I use 'em round-robin style—taking fresh sheets from the *bottom* of the pile every time—to equalize wear."

My tip-off when you must buy sheets.

"Of course, you won't buy unless you're in desperate need! But when your linen-cupboard is

really bare, remember this: smooth, dreamy-soft Cannon Percales cost just about the same as heavy-duty muslin. And there are 25% more threads to the inch in Cannon Percales than in the best muslin—wonderful for wear!

"And Cannon Percales save money if you send your wash out at average pound laundry rates—because percale's lighter. Easier to do at home, too!"

My best words of advice.

"Don't buy sheets unless you honestly have to! If you *do*, be sure to pick a name you can trust for all the things you can't see for yourself in a sheet. Take the Cannon name—you've seen it on those wonderful Cannon Towels! It's every bit as dependable on sheets!

"One last reminder. Whether you buy new Cannon Percale Sheets or own some already—resolve to add *years* to their life by proper care."

Cannon also makes an economy muslin sheet—well-constructed, long-wearing—a splendid value!

Cannon Percale Sheets

CANNON Made by the makers of Cannon Towels and Hosiery

6

FIGURE 24

August 31, 1942, Munsingwear placed a full-page ad offering nine tips on prolonging the life of all manner of underwear, both men's and women's, each pointer accompanied by a rather cute drawing, and on May 31, 1943, also in *Life*, but in a much smaller ad and much more briefly, Maiden Form told women how to get the most wear out of their brassieres, heading the ad with the familiar slogan, "Use It Up, Wear It Out, Make It Do!" but, in those "pre-lib" days, omitting "Or Do Without!" Also for women, Mojud Hosiery described how to get the longest wear from its rayon stockings in an ad in *Life* on November 30, 1942 (except on the Black Market nylon was long gone by then for military uses, primarily parachutes).

A few ads regarding some random products will illustrate the extent of the concern for conservation in the face of the absence or shortage of consumer goods. On June 16 and July 27, 1942, in *Life*, the Wilson Sporting Goods Company filled two different ads with specific advice on prolonging the usefulness of everything from golf clubs to footballs. In *Life* on November 8, 1942, Eveready explained how to conserve flashlights and batteries. In *Look* on February 9, 1943, Gem Razors and Blades offered ways to prevent damage to their no-longer-manufactured safety razors (there were still blades aplenty), and on October 19, 1942, in *Life*, Mennen urged men to buy shave cream in jars rather than tubes to help conserve the tin so vital to war work. The tin shortage was so severe and the need for tin so great that six months before the Mennen ad the War Production Board ruled that people buying shaving cream or toothpaste in tin tubes "had to put a used tube along with their cash on the counter" (*Business Week* 4 Apr. 1942: 8). The tubes collected by drug stores and other retailers were to make up for and, ideally, eliminate the estimated "25 tons of tubes that are discarded daily" (*Business Week* 14 Feb. 1942; 18).

Virtually all conservation ads in the leading general-interest magazines were aimed at civilian consumers. But there was also a small group that targeted the business community, all—with the exception of ads on how to keep one's Mimeograph machine up and running—dealing with one particular article—typewriters. Some of these ads had a character, and an angle, all their own. During the war, America's three leading typewriter manufacturers—Underwood, Smith-Corona, and Royal— were not, of course, manufacturing typewriters but were engaged in various kinds of war production. Accordingly, the ads of all three companies (very few by Underwood, incidentally) focused on how individuals and businesses could keep their typewriters in good working order so that they would hold up until new machines could be produced. But in the late summer and fall of 1942 a new dimension was added to the Royal and Smith-Corona ads typified by the words in Royal's ad in *Life* on August 24, 1942, headed, "Brother can you spare a typewriter to help win the war?": "We're not *selling* Royal Typewriters today . . . WE'RE BUYING 'EM! The United States Government is in urgent need of 600,000 typewriters—for use by the Army . . . the Navy . . . the Air Corps . . . the Marine Corps. These machines are needed for speeding up war production and the movement of supplies—transmitting orders to troops on land . . . ships at sea . . . even planes in the air. The typed message is the fastest, most reliable means of written communication! *Typewriters are essential to Victory!*" (103). This ad and the others by both Royal and Smith-Corona explained their buy-back scheme in which all standard (not portable) typewriters of their own manufacture made since January 1, 1935, would be purchased at their 1941 trade-in value regardless of the shape they were in, to be reconditioned and sent to the government for distribution to the armed forces. This program appears to be the only case of conserved, still usable equipment—not scrap—going directly into the business of fighting the war.

"Get in the Scrap!"

In 1942 Bing Crosby promoted scrap drives on the radio with the song "Junk Ain't Junk No More ('Cause Junk Will Win the War)" (see Jones 203). During World War II, junk, scrap, salvage, or what we call recyclables today were big business, with war industries depending heavily on scrap metal, rubber, paper, and kitchen fats for the production of everything from bombers to bullets. And when Fats Waller sang the hilarious "(Get Some) Cash for Your Trash," which he wrote and recorded just weeks after Pearl Harbor, he was actually serious, since households, factories, and farms didn't have to just donate their scrap but could sell metal, rubber, and paper to junk dealers and brokers throughout the war. Housewives could exchange kitchen fats at the butcher's for either cash or ration coupons.

That the wartime need for scrap was real and critical is made manifest by *Business Week* publishing no fewer than fifteen long articles on it between February 14, 1942, and January 20, 1945, as well as numerous short blurbs about scrap in the magazine's weekly columns of business-news briefs. A journey through the articles reveals detailed information about kinds of scrap, its need in various industries, the ups and downs of the junk business, the successes and failures of various scrap drives, and the critical shortage of scrap, primarily iron and steel, at various points in the war. Also, some little-known, fascinating facts about scrap turn up, like a drive for obsolete door keys in the fall of 1942 that yielded 200 million of them turned in at collection points. That number of keys translated into "over 3,000,000 lb. of scarce copper, zinc, and nickel, plus significant amounts of not-so-scarce lead, iron, and steel," all of which would go into the production of war materials (*Business Week* 16 Jan. 1943: 59). But the most pertinent information in these articles is that war industries depended first on industrial scrap for its quantity and quality, second on farm scrap, and only third on household drives that "yield mostly inferior scrap and are a headache to scrap dealers because, on the whole, it is light and mixed with other metals requiring an unusual amount of preparation" (*Business Week* 3 Oct. 1942: 19). Still, in national magazines, only an occasional ad sent out a call for industrial or farm scrap. Most ads for industrial scrap appeared in industry trade papers, and most for farm scrap in local rural newspapers and magazines. Inexplicably, not one ad calling for farm scrap appeared in *Farm Journal* during the entire war. On the other hand, in the large-circulation magazines, appeals for the supposedly "inferior" household scrap were legion, many clustered together at certain times during the war, suggesting they were parts of coordinated, large-scale advertising campaigns for domestic scrap.

Yet it's clear that the War Advertising Council did not coordinate the large number of scrap collection ads placed in magazines by commercial advertisers during the summer and fall of 1942, except in a very indirect way. At that same time, the Council was presented with one of its earliest and biggest challenges from the Office of War Information, the Bureau of Industrial Conservation, and the Office for Emergency Management—to organize advertising support for a widespread "general salvage campaign" (*Business Week* 27 June 1942: 20). Following its accustomed modus operandi (see Chapter 1 and *Business Week* 3 July 1943: 82–83 for more details), the Ad Council itself initially examined the problem and recommended ways to best approach it. It then turned over the matter of scrap drive ads to a single (volunteer) agency, Leo Burnett, to map out a general advertising campaign and suggest sample copy for ads. This done, sponsorship for the campaign had to be found, not just for print advertising but for radio spots as well, but the task of scrap drive ads was so huge that no single manufacturer was willing to accept the administrative or financial burden. The campaign finally fell into the category of "association advertising" when the American Iron and Steel Institute picked up the primary sponsorship with the Automotive Safety Foundation coming along for the ride (see *Business Week* 27 June 1942: 20). As was the Council's policy for all campaigns it spearheaded, the sponsor chose an ad agency to work with (usually one it had worked with before), in this case McCann-Erickson. What all this means is that two trade associations placed every ad in the Council's campaign for the government's scrap drive in the summer and fall of 1942, while those placed by commercial advertisers were strictly independent efforts.

In the leading national magazines no scrap ads appeared during the pertinent months placed by the American Iron and Steel Institute and/or the Automotive Safety Foundation. The closest that any ads come are a mere one or two very prosy ones scattered in *Life*, *Time*, and *Business Week* between late July and late September 1942, each ad a slight variation of the same copy and each bearing a small photo of Donald M. Nelson, chairman of the War Production Board, smoking his pipe. Not at all eye-catching, these wordy scrap appeals all included at the bottom, "This advertisement paid for by the American Industries Salvage Committee" and "This message approved by Conservation Division [of the] War Production Board" (*Business Week* 22 Aug. 1942: 59). The index of advertisers in *Business Week* lists the ad agency as well as the advertiser of each ad, revealing that the agency responsible for these mundane ads—far less appealing than any scrap ads by commercial advertisers—was none other than McCann-Erickson, the agency employed by the American Iron and Steel Institute for the campaign launched by the War Advertising Council. Apparently the Institute created the Industries Salvage Committee as the nominal sponsor of its scrap ads. Given the infrequency and poor quality of these ads in major national magazines, one can only hope that the $2 million price tag for Washington's scrap campaign was better spent on ads in newspapers or on the radio. But whatever the case, the Council's campaign on behalf of the government's urgent request for scrap was indirectly the impetus for commercial advertisers to make their own voices heard simultaneously, frequently, and usually better—thus the numerous commercially sponsored scrap ads during the same time frame.

Between May 11 (more than a month before the Ad Council's campaign began) through November 16, 1942, in *Life*, *Collier's*, *Newsweek*, *Time*, *Business Week*, *Ladies' Home Journal*, *Esquire*, and the *Post*, advertisers as diverse as Republic Steel, Johnson's Wax, Black & White Scotch, United States Rubber, and International Harvester made impassioned appeals for household scrap, a few companies making a pitch for industrial and farm scrap as well. While the goal of all these companies' ads was the same, the similarity among scrap ads pretty much ends there, with their methods of cajoling home front civilians to "Get in the Scrap!" displaying as much imagination as urgency. Johnson's Wax titled the earliest scrap ad "SPRING HOUSE CLEANING 1942—FORWARD MARCH WITH THE SCRAP BRIGADE!" (*Life* 11 May 1942: 42–43). The two-page spread featured a mother and young daughter dressed exactly alike—typical of mother–daughter duos in war ads—first seen marching with brooms over their shoulders. In seven other photos they combine spring cleaning with clearing out junk of every description, mostly from the basement and attic. United States Rubber took a totally different approach in a two-page ad in *Life* on July 20, 1942, focusing on what scrap helps make for the war, such as "Subs and ships are 50% scrap metal, Scrap rubber makes tires for trucks and jeeps, 1 old radiator makes an aerial bomb, 1 refrigerator makes 3 machine guns" (74–75). In *Newsweek* on September 28, 1942, an ad titled "Are you HOARDING?" by the John A. Roebling's Sons Company baldly appealed to readers' guilt: "[. . .] you are hoarding . . . IF, in your yard, or in your attic, or in your basement, you are allowing a pound—yes, *one pound*—of iron or steel or other metal to lie, wasted, while American furnaces shut down for lack of it . . . IF, on your farm you are allowing old tools or equipment or junk to rust to nothingness, while American boys click triggers on empty guns" (57).

Most of the 1942 scrap ads by commercial advertisers stressed scrap in general or metal in particular, but a few focused on rubber, and these were as varied in their approach as the others. In *Collier's* on September 12, 1942, the Black & White Scotch Scottie and Westie are rolling around in an old tire before turning it in: "Don't wait another day! Turn in every scrap of rubber you can find—to your local salvage agency" (40). United States Rubber struck a grim and thoughtful note in the October 1942 issue of *Esquire*. A drawing of a downed American flier bobbing about in the water in a rubber life jacket was captioned "Thanks for the Rubber that Saved his Life!" The copy asked people not to let up since rubber and other scrap will be "continually necessary until the war is over" (3).

During the same months in 1942 that the War Advertising Council directed Washington's general salvage campaign, its $2 million budget paid for by sponsoring trade associations, the Council also launched a separate campaign for "educating the housewife to save fats and greases," sponsored by another trade association, Glycerine and Associated Industries, with an advertising budget of $500,000 (*Business Week* 27 June 1942: 20). But this time no commercial advertisers in the major national magazines rode the coattails of the campaign, even as critical as kitchen fats were for making glycerine, which in turn was vital for the production of gunpowder and other ammunition. Only in 1943 and '44 did commercially sponsored kitchen fats ads appear. Among the earliest was one of Calvert's "Metropolitan Moments" cartoon ads in the March 1943 *Esquire* in which the affluent moustached gentleman proclaimed, "We're Saving All Our Fats and Greases / To Blow the Axis All to Pieces" (163). In *Life* on August 16 and the *Post* on August 28, 1943, the Statler Hotels more seriously explained to housewives why the fats they should save were more important than "the comparatively large quantities of fats and grease which the 42 kitchens of the 8 hotels in the Statler organization carefully salvage, plus that saved by all the other hotels," simply because there were more women cooking in more homes, and, hence, generating more fats and grease than all America's hotels put together (*Life* 39; *Post* 99). A kitchen fats ad in *Life* on April 3, 1944, is not only a vigorous and humorous promotion for saving fats and grease but also a superior example of how a Double-Barrelled ad can effectively both get a war message across and sell a product. The ad (see fig. 25) is one in Sanka Coffee's cartoon-and-dialogue "War Conscience" series in which a particularly insistent and aggressive personified Conscience goes after a housewife for neglecting one of her "War Jobs"—always a housewife who's too sleepless, stressed out, or wired from caffeine to pay much attention to anything (52).

Calls for scrap in advertising can be useful barometers of what materials were in critically short supply at different times during the war. For example, throughout all of 1943 and on into January 1944, there were renewed calls for metal, but most specifically for tin, in magazine ads placed by such companies as Westinghouse, Martin Aircraft, Campbell's

"YOU PINCHED ME!"

War Conscience: Certainly I pinched you, dearie. I'm your new Wartime Conscience. And if you keep throwing out perfectly good kitchen fate that way, I'll have you black and blue all over in a week.

Woman: Black and bl—! Why—! I'll—

War Conscience: Tut, Madam! Do you realize that your Government needs that Waste Kitchen fat of yours so badly for ammunition that it's willing to give you two whole meat points, for just a pound of it? Do you—?

Woman: Certainly I realize it. But do you know I didn't sleep a wink last night, just because I had one measly cup of coffee for dinner? And do you realize

maybe a person forgets her War Duty sometimes when she's tired or something?

War Conscience: Personally, Madam, I don't care how tired you get! Your Government needs you to do your War Job, and I'm here to see you do it. And as far as not sleeping goes—hasn't anybody ever told you about caffein-free coffee?

Woman: What?

War Conscience: Caffein-free, dear. Take Sanka Coffee, for instance. 97% caffein-free. Lets you sleep and sleep and *sleep.* And flavor! Madam, this Sanka Coffee is

the strawberry shortcake of the coffee world! It is the coffee that eliminates the man who says he can't get a good cup of coffee. It's the crème de la crème for the woman who's kept awake by caffein.

Woman: Really?

War Conscience: Certainly, dearie! Try it …but remember this…Sanka Coffee may let you sleep, but *I* won't if you fall down on your Wartime Job! That's all, Sister!

A Product of General Foods ★ Listen to the Kate Smith Hour every Friday evening. CBS Network.

FIGURE 25

Soup, and Green Giant. The first two needed tin for war production, the second two packaged their products in tin cans that should be saved for the junk dealer and not thrown away. While I have found no evidence that the Ad Council organized a campaign for saving waste paper, it's striking that between late February 1944 and mid-September 1945, commercial advertisers placed no fewer than fourteen ads in all the major magazines except *Look* and *Farm Journal*, calling for saving and turning in waste paper and cardboard to be reprocessed for military purposes. That number of ads in a comparatively short period of time suggests there was an actual, impending, or projected paper shortage during those months. The range of advertisers stressing the urgent need for paper is extremely broad, with only a few like the Container Corporation of America and Kimberly-Clark engaged in the making of paper products themselves. Others included (yet again) Black & White Scotch, Hart Schaffner & Marx, *McCall's Magazine*, Dole, Ansco Films and Cameras, Sanka, and Unguentine. That the paper situation was acute is indicated pointedly yet humorously in an ad by Taylor Instruments in *Business Week* for May 27, 1944: "It's enough to make an editor weep. But the thing to do with this magazine (after reading it) is give it to your local Waste Paper Drive" (97).

It almost goes without saying that scrap drives aided home front efficiency in very material ways, especially from the standpoint of war production. Yet numerous other ads pointed out many more ways, some seemingly inconsequential but actually not, in which civilians could help make the home front a more efficient component of the overall fighting machine.

The Spirit of Efficiency
Analogous to the familiar "If you're not part of the solution, you're part of the problem," the attitude of some especially emphatic war ads was "If you're not helping home front efficiency, you're obstructing it." A number of such ads appeared in business-oriented magazines like *Time* and *Business Week*, but their copy makes it apparent that the ads were addressed not just to war industries but to the entire American public. Aside from a statement at the bottom about how its main copy related specifically to the ad's sponsor, York Refrigeration and Air Conditioning, the entirety of that copy was simply "If it won't help WIN THE WAR for-

get it!" (*Time* 5 Oct. 1942: 47). In *Business Week* on December 12, 1942, an ad by the Philadelphia Textile Finishers paraphrased that sentiment, making it perfectly clear to whom it was addressed: "How many more will die before the 'People of the United States' deliver the goods needed to win this war? Whatever you are doing, if it does not help win Victory, better skip it" (4). Two weeks earlier, that same advertiser placed another ad in *Business Week* on November 28 in which the art depicted a line of eight people—seven men and a woman—queuing up to buy tickets from the "Life & Business as Usual Excursion Company." The ticket-seller was a leering skeleton, and the ad was headed "THESE PEOPLE ARE LOSING THE WAR!" The copy enumerated seven types of Americans obstructing full home front participation, including "CAPITALISTS—using it to make large profits. WORKMEN—killing time . . . doing careless work . . . staying away from the job. MR. and MRS. PUBLIC—hoarding . . . and scheming to get sugar, gasoline, tires . . . and griping because there are no bananas for banana splits" (23). A more positive note for full home front efficiency was struck by Duo-Therm Fuel Oil Heaters in the February 1944 *Farm Journal*, showing how *every* member of a farm family was supporting the war effort, including, "*Dad*, short of help, increased his dairy herd, organized a machinery pool, headed up War Bond drive. [. . .] *Daughter Sue* a Nurses' Aide in town; four-time donor to the blood bank; works at the USO" (77). One last example of this general push for home front efficiency is also a splendid example of how sentiment—extremely moving sentiment—could serve the cause of wartime causes well. In the Weatherhead Company ad on the back cover of *Business Week* for October 9, 1943, the art depicted a young girl looking upward as a medal on a ribbon was placed around her neck. That medal, the copy reveals, was the Congressional Medal of Honor bestowed posthumously on little Nancy Jane's father who was "killed in action at the victorious Battle of Midway" (see fig. 26). The emotional tug of the copy describing the presentation and what the loss of her father means to Nancy Jane is positively heartbreaking at the same time that it leads in perfectly to the ad's conclusion, "Every single second lost today on our production lines . . . every hoarded bit of food, rubber, and metal . . . every moment of complacency or face-saving or temporizing . . . means more children become fatherless. Each of us owes something to Nancy Jane's dad . . . and to Nancy Jane!"

A medal for Nancy...

LITTLE Nancy Jane is only six. She stood alone, with all the inborn dignity of childhood, in that historic room amid the admirals, the senators, the great and near-great grown-ups.

She heard a deep, resonant voice say:

"For conspicuous gallantry over and beyond the call of duty, the Congress of the United States of America awards the Congressional Medal of Honor to Marvin Clayton — Lieutenant-Commander, United States Navy—killed in action at the victorious Battle of Midway."

And then a blue ribbon passed over her head. And looking down, she saw a gold medal at the end of the ribbon nestling against her dress.

Little Nancy Jane is only six. She's too young to understand the words of the citation—not quite old enough to realize that this blue-ribboned gold medal is the highest honor our nation can bestow on its heroes.

But not too young to know that never-more will she feel those strong, gentle hands tucking in her blanket ...or hoisting her high in the air for a morning kiss... or patiently guiding her pencil as she scrawls a birthday greeting to Grandma!

Little Nancy Jane is only six— and fatherless! However long actual fighting goes on—this war means sacrifice for little Nancy Jane for the rest of her life!

Every single second lost today on our production lines...every hoarded bit of food, rubber and metal... every moment of complacency or face-saving or temporizing...means more children become fatherless.

Each of us owes something to Nancy Jane's dad... and to Nancy Jane!

The men and women of Weatherhead this message. Most of us have near rel uniform ... sons, husbands, brothers ... daughters, too. Our task is not dramatic... vital to every single big weapon. For yea been making for peacetime purposes fittings and devices we are making today. responding to the urgent war needs of t we have found ways of producing them quantity than ever before— more than every twenty-four hours! So, you see, a also one of the great weapons for win war and for building the kind of world fighting for.

Albert J. Weatherhead

Weatherhead
THE WEATHERHEAD COMPANY · CLEVELAND, OHIO
Headquarters for fittings, hose assemblies, hydraulic devices and essential machine parts
Plants: CLEVELAND; COLUMBIA CITY, IND.; LOS ANGELES; ST. THOMAS, ONT.

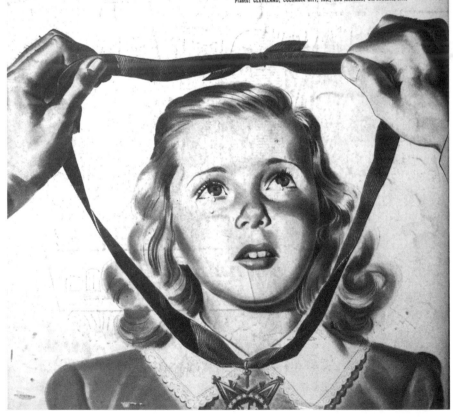

FIGURE 26

Products for Efficiency

Most ads dealing with home front efficiency urged specific ways for the public to help. A much smaller number merely sold products their advertisers claimed could help the home front run more efficiently, most of them legitimate enough, some rather more dubious. These ads didn't seek public participation, except to buy the manufacturer's merchandise. Products for increasing war workers' efficiency through better health and nutrition were already covered in Chapter 3, but advertisers of some of these same and other products also placed ads promoting their goods as aids to home front efficiency generally. One of the most prolific of these companies was Kellogg's. While not neglecting the nutritional value of its corn flakes and other cereals, beginning in 1943 Kellogg's ads began to emphasize how cereal could free busy wartime families for volunteer work, jobs, and other commitments: Kellogg's Corn Flakes "Save Time—They're Ready to Eat! Save Fuel—No Cooking Required! Save Work—No Pans, Skillets to Wash!" (*Life* 6 Sept. 1943: 66). Similarly, also in *Life*, on January 25, 1943, Swift's Premium Frankfurts [sic] hyped hot dogs for efficiency: "SAVE TIME—FUEL! Swift's Premium Frankfurts need to be *heated* (not cooked) only 7 minutes. This saves cooking fuel and your time" (9). And the H. J. Heinz company ran a photo spread in *Life* on April 2, 1945, depicting seven people ranging from war workers to volunteer War Bond saleswomen eating on the job for efficiency's sake, and describing how Heinz makes that eating better with everything from canned soups to condiments (20). Turning from food to clothing, Pendleton Woolen Mills boasted that since the health of all war workers and volunteers was critical, warm, strong Pendleton Shirts were the choice of "thousands of civilian defense guards, air raid wardens and men in war industries" (*Life* 16 Nov. 1942: 108), and, for women, Spirella was only one of several manufacturers of ladies' "foundation garments" that sang the praises of their corsets and girdles for keeping the body properly aligned when on one's feet for hours as a plane spotter, air raid warden, or riveter (*Ladies' Home Journal* March 1942: 164).

Of the products-for-efficiency ads, some that seem most legitimate came from makers of automotive supplies. In *Life* on November 30, 1942, B. F. Goodrich took out a full-page ad to promote a gadget called the Speed Warden. Attached to the accelerator, the gizmo would prevent a car from going beyond the wartime speed limit of 35 m.p.h., thus making more efficient use of gasoline and tires. All that for only a dollar, plus installation "if you wish for a small charge" (17). Rather more mainstream, an ad for Exide Batteries in *Life* on February 21, 1944, showed a woman in a visiting nurse's uniform next to her car bearing a "C" ration sticker on its windshield, the C designating doctors, nurses, and other essential home front professionals who were allowed more gas than the average driver. "A C sticker is a serious responsibility" begins the copy; "If the use of a car is essential, it's up to the owner to keep it in tip-top operating condition. Wartime America needs its automotive transportation" (128). The ad then recommends having a car's battery checked every two weeks, recharged if necessary, and replaced with a new Exide battery only when *absolutely* necessary. Of the many battery ads in leading magazines, this is the only one that emphasized efficiency for essential civilians. Finally, while not selling anything, two makers of buses, the White Motor Company and GMC Truck & Coach Division, proudly displayed their role in home front efficiency by describing their buses' mass transport of workers to and from war plants and shipyards in the *Post* on August 8, 1942, and February 11, 1943, respectively.

Efficiency Is a Lot of Little Things

Possibly because they weren't as widely publicized as buying War Bonds, giving blood, or collecting scrap, a lot of little things civilians should do to improve stateside efficiency never made it into any general books about the World War II home front. To be sure, the number of ads promoting this grab bag of small actions and gestures was far fewer than those for the "big" campaigns, but they were no less fervent in their appeals, attesting to the vital importance of these matters during the war.

Some of the items seem so obvious as to hardly have needed advertising to heighten public awareness of them, preventing nonindustrial accidents for one. But apparently Americans during the war were just as careless or preoccupied in their cars, in their homes, or just walking down the street as they are today, and, accordingly, needed some pretty harsh reminders that casualties to both people and property were roadblocks to home front efficiency. Quite a number of ads, most by insurance companies, were ready and eager to do the reminding, such as the following two. Heading its ad in the *Post* on June 27, 1942, "Accidents help the enemy," the Lumbermens Mutual Casualty Company minced no words: "We can't all fly bombers or man machine guns to help win . . . We can all get together at home to help cut down on accidents . . . An accident today—in car, home or factory—is just a polite name for sabotage. The idea behind sabotage is to wreck men and materials, to throw away time. The idea behind an accident is exactly the same" (42). The ad pointed out that "it takes more than just driving slowly to cut down on automobile accidents. Even more important, it takes driving thoughtfully," following that statement with specific tips for safe driving. Equally strong was the language in the American Mutual Liability Insurance Company's ad in the *Post* on January 16, 1943: "No . . . not in North Africa . . . or the Aleutians . . . or at Guadalcanal. They died . . . one hundred thousand American men, women and children last year . . . accidentally . . . under the wheels of automobiles, in the flames of burning homes, from falls, infections, poisoning. No, they didn't perish at the war front . . . they died at home for want of safety" (47). Stressing that most accidents can be prevented, American Mutual devoted the rest of the ad to encouraging people to write for its free book on accident prevention, "War Edition of *Watch*."

Then there was the matter of keeping healthy. Diverse advertisers, some attaching their messages to selling products, some not, got out the word on the need for good health. Dr. West's Toothbrushes declared, "Here's the single biggest thing—the greatest contribution you can make to your nation at war: Get healthy. Keep healthy. Strength is our supreme national resource now or ever" (*Life* 24 May 1943: 9). In *Collier's* on September 25, 1943, the Metropolitan Life Insurance Company devoted a full page to the subject of foot health and how it affects the whole body in wartime or anytime. And Dixie Cups, always alert to public health issues and the role of disposable drinking cups, warned in *Life* on March 16, 1942, "Illness, contagion must not be permitted to slacken our speed—or weaken the staggering blow our nation has set itself to deliver. Common colds, influenza, trench mouth and the like must not black out the work of thousands of willing hands. And health officials everywhere tell us that these illnesses are most commonly spread by indirect mouth-to-mouth contact at the common drinking place" (118).

Also in the sphere of health care, the number of doctors, dentists, nurses, and pharmacists needed by the armed forces created a serious shortage of these professionals to serve the home front. Several advertisers addressed the problem with ads showing how ordinary people could help alleviate the strain and increase the efficiency of too few health care workers doing too much work. In *Life* on March 29, 1943, and again in the May 1943 *Farm Journal*, Mennen combined a series of "rules" for baby care by mothers with advice about dealing with doctors, such as "Don't call the Doctor to your home unless absolutely necessary. Whenever possible, take your baby to the doctor's office," and "Phone Doctor early in day (early morning if possible), to help him plan his calls with minimum use of time, gasoline, tires, etc." (*Life* 52). Simmons Beautyrest Mattresses went even farther in suggesting home care not just for baby but for the whole family in the face of the doctor crunch, by encouraging women to take Home Nursing Classes so they could deal with many health problems on their own (*Life* 20 Sept. 1943: 83). Ways to help one's dentist were offered by Ipana Tooth Paste in the *Post* on June 3, 1944, advising people to schedule appointments well in advance and keep them; "If you must break your appointment—do it promptly" (1). The ad also advocated regular checkups to catch problems before they might require "prolonged treatment" and to give teeth proper care between dental visits. "He's Helped You Many Times . . . Now Your Druggist Needs Your Help" proclaimed the Owens-Illinois Glass ad in *Collier's* on January 1, 1944, listing five ways to make the life of the overworked wartime pharmacist easier, including allowing as much time as possible to have prescriptions filled and shopping in person whenever possible so that the drugstore could save deliveries for emergencies (inside front cover).

These ads were one-shot pleas to help make home front health care more efficient, but Wyeth, the pharmaceutical company, created a campaign of at least eight ads in *Life*, *Time*, and the *Post* from February 21, 1944, through November 19, 1945, explaining the shortage of doctors and how to help. Wyeth's ads are consistently attractive and imaginative in their art and copy—sometimes warm, sometimes frankly factual, sometimes sentimental, and sometimes even whimsical as in the *Life* ad on July 14, 1944, in which a pigtailed little girl in a doctor's waiting room looks up at the nurse behind the desk and says, "I want an appointment to see my Daddy!" (65; see fig. 27). The copy, of course, explains that "this little girl's daddy is a doctor. He has precious little time for his family or anything other than doctoring these days." With so many doctors in the military, each home front physician was left with an average of 1,700 people to care for. This ad, like all of Wyeth's, concludes with four simple ways to help the doctor when you need him: "Phone him first. Go

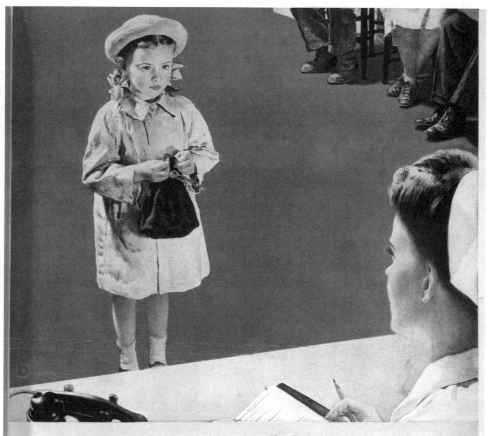

"I want an appointment to 'see my Daddy!'"

"I HARDLY EVER see him any more. Mommy says it's because of the war. But Daddy's not a soldier. So *why* can't I see him?"

This little girl's daddy is a doctor. He has precious little time for his family or anything other than doctoring these days.

For today nearly half our doctors are serving with the armed forces. So, the home-front doctor has twice as many folks to care for . . . an average of 1700 people dependent upon his being available day and night.

Just as it's up to him to do more and more, it's up to *you* to do all you can to help him. Won't you,

whenever you think you need him, remember to do these four helpful things?

PHONE HIM FIRST. Tell him briefly exactly what's wrong. Let him decide whether he should come to see you, or you should go to him.

GO TO HIM—whenever you are able. House visits take time when someone else may need him urgently.

KEEP YOUR APPOINTMENT promptly, don't postpone it; make it at *his* convenience so that he can plan his crowded hours better.

FOLLOW HIS ADVICE TO THE LETTER—so that your trouble doesn't drag on, get complicated, or need extra attention.

★ ★ ★

ONE OF A SERIES of messages published as a public service by Wyeth Incorporated, Philadelphia, illustrated by Douglass Crockwell. Wyeth Incorporated, pioneer pharmacists since 1860, are relied upon by your physician and druggist for quality, precision, and ethical standards in pharmaceuticals, biologicals (including penicillin and blood plasma), and nutritional products.

SAVE YOUR DOCTOR'S TIME IN WARTIME!

FIGURE 27. Reprinted by permission of Wyeth.

to him—whenever you are able. House visits take time when someone else may need him urgently. Keep your appointment. Follow his advice to the letter—so that your trouble doesn't drag on, get complicated, or need extra attention."

Health care workers weren't the only ones who needed extra help from the public to maximize their efficiency during the war. So did grocers, among others. Large self-service supermarkets were still relatively new and not yet common in many localities during the war years. In the majority of neighborhood grocery stores, shoppers (mostly "housewives") would tell the grocer or one of his clerks what items they wanted, and the grocer or clerk would take them down from a shelf and bag them along with the rest of the shopper's order. I can vouch for this as the prevailing modus operandi in suburban groceries, since I well remember going often with my mother to Smithfield's in the "business district" of Wilmette, Illinois, and watching this labor-intensive procedure for grocery shopping. And, on top of that, there were no prepackaged meats to speak of during the war, so at the meat counter the shopper made her request, showed she had enough ration points, and the butcher cut each piece of meat to order. Small wonder that a few advertisers came up with ways for shoppers to help make the work of grocers and their employees easier and more efficient. In the December 1942 *Ladies' Home Journal*, Del Monte promoted the idea of weekly meal planning and shopping: "It saves your time—saves your tires—saves your gas. And helps your grocer give you better service too! [. . .] Remember to shop early in the week, too—and early in the day. *Both* help your grocer give you better service" (38). While repeating some of the same pointers much later in the war, Ivory Soap added a few more ways to help the grocer: "Have ration points handy—it saves everybody's time. Use a shopping bag—or carry parcels unwrapped. Return paper bags. They're scarce. Make up a shopping list in advance" (*Post* 1 Jan. 1945: back cover).

Volunteers and Kids for Efficiency

There's no way of knowing how many men and women did these simple things and others to help the home front run more smoothly. But what *is* known is that enormous numbers of them participated in more structured volunteer work—twelve million in activities related to civilian defense alone just by mid-1943. Another three million women volunteered with the Red Cross, and millions more through American Women's Voluntary Services, the Crop Corps and Women's Land Army (see Chapter 4), and other agencies, not to mention another million or so who served coffee and doughnuts in USO canteens (Lingeman 59). Both men and women volunteered to sell War Bonds, staff local draft boards and ration offices, and so forth. The more Americans who volunteered for such work, the fewer paid staffers would need to be involved, freeing their time for other matters, and, once again, stepping up the efficiency of the home front. Virtually no ads appeared in the leading national magazines calling for volunteers except for those recruiting agricultural help through the Crop Corps and a few dealing specifically with volunteer work by women (see Chapter 8). Some ads paid brief or casual tribute to people already volunteering, but in my database of more than 5,000 ads, just two appealed for volunteers, one implicitly, the other more directly, both in March 1942. The Chesapeake and Ohio Lines ad in *Newsweek* on March 23 finds Chessie, the railroad's ubiquitous "calendar cat," asleep (Chessie's almost always asleep in C&O ads) in the center of a large (fictional) Civilian Defense emblem labeled "Sleep Warden." She's encircled by smaller insignia of fourteen (actual) units of Civilian Defense, among them Emergency Food and Housing Corps, Messengers, Auxiliary Firemen, Air Raid Warden, and Nurses' Aides Corps. All the copy states vis-à-vis Civilian Defense is "Like thousands of other Americans, Chessie has volunteered for Civilian Defense Service," while her "Old Man" Peake, a big husky tomcat we'll meet soon, is off fighting in the war (69). Implied is something like "if Chessie can volunteer to help her country, so can you." Earlier that month, on the 7th in the *Post*, Smith-Corona featured a high school girl in skirt, sweater, bobby sox, and saddle shoes, lying on the floor doing homework and saying, "Help win the war? . . . ME?" To which the ad's copy replied, "Indeed, yes, young lady, you and some eleven million other girls in this country of ours. How? In all the countless ways that women always find. The Red Cross wants you. Volunteer workers are wanted in civilian defense, in under-manned draft boards, in auxiliary services for men in uniform, in vital social service work" (49). With the exceptions noted above, these two ads are the only ones in leading magazines that recruited volunteers. Yet this isn't too surprising. The government and agencies like the Red Cross mounted massive poster campaigns for volunteers, and, since most people volunteered close to home, most print advertising for volunteers was in local newspapers. Advertisers didn't think volunteerism unimportant. They just put their advertising dollars and ideas where the ads would do the most good.

Even with millions of men and women employed in war industries or engaged in volunteer work, one more segment of the population remained to be tapped in order to achieve universal participation in stepping up home front efficiency—America's children. Throughout the war, children were some of the most persistent and voracious scrap scavengers, whether on their own, teamed up with other neighborhood kids, or in more structured groups like the Boy Scouts. Millions of children also raised millions of dollars by buying War Stamps in their schools. But there were still more ways that kids could help the overall home front efficiency, as some advertisers were quick to point out, mostly by relieving their parents—primarily their mothers—of some of the tasks at home so they could devote more time to their war work or volunteerism. Carnation Milk and H. J. Heinz both produced Double-Barrelled ads that sold their products as much as promoted this idea, but the war message wasn't slighted in favor of the selling. "Milk-rich dishes to make housework easier for the crop of young cooks pinch hitting in America's homes. Many a 'teen age girl flies home from school . . . pops into an apron . . . and cooks the dinner, while Mother is making war munitions" (Carnation, *Life* March 8, 1943: 53). Heinz produced a full-page photo spread of young cooks cooking in *Life* on March 3, 1945, two of the photos captioned "Modern mothers, engaged in numerous wartime activities, confidently turn over kitchen chores to the children!" and "Dinner's on when mother's home from the Red Cross. Junior salvages the empty tin while sister heats Heinz Vegetable Soup with Beef Stock" (24). But it was the Scott Paper Company that really carried the banner for children helping in the home. A series of at least four ads full of cute drawings in *Life* between September 14, 1942, and March 1, 1943, described the chores kids could take over from their war-working parents. Scott even offered children an "Official Clean-Up Warden Arm Band" for assuming such responsibilities. Each ad featured things kids of different ages could do to help, from putting toys and clothes away for the preschool crowd up to washing dishes and floors and vacuuming for junior high or high school students. And, much to its credit, Scott relegated selling its toilet tissue and paper towels to a small, insignificant corner of each ad.

One advertisement for increasing home front efficiency along with the self-esteem of thousands of Americans is so anomalous that it can't be categorized and yet is certainly worth remembering. On January 18, 1943, an ad appeared in *Life* in the form of a letter to shipbuilding and airplane magnate Henry J. Kaiser from Dean Babbitt, President of the Sonotone Corporation. Beginning by citing Kaiser's recent well-publicized push for 25,000 more workers for his shipyards, Babbitt pointed out that of the five million hearing-impaired Americans, at least half a million had the skills and ability to work in shipyards, airplane factories, and, by implication, other critical war industries if only they wore a "properly fitting hearing aid" (17). And, no, the letter didn't sell Sonotone hearing aids but instead declared, "This is no time for selfish, competitive thinking. I honestly don't care which hearing aid a man buys, as long as he buys one if he needs it, and gets back to his full, fighting efficiency."

"A Slip of the Lip Can Sink a Ship"

More than just the title of popular swing tune recorded in 1942 by Duke Ellington's Orchestra with vocal by Ray Nance, that phrase expressed the very real concern of the military and government about rumor control and preventing critical war information, however small, from getting into the hands of the enemy. Poster campaigns and considerable magazine advertising by commercial advertisers made civilians aware of the importance of this issue and asked for their cooperation by not spreading anything anyone knew about war production, troop movements, or other sensitive matters, and by not even listening to rumors, let alone passing them on. The need for the public's cooperation in rumor control may at first seem remote from home front efficiency, but both efficiency and conservation in fact lay at the heart of trying to keep every military secret precisely that—secret. Leaked information could allow saboteurs to blow up a war plant or lead a German U-Boat to where it could sink an American troopship. In each case, loose talk would have led to disasters that impeded the efficiency of war production, wasting vital materials and the lives of men and women needed to fight the war.

Rumor control ads in national magazines began early, in May 1942, and stayed around until comparatively late, the last appearing in December 1944. One can only hazard a guess as to why no more appeared after that, but one reason may be that since there had been no significant instances of stateside espionage or sabotage since the war began, by the winter of 1944 both the government and private advertisers that got out war messages may have felt that rumor control was well in hand and turned their attention to other matters. Whatever the case, during the time that such ads appeared, about two dozen different ones were published in the leading magazines, and their approaches were as varied as the advertisers sponsoring them. Cuteness was the approach when the Black & White terriers, their little ears perky and alert, said "SH-H-H! The enemy has big ears," the rest of the ad in *Newsweek* on December 14, 1942, warning, "Guard your speech. Don't talk to strangers about the War. Don't spread rumors. And above all—don't ask questions dealing with vital war information" (97). Beyond cute were the outright funny O. Soglow cartoon ads placed in *Life* by Topps Gum. On February 14, 1944, a "foreign-looking" spy's head pops out of a garbage can to listen to a war plant guard whispering to a pretty girl, the ad captioned "Don't talk chum, chew Topps gum," just about as succinct a Double-Barrelled war message and product pitch as one could hope for (105). The Smith Bros. Cough Drops ad in *Life* on November 29, 1943, squelched rumors and sold cough drops almost as simultaneously: "KEEP YOUR MOUTH SHUT! DON'T GOSSIP—it spreads rumors! DON'T COUGH—it spreads germs!" (115). Other advertisers publishing anti-rumor messages were as diverse as Hartford Insurance, Budweiser, Gaines Dog Meal, and three whiskey manufacturers—Calvert, Seagram's, and Corby's. Their ads ranged from solemn copy-heavy presentations by Hartford and Budweiser to just an Uncle Sam billboard cautioning "QUIET about troop movements, ship sailings, war equipment" in the art of the Gaines ad, the copy itself just selling dog food (*Life* 26 June 1944: 71).

But of all companies warning against spreading rumors or authentic information, one virtually made the campaign its own, placing twelve of the twenty-four rumor control ads in the major national magazines. The John B. Stetson Company, one of America's leading manufacturers of men's hats, was well positioned for this. The old adage about secrecy, "Keep it under your hat," became in each ad "Keep it under your Stetson." Reinforcing the slogan were some brilliant art and copy. Some of the ads were brief photo stories showing how scraps of information could give the enemy all it needed to torpedo a ship or take the surprise out of an Allied surprise attack. Some were sentimental, such as a large painting of a little girl leaping into her returned father's arms, her mother just steps behind her, captioned "Let's bring him home quicker!"

(*Collier's* 11 March 1944: 65). The idea of the copy was that the less the enemy knows, the sooner we can end the war, the Stetson rumor slogan appearing in large type at the bottom. Still others were nearly all art, more powerful than sentimental. The picture in the last of the Stetson ads shows a soldier in combat gear visiting another soldier's grave, headed "The Less Said, the Less Dead." With the Stetson rumor slogan at the bottom, that comprised all the copy (*Life* 30 Oct. 1944: 79; see fig. 28). Some Stetson ads sold hats in two to four lines of small type at the bottom, but, by and large, the vital war message was the raison d'être of all of the company's war ads.

"Room for 1 More"

As in the campaign for rumor control, home front efficiency and conservation were inextricably linked in promotions for ride sharing or carpooling. Several men in a neighborhood going to work together, whether in a war plant or otherwise, several women doing their shopping in a single car, or several children on the block being driven to school by just one parent was a more efficient mode of transportation than if each of these people traveled separately. Not only that, the more people riding in the fewest number of cars would go a long way toward alleviating the tremendous wartime overcrowding on trains, buses, subways, and trolleys (streetcars), and, in major cities, would make more taxicabs available for those who had no other convenient means of getting around. At the same time, carpooling would conserve all the drivers' rationed gas allocations, prolong the life of their virtually irreplaceable tires, and reduce the wear and tear on their equally irreplaceable cars. Accordingly, a number of advertisers urged drivers to always find, in the words of the sign on the dog owner's car in the Black & White Scotch ad in *Life* on December 6, 1943, "Room for 1 more" (87).

Not surprisingly, the first ads advocating ride sharing came from rubber companies, beginning as early as June 1942, with United States Rubber placing a two-page spread in *Life* and two different full-page ads, one each in *Time* and *Ladies' Home Journal*, during just that month alone. B. F. Goodrich came on board in July with a single ad repeated in *Life* and *Look* about a week apart. The U.S. Rubber ads in *Life* and *Time* were the most elaborate, not just in 1942, but during the whole campaign, which continued well into 1945. Illustrated with line drawings of various means of transportation, the two-page ad in *Life* on June 15, 1942, contained

The Less Said, the Less Dead

Keep it under your
STETSON

FIGURE 28. Reprinted by permission of The John B. Stetson Company.

separate paragraphs describing how trolleys, buses, trains, and taxis "can't do it alone," followed by four more illustrated paragraphs showing how some people, "but not enough," already had organized pools to drive to the train, to shop, take the kids to school, or drive all the way to work. The rest of the ad described how war plants, other companies, and neighborhood groups could organize carpooling plans to maximize travel efficiency. Included was a sample of a card for drivers to fill out with information about their cars, how many passengers they could take, at what times they traveled, and so forth, to be used in organizing such large-scale ride sharing (10–11). The one-page ad in *Time* on June 1, 1942, was a somewhat scaled-down version of all this material plus a long, detailed paragraph for plant managers on how to take a census of employees' cars and organize driving pools (49). Cluttered, yes, and certainly no prize winners for design layout, still these ads show how seriously U.S. Rubber took the matter of ride sharing as a partial solution to conserving rubber and gas and providing more efficient home front transportation for everyone.

Targeting a different audience, U.S. Rubber took another approach to carpooling in the June 1942 *Ladies' Home Journal*. Against background pictures of cars used by groups of people for work, school, shopping, and defense (a car full of volunteer Nurses Aides in front of a hospital), the copy was a phone call by a woman to her neighbor, talking about carpooling in terms of patriotism and conservation: "And what is this kind of patriotism? Simply a matter of saving the neighborhood's transportation by pooling the mileage left in six sets of tires. Pooling our mileage helps every family on our block keep within the weekly allowance on its tire mileage budget chart," a chart devised to predict how much wear was left in tires based on the number of miles driven (61). In July, B. F. Goodrich made a straightforward pitch for ride sharing by pointing out that "even our Army is finding ways to do its job with less rubber" and that although Goodrich itself was one of the pioneers in developing synthetic rubber, its civilian use would be a long time coming, so people had better conserve whatever tires they had any way they could (*Life* 6 July 1942: 1; *Look* July 14 1942: 5).

In the main, carpooling ads later in the war simply repeated the same kinds of messages in different ways, although one by Pabst Blue Ribbon Beer added a rather charming note in remarking how ride sharing helped improve national unity on the neighborhood level, "For neigh-

bors who formerly were little more than nodding acquaintances are beginning to drop in evenings for a game of bridge" (*Collier's* 25 Jan. 1943:
31). But transportation efficiency and conservation of gas and tires remained the driving force in carpooling ads even into what proved to be
the last year of the war: "When four drivers join a share-ride club, they
quadruple the mileage from every gallon of gas and every set of tires.
Simple—but what a tremendous saving!" (Hudson Motor Car Company, *Collier's*, 24 Feb. 1945: 35).

Lodging, Travel, and Telephones

Of all the ways in which civilians could facilitate greater home front efficiency, none generated more advertising over a longer period of time
than the related areas of hotel accommodations, bus and rail travel, and
telephone communications. What's more, only four advertisers accounted
for roughly 140 of the 160 *different* ads encouraging greater public cooperation to make these essential features of life on the home front run
more smoothly: Bell Telephone System (58 ads), Pullman (47), Greyhound (22), and Statler Hotels (13). And while hotels, sleeper cars on
trains, and interstate bus travel appear to have little in common, in fact
the ways that Mr. and Mrs. Home Front could help them all provide better service for civilians and the military alike were remarkably similar.
Only how people could expedite long distance telephone service was
rather different, but as vitally important, if not more so.

The war demanded significantly increased travel by industry and
business executives, engineers, scientists, and others in the higher eche-
lons of war production, which in turn necessitated a greater number of
hotel rooms available in such key "war centers" as Washington, D.C., Detroit, and New York City. The Statler Hotel chain, with hotels in those
three cities plus Boston, Buffalo, and St. Louis, devoted over half of its
ads during the war to how people could help ensure that the greatest
number of hotel rooms would always be available and no unused rooms
be wasted. The Statler "Golden Rule for Wartime Travelers," which by
extension applied to anyone needing accommodations at any hotel in
the country, boiled down to three simple things to do (expressed slightly
differently in different Statler ads): "1—Make reservations in advance,
specifying hour of arrival and date of departure. 2—Cancel unwanted
rooms promptly. 3—Release rooms as early as possible on day of departure." That version of the rule is from a Statler ad, the rest of which, for

my money, is the most hilarious wordless cartoon ad of war years, thanks to the unlikely room service waiter in the final panel (*Life* 11 Sept. 1944: 43; see fig. 29). Only one other hotel, New York's Hotel New Yorker, echoed Statler's advice to travelers, prefacing it with radio comedian Fred Allen saying, "When GI's and civilians on war business are unable to secure hotel rooms because some thoughtless civilian ties up more space than he needs, stays longer than necessary, and reserves rooms but never claims them—brother, that's not funny!" (*Newsweek* 23 Apr. 1945: 103).

Long before the Greyhound bus line was telling travelers, "Leave the driving to us," the company's primary slogan was "See America Now," or at least it was before Pearl Harbor, after which it quickly changed to "SERVE America Now—so you can SEE America Later!" (*Ladies' Home Journal* Sept. 1942: 120). Like some ads by railroads, next to be discussed, a few of Greyhound's focused entirely on how the bus line itself was helping make stateside travel more efficient for military personnel, war workers, farm workers, and others fighting the good fight here at home. But not many Greyhound advertising messages were purely self-congratulatory, and even most that were also included tips on how bus riders could do their part for the greater efficiency of intercity bus travel. The ads varied the pointers a bit from time to time, but this list from *Collier's* on September 26, 1942, is typical: "Travel on Tuesdays, Wednesdays, Thursdays—leaving week-ends for men in uniform and war workers. Take as little baggage as possible. Get trip information from Greyhound agent, in advance. Be at bus station early. Don't take unnecessary trips" (103). Other Greyhound ads discouraged people from traveling purely for pleasure, but if they did, to avoid peak summer travel months. And all bus travelers were asked to accept "occasional inconvenience or crowding with good nature" (*Post* 11 Sept. 1943: 81). Periodically Greyhound ads even thanked the public for "responding willingly to suggestions for making the most patriotic use of wartime travel" (*Post* 27 March 1943: 67).

Quite a few railroads advertised in national magazines during the war, among them the Chesapeake & Ohio Lines, the Pennsylvania Railroad, the New York Central, the Seaboard Railway, and the New York, New Haven, and Hartford Railroad, all of which made home front efficiency a highlight of their ads. Each of these railroads approached the matter in one or more of three ways: demonstrating how the advertised railroad, or, more generously, *all* American railroads, expedited the in-

FIGURE 29

creased wartime volume of both freight and passengers; explaining to potential travelers the reasons for delays, or less frequent or less luxurious trains than before the war; and appealing to passengers to take steps to help improve the efficiency of rail travel. For example, of four New York Central ads in *Life* during 1943 and 1944, two were wholly about how that railroad expedited home front efficiency, one on page 71 on May 22, 1944, illustrating in detail how a train's "post office on wheels" sped the delivery of vital wartime mail, the other, on page 47 of the issue for July 24, 1944, describing the layout and functioning of Army Hospital Trains. The New York Central's ad on November 11, 1943, on the other hand, combined a description of what makes a dining car run smoothly with a few suggestions for travelers: "If you have to wait for a seat, please remember that dining cars, too, have a war job to do"; and, because of the large numbers of military personnel traveling, "To give them room, plan trips *you* must make for mid-week" (61). An ad about the workings of Grand Central Terminal in New York City devoted more space to advice to passengers than to the terminal itself, including "To save holding up ticket lines, get information *in advance* from [the information] booth or by telephone" and "Someone (perhaps a soldier on furlough) may have to wait over for a later train if *you* fail to cancel an unwanted reservation. These days, cancel reservations the *minute* your plans change" (*Life*, 12 July 1943: 53).

A representative ad restricted to telling people why wartime rail travel might not be all they were accustomed to before the war is that of the Chesapeake & Ohio Lines in *Time* on December 27, 1943, in which Peake the cat in his military gear looks longingly at a picture of his "pinup cat" Chessie (sleeping as usual) (/, see fig. 30): "Time and distance separate us from a lot these days including the kind of travel accommodations the railroads used to be able to give, before they undertook the transport of the largest army and navy in history and the supplies needed to keep them fed and in trim."

One more railroad ad deserves mention if only because it won *Advertising & Selling*'s "medal award for a newspaper advertisement of a national institution" for 1942 and became something of a sensation among the general public (*Business Week* 6 Feb. 1943: 68). Created by Nelson Metcalf, a thirty-year-old copywriter with the Boston advertising agency of Wendell P. Colton, the ad for the New York, New Haven, and Hartford Railroad titled "The Kid in Upper 4" eventually got to suggesting ways

His Pin-Up Girl!

TIME and distance separate us from a lot these days—including the kind of travel accommodations the railroads used to be able to give, before they undertook the transport of the largest army and navy in history and the supplies needed to keep that army fed and in trim.

So maybe you'd like something to pin up, too—to remind you that the railroads, when this is all over, will again bring you the safest, most comfortable, most enjoyable transportation that your travel dollar can buy.

Here is the new C & O calendar for 1944. Because of the paper shortage, there may not be enough to go around. So if you'd like one—illustrated with the painting above—better write and reserve one for yourself right away!

CHESAPEAKE AND OHIO LINES

3312 Terminal Tower · Cleveland 1, Ohio

FIGURE 30

for train travelers to accommodate the needs of soldiers on the same train, such as "If there is no berth for you—*it is so that he may sleep*" (*Life* 21 Dec. 1942: 21). But the bulk of Metcalf's copy consisted of the young soldier's thoughts in his berth, his mind replaying images of home, his mother and father, his girl, his dog, and other trappings of nostalgia and sentiment just prior to his being shipped overseas. The ad originally ran in just two newspapers, but Elmer Davis, OWI chief, was so taken with it that he persuaded the New Haven (as the railroad was generally called) to give it wider circulation, whereupon it ultimately ran in two hundred newspapers and a dozen national magazines (see *Newsweek* 11 Jan. 1943: 58, 60). It became so popular that ten thousand color posters of the originally black and white ad had to be printed to fill requests for it. Metcalf's ad was probably such a sensation simply because it was one of the first ads of its kind, but today it seems pretty innocuous compared to the even more sentimental, nostalgic, and generally moving war ads that would follow before the war was over, a great many of them far more powerful than "The Kid in Upper 4." In fact, even in its own day, the sequels that tried to capitalize on the first "Kid" ad, such as "The Kid in the Convoy" (*Life* 26 Apr. 1943) and "The Kid and His Letter" (*Life* 28 June 1943), caused no stir whatever, either in the ad industry or among the public.

By far the most frequent, prolific, and creative advertiser encouraging the public's cooperation for more efficient wartime rail travel was not a railroad but the company that owned, managed, staffed, and leased to railroads most of the sleeping cars for long distance train travel—Pullman. Of Pullman's fifty-three ads in the leading magazines that spanned the length of the war, fully forty-seven dealt in whole or in part with cooperation by train travelers. Rather remarkably, each of the forty-seven ads included different art, and, in the main, different copy as well. The only constant, whether in the body of the copy or as a separate list at the end, were the specific ways travelers could help facilitate more efficient train travel, especially on Pullman sleeping cars, as in the list in the Pullman ad in *Life* on July 17, 1944: "1. Don't reserve Pullman space until you are *sure* that you will need it. 2. Cancel promptly when plans change—so someone else can use the Pullman bed reserved for you. 3. Take a berth or small room when alone, leaving drawing rooms and compartments for two or more. 4. Travel light—leave extra luggage home or check it through to your destination. 5. Don't go unless your trip is *necessary*" (56). Other Pullman ads gave specific reasons for some of these things, which can be summarized by the fact that about half of Pullman's sleeping cars were in use on troop trains and the other half trying to accommodate about twice as many passengers as before the war. As for the ads' variety and creativity, some described how Pullman sleepers were used as ancillary wards on army hospital trains, others discussed the needs of the military on regular passenger trains as well as troop trains, in one a mother explained to her young son why his father had to travel so much (war work), and some were simply and charmingly sentimental, such as the ad in *Life* on December 20, 1943, in which a twelve-year-old boy, accompanied by a rather manic-looking dog, types a letter to his grandmother to explain why the family won't be visiting her this Christmas, the copy replete with some wonderful misspellings (46: see fig. 31).

Of all advertisers placing home front efficiency ads, only one produced more than Pullman, and even more frequently. Like the Pullman ads, the variety in the artwork seems almost infinite throughout Bell Telephone's fifty-eight ads—most of them in *Life*—asking the public to help keep long distance service running smoothly, a message absolutely constant in the ads: "Please give a clear track to the war effort by confining your Long Distance calls to those that are really necessary" (*Life* 17 Aug. 1942: 3). Some ads included more details and refinements, but that one sentence was the rationale given all civilian home front callers for staying off long distance lines except when they had to: War calls come first and absolutely must get through. Some of the Bell ads took a moment to explain why no new long distance lines could be built—"We can't build new lines [. . .] because copper, nickel and rubber are shooting, not talking, materials right now" (*Life* 14 Sept. 1942: 3). But in an era when, we must remember, all long distance calls (and even local ones) went through a telephone operator, most Bell ads contented themselves with briefly telling people how to keep the lines clear: "You can help by—Knowing the number you want to call. Calling in the less busy hours—before 10 A. M. and after 8 P. M. for example" (*Collier's* 30 May 1942: 10); because of the high volume of war-related calls, "we ask you not to put through a Long Distance telephone call to Washington unless it is absolutely necessary" (*Life* 31 Aug. 1942: 1); "Help keep war-crowded circuits clear on December 24, 25, and 26" (*Life* 6 Dec. 1943: 3); "Please limit your call to 5 minutes" (*Collier's* 10 June 1944: 35, and in numerous other ads). The art ranged from a cartoon of hoards of people madly

"Dear Grandma: This is instead of Me."

"We are not coming to visit you this Christmas because Dad says it would be unpatriotick.

"He has to travel some, you know, on account of his war business. So he knows what it's like on trains. They are so crowded now, he says, that we wouldn't have near as much fun traveling as we used to. Besides, we would be taking up room that other folks need lots worse than we do.

"I see what he means by that because if my brother Tom was in training camp instead of on some island I can't spell—and if he could get a furlow—I'd hate to think some 12 year old like me was doing him out of a place to sleep on his way home.

"Or, if Dad has to go to the munishuns plant again during the hollidays, like he says he might, it wouldn't be fair for someone just going to their Grandmother's to have got Pullman beds and maybe none left for him—so he would have to sit up all night and get there too tired out to do a good job.

"So I have just rapped up your present to mail and you will get it and this letter *instead of me* on Christmas.

"Incidentally, my present from Dad is going to be the best ever and I already know what it is. He figured out what the whole train trip would cost—Pullmans and everything—and is taking that money to buy me and Mom and him each a whopper of a War Bond!

"Isn't that keen? Won't I be proud? Bet you it's a bigger one than any of the other kids have got!

"Well, Grandma, I must close now, so lots of love and Merry Christmas and Sport just licked my ear to say the same for him."

* * *

With thousands of servicemen on furlough added to the 30,000 who go *Pullman* on mass troop movements every night, trains will be *doubly* crowded. So it is *doubly* important to ask yourself: "Is my trip necessary?"

If it is, try to go *Pullman*, by all means, for you'll not only get the *sleep* going you need to *keep* going at your essential job, but you'll leave coach space for those who can't afford the privacy and comfort you'll enjoy.

PULLMAN

For 80 years, the greatest name in passenger transportation—your assurance of comfort and safety as you go and certainty that you'll get there

FIGURE 31

FIGURE 32. Courtesy of AT&T Archives and History Center.

rushing along long distance wires at Christmastime to a photograph of shirtless soldiers setting up a phone communication switchboard in New Guinea. In between were numerous drawings of the little Bell telephone man doing and saying many different things, as in his plea for civilian co-operation on page 3 of *Life* for October 12, 1942 (see fig. 32).

Between practicing conservation, participating in scrap drives, and, in general, doing what they could to foster greater home front efficiency, wartime Americans had a lot on their plate and on their mind. It's no wonder then that numerous ads offered ways to keep up home front morale as well as the morale of the armed forces—all the subject of the following chapter.

SODA POP, LETTERS, AND CIGARETTES MORALE OVERSEAS AND AT HOME

Just as Napoleon said, "une armée marche à son estomac"—an army marches (or travels) on its stomach—it's equally valid to say that armed forces fight effectively only in proportion to their level of morale, whether that of an entire fighting unit collectively or of each and every serviceman from raw recruit to top brass individually. Moreover, in a modern, mechanized war like World War II, our fighting fronts' efficiency depended not only on the troops' morale but also on that of home front industry, agriculture, and individual civilians doing all they could to support the war and the morale of our boys fighting it. With civilians expending so much effort in these activities, their morale too often needed a lift. Advertising played a large role in morale boosting for both civilians and servicemen. But having said that, one runs up against a question needing an answer right at the start.

What *Is* Morale Anyway?

Most standard definitions of "morale" are not descriptive of what constituted it for either the military or the home front during the war. Take, for example, *Webster's Third New International Dictionary* and Princeton University's WordNet. Both define morale as a state of psychological well-being based upon one's sense of confidence, usefulness, and purpose, and both *Webster's* and Princeton define "well-being" as being happy, healthy, and prosperous. But no matter how high his morale was to take out a Japanese machine-gun nest on Saipan, a marine pinned down by enemy sniper fire could hardly have felt a state of well-being. Nor could his mother, wife, or sweetheart back home, worrying daily how and even where her marine was. Yet such women had a kind of morale that kept the home front running. Ergo, definitions of morale that include well-being and happiness just don't work for the war years.

One definition, with embellishments, *does* describe the primary type of wartime morale, simple as it is. While, I confess, I was Googling for meanings of morale, I came across the following one at a website with the URL http://www.business-words.com/dictionary/M.html. Other than a sentence illustrating the word's use, this lexicon's entire entry for morale was "spirit or attitude." As such, morale is fluid and can range within anyone from high to low, good to bad, depending on whatever affects that person's spirit positively or negatively, which accounts for advertising and other media's efforts to sustain or raise morale at home or on the front lines. The optimal spirit or attitude needed by both civilians and servicemen was a resolve to face whatever was thrown at them smilingly, courageously, and without despondency or hopelessness. Put another way, morale was the spirit or attitude instilled in people by a goal to be achieved, that morale in turn fostering their capacity to achieve that goal.

A second sense of morale during the war was more casual, yet extremely important, especially to GIs abroad. This was the occasional and fleeting lifting of one's spirits by something as small as smoking a favorite brand of cigarette or hearing a Glenn Miller tune over the short-wave radio. This sort of morale lifting may seem trivial, but the armed forces considered its value immeasurable. The need for such morale boosts lay behind the many USO Service Centers and "Stage Door Canteens" around the United States where GIs could drop in to eat, have coffee and doughnuts, or chat and dance with a pretty girl. On a grand scale it lay behind the USO and other groups sending tours of popular singers, big bands, movie stars, and radio personalities to entertain troops from North Africa to the South Pacific. This kind of morale was also the rationale for advertising products said to lift GIs' spirits, even briefly.

War ads almost never tried to define morale, although one series of over twenty-five of them over nearly the entire length of the war in *Collier's*, *Time* and, mostly, *Life* did a fine job of *describing* it. The Brewing Industry Foundation—trade association of American breweries—sponsored the series, each ad's picture captioned "MORALE IS A LOT OF LITTLE THINGS." The ads enumerated home front civilians' versions of the kinds of little things that momentarily lifted the morale of servicemen just discussed. The opening copy of the first ad in the series, in *Life* on June 15, 1942, is typical of the rest. After an illustration of a pipe-smoking man sitting with his fishing gear around him, it began: "If you're a man, it's a shine on your shoes . . . the sweet feel of a fly rod in your hand. It's your favorite pipe . . . your roses . . . that old hat your wife tried to throw away last fall. If you're a woman it's a tricky new hairdo maybe . . . or a change of lipstick. Morale is a lot of little things like that. People can take the big bad things . . . the bitter news, the bombings even, if only a few of the little, familiar, comforting *good* things are left" (67). While the series really meant that little things like that *helped* morale, rather than *were* morale, it's not worth quibbling over the point since it doesn't invalidate the emotional charge or effectiveness of the ads. The second part of every ad in the series turned to selling with the identical words, "It happens that there are millions of Americans who attach a special value to their right to enjoy a refreshing glass of beer," as one of their "little things" to help their morale along. These Double-Barrelled ads skillfully, and strongly, put their war message first and their sales pitch second.

Without ever mentioning the word, one singular ad eloquently articulated the deep meaning of morale in wartime, especially on the home front, and most especially for home front women. In *Life* on July 10, 1944, a Belmont Radio ad featured a large illustration of a youngish-looking mother watering houseplants, a flag with two Service Stars behind her. Except for the company's name and address, the ad's entire copy ran as follows: "When she said goodbye to her two young sons it was with a smile that never faltered . . . a smile that told them not to worry about her . . . she would be all right. And she will continue to show this spirit to the end . . . in willing acceptance of war's daily trials, in uncomplaining sacrifice, in always cheerful, encouraging letters. With courage that has inspired mothers since time began, she is helping her sons do their parts as men. And she is doing hers as mothers have always done. It is she who sets the pace in Red Cross Work . . . who helps meet quotas in War Bond drives . . . who is among the first to volunteer for every worth-while cause. It is she who keeps America the home of the brave. With our hands and dollars, *let's all help keep it the land of the free!*" (89).

Three Cheers for Our Side

Even excluding the numerous ads in Chapter 7 specifically intended to boost civilians' morale about shortages and rationing, from early 1942 until months after the war was over nearly a thousand "morale ads" of other varieties appeared in just the ten national magazines examined here. Although there were other kinds as well, three types of morale ads predominated: those promoting products for their supposed or actual capacity to boost the morale of servicemen, the home front, or both; those encouraging civilians to help sustain or increase the morale of men and women in the service by doing things other than buying and mailing them such products; and those ads that were intrinsically intended to lift the morale of their readers on the home front and in the service. Of the last type, one of the most potent was advertising paying tribute to the various branches of the armed forces, its function and effect expressed well in a Young & Rubicam ad in *Newsweek* on October 16, 1944: "A good and useful purpose is served by war advertising devoted to specific branches of the front-line services. [. . .] it is helpful in two ways: First, it builds morale in the Services by showing recognition and awareness of specific jobs being done and dangers being faced. Second, it builds morale at home by creating an informed public and keeping alive in the public mind the actualities of war. [. . .] With each day that passes, our men overseas are a little more cut off from home. There's a little more chance that they may feel 'forgotten' . . . feel that their bloody tasks are being taken for granted back home. The need to combat this feeling increases daily . . . regardless of our progress or lack of progress in the war. The same increasing need exists to combat civilian apathy . . . to keep the public aware of the war in terms of the lives and deeds of those who are fighting it" (47). Along with military tribute ads there were ads saluting civilians; those commending war workers and farmers have already been discussed in Chapters 3 and 4, respectively, and those saluting women in the service and on the home front are in Chapter 8, which is devoted entirely to womanpower. A few other random civilian tribute ads will follow a look at those for the armed forces.

Military tribute ads weren't many but they were sincere, none of them selling a product. Even those placed by the Oldsmobile and Pontiac divisions of General Motors weren't really self-serving when toward the end of most ads they briefly described some of their war production, not to brag but to say they were glad to be able to help build some of the materiel that made combat troops' jobs a little easier. Most advertisers sponsoring tribute ads did so only once or twice, but two ran fairly extended series. Pontiac was one of those. Without counting its tributes to servicewomen or nurses, between July 7 and October 31, 1944, Pontiac sponsored six ads in the *Post, Newsweek, Collier's, Time, Life,* and *Look* honoring, in sequence, the Marines, the Army, the Merchant Marine, the

Army Air Force, Naval Aviation, and the Coast Guard, placing each ad only once in a different magazine, with no duplications. Each ad featured a large, rather idealized portrait of a man in each service by illustrator Bradshaw Crandell, and the copy consisted of a brief history of that service and/or its role in the present war.

Most service tribute ads commended an entire branch of the armed forces, only a few honoring specialized groups within the whole. The series of over six Hammond Organ ads entirely in *Newsweek* from early summer through late fall 1944 did precisely that. Through a vivid drawing and brief true-life narrative, each ad commended not just the spiritual guidance but also the courage and heroism of a military chaplain in combat. Prior to the Hammond Organ series, Willys-Overland, primary maker of the ubiquitous Jeep, placed a one-shot tribute to chaplains in the *Post* on January 1, 1944. This ad also narrated one chaplain's heroics under fire, but a battle-scarred Jeep played nearly as big a part as he in getting two wounded soldiers to safety behind the lines for medical treatment. Just a few other specialized units of the service came in for praise via magazine advertising, and in two of the three most conspicuous cases, it's very clear what motivated the advertiser to place such an ad. In *Collier's* on February 24, 1945, homage was paid to those relatively unsung troop- and cargo-carrying fliers, the Air Transport Command, Naval Air Transportation, and Troop Carrier Command. Paying that homage was Douglas Aircraft, builder of many of the troop transport and cargo planes. Similarly, it's obvious why two vivid tributes to the members of the U.S. Army Medical Department were placed (with no selling) in the *Post* on September 25 and *Newsweek* on September 27, 1943, by Johnson & Johnson, "the world's largest makers of surgical dressings" (*Newsweek* 5; *Post* 87). The only other group within the military to receive tributes from advertisers was so huge that it sometimes seems to have comprised the entirety of the U.S. Army, but the U.S. Infantry was only one of its parts. During the summer and early fall of 1944 (the year of most tribute ads), Camels, Plymouth, and Veeder-Root Incorporated each placed an ad saluting the infantry. Just a portion of the Veeder-Root copy illustrates the morale-building cheerleading in such ads for both the military and the home front: "Who says a private doesn't rate a salute? Well, here's one to the Infantry . . . the boys who hammer their way into enemy ground, tear it loose, and nail it down for keeps. They're the forces of attack, the forces of occupation, the final force of victory. The Infantryman calls himself a 'dogface.' History calls him 'King of Battles.' And, when the chips are down, whatever the odds, you can count on him every time" (*Newsweek* 7 Aug. 1944: 16).

Even fewer than military tributes, advertising's praise for people stateside was invariably for those whose contributions to the war effort were vital but, for the most part, went largely unnoticed. Two of these ads saluted home front women, not in the military and not necessarily even in war work. The more general was a two-page spread by Red Cross Shoes in *Life* on September 14, 1942, commending "Today's American Woman," "For her smiling cheerfulness in adapting herself to a sudden 'new way of life' * For her genius in rearing a family and running a home . . . and finding hours for volunteer work * For the enthusiasm and tireless energy with which she attacks her war work jobs * For the amazing efficiency with which she does them * [and] For managing— with all her busy life—to be fresher and lovelier and more charming than ever" (66–67). The ad then went on to sell shoes to the lady! An unusually emotional tribute ad that sold nothing was placed by North American Aviation in *Look* on April 4, 1944, praising mothers of fliers in the Army Air Corps: "You've hitched your heart to a star, the white star that marks your son's ship [. . .] You have loaned your son to fight for his country, his God. You sent him tearfully, perhaps . . . but your eyes were shining, your head was high" (75).

Two home front tribute ads saluted people very harried by the day-to-day hassles of their jobs. In a Cannon Percale Sheets ad in *Life* on April 30, 1945, the more unusual of the two salutes was given in first-person address by a woman shopper, starting out, "C'mon gals—it's our turn! Yep—our turn to treat to compliments! And who gets 'em? Who's been *earning* 'em ever since the war started? Why, who but our really swell department stores—all over the country" (16). We then discover it's not the department stores per se that merit the praise but "the extra-busy salespeople! There's not enough help to go round, these days—yet they manage to be in two places at once and still keep smiling!" along with "the new helpers-out! Lots of gals who never sold before are trying like sixty to do a good job." Thanks to Cannon Mills they finally got some of the recognition they deserved. As did America's grocers, courtesy of the Pillsbury Flour Mills Company on September 18, 1943, in the *Post*. Once again the copy was a first-person address, this time by the grocer himself: "Oh sure, I'm short of help and all that. My customers, often as not, don't get the very best of service, even though I do put in sixteen hours a day. But do you hear any squawks from them—or from me? You don't and you won't" (106). One civilian tribute ad was to a person who, if multiplied by all others like him, literally ran into the millions—the Victory Gardener. In *Collier's* on March 18, 1944, Calvert Distilleries sponsored an ad honoring Victory Gardeners that is striking in every way. As one of the ads in Calvert's "Salute to a Clear-Headed American" series, the art is a bas-relief sculpture of a Victory Gardener tending his plants, and the accompanying copy an eloquent, unrhymed, and unclichéed poetic tribute to him (31; see fig. 33).

"Have Yourself a Merry Little Christmas"

The 1944 M-G-M musical *Meet Me in St. Louis* was set in 1903, but Hugh Martin and Ralph Blane's song "Have Yourself a Merry Little Christmas" deliberately resonated with the ambivalent thoughts and feelings of the contemporary home front at Christmas, as in the song's stoic but gloomy conclusion about the war's uncertainties: "Someday soon we all will be together *if the fates allow*, / Until then we'll have to muddle through somehow, / So Have Yourself a Merry Little Christmas *now*" (emphases supplied). Such a dark Christmas song during World War II isn't surprising since those alone, separated from family and friends, or dislocated geographically from familiar and safe surroundings at Christmastime can feel lonely, melancholy, or depressed. Susceptible to such dark moods during wartime Christmases were GIs overseas or in stateside camps away from families and sweethearts, and folks at home facing their first (or yet another) Christmas without their GI son, daughter, husband, wife, or lover. Hence, at Christmas military and home front morale needed special lifting. Wartime seasonal advertising shows that the ad industry was well aware of this and did what it could to help.

The war's Christmas morale ads form something of a microcosm of the three predominant forms of all morale advertising: those selling products to boost GI morale, those encouraging civilians to help boost it, and those designed to help a civilian's morale by just reading the ad. By and large, ads selling Christmas gifts for GIs were pretty perfunctory. For example, beneath a nearly full-page illustration of a girl holding a candy box and kissing a soldier captioned "Take her the candy that's sure to thrill her heart!" a tiny sidebar in the bottom left corner of the Whitman's Candies ad in the *Post* for November 21, 1942, also suggested, "This

FIGURE 33

Christmas Remember Your Service Man! . . . Wherever he is . . . in camp or base . . . this Christmas give his spirits an extra boost with Whitman's" (8). Similarly, in *Time* on October 4, 1944, the Personna brand of razor blades took out a half-page ad illustrating three different gift sets of razor blades in different price ranges, since "Soldiers want blades, *need* blades" (73), and, of course, by implication, the blade they wanted was Personna. Of all the Christmas selling ads, the only one with a genuine message touching on the morale of an absent GI was by the Gruen Watch Company in *Life* on November 20, 1944. Simultaneously, the ad suggested Gruen watches as Christmas presents for the military — overall a skillful and effective Double-Barrelled war ad. A more than half-page painting depicted a WAC sergeant in the tropics against a background of palm trees. She looks thoroughly military but also scarcely able to hold back her tears. The caption read, "For a minute I was home . . . and it was Christmas Day!" (72). The copy began, "She'd tried so hard to hold the memories back . . . they'd be lighting the candles now . . . or opening the presents. How far away it seemed. But one thing helped . . . the lovely watch with the tender words on the back. She looked at it a thousand times . . . and suddenly she was home for Christmas." If wartime readers of this ad were as susceptible to nostalgia as I am, it must have resonated with feelings and images they could all relate to (see fig. 34).

Many Christmas morale ads focused on what home front civilians could do to sustain high morale in absent GIs. At bottom, most such ads gave practical advice and suggestions, and yet in almost every one of them emotion and sentiment weren't far behind, frequently in an appeal that worked on the reader's guilt as an impetus to action. Typical of such ads were two just about a year apart encouraging folks at home to mail Christmas packages to GIs overseas by October 15 to ensure they arrived by December 24. In a sidebar to an ad for Birds Eye frozen vegetables in *Life* on October 9, 1944, popular singer Dinah Shore had this to say about anyone's son, husband, father, brother, or sweetheart overseas: "Ever since he was a little boy, Christmas has been the big day in his life. And *this* Christmas he'll be broken-hearted if he doesn't get that Christmas present from you, and on time. So . . . don't wait another day! Mail that Christmas package to your boy *today!* The deadline for mailing Christmas packages overseas is October 15. Only a few days left. Don't wait. Remember what Christmas means to him!" (40). In the *Post* on Septem-

For *a minute I was home... and it was Christmas Day!*

She'd tried so hard to hold the memories back...they'd be lighting the candles now...or opening the presents. How far away it seemed! But one thing helped...the lovely watch with the tender words on the back! She looked at it a thousand times...and suddenly, she was home for Christmas! What better gift could you find...to say the things you'll want to say this Christmas...than a fine watch? May we suggest that you choose the Precision Watch...Gruen, because it has been America's choice for precision since 1874... Gruen because it was voted "America's best-styled watch" by leading fashion designers. Why not ask your Gruen jeweler to show you the many beautiful models still available. And remember ... your choice would be greater if we weren't doing everything we possibly can for Victory!

While we have been manufacturing large quantities of vital precision instruments for war, we also continue to produce fine Gruen Watches for civilian use ... but of course the demand for these watches far exceeds production possibilities today.

THE PRECISION WATCH

GRUEN WATCHES from $29.75 to $250; with precious stones to $4,000. Prices include Federal Taxes. The Gruen Watch Company, Time Hill, Cincinnati, Ohio, U. S. A. *In Canada:* Toronto, Ont.

BUY A GRUEN WATCH...BUT BUY A WAR BOND FIRST

"PRECISION" AND
"THE PRECISION WATCH"
ARE THE REGISTERED TRADE
MARKS OF THE GRUEN WATCH COMPANY

GRUEN...MAKERS OF THE PRECISION WATCH...AMERICA'S CHOICE SINCE 1874

FIGURE 34

ber 29, 1945, with plenty of GIs still overseas, the guilt inducers in a Big Ben Westclox ad were all in the first sentence, "To your man overseas your Christmas package will be the one bright spot in a lonesome day," and in the last, "Do this and you'll bring Christmas cheer to a lonely heart." (45). In between were instructions on how to pack and address overseas packages and a reminder of the mailing deadline. Other ads suggesting ways to brighten up a serviceman's holiday were more upbeat, less guilt-laden. As part of its long series of ads captioned "Visit him every week in snapshots," for Christmas 1942, Kodak placed one in the *Post* titled "Pay him a Christmas visit in snapshots," declaring that "Snapshots, more than anything else, can gather up the very spirit of the home Christmas — the faces, the scenes, the incidents — and deliver it to a distant shore or ship or camp" (back cover). Lest one think that this ad and the others in the series were just Kodak's devices to sell film, none of the ads plugged purchasing Kodak film specifically, but instead emphasized what photos from home do for GIs' morale. Speaking of home, and much closer to it, a Pullman ad in the *Post* on December 16, 1944, came up with a way for civilians to raise the morale of service personnel stateside by doing absolutely nothing. The ad asked, "Want to give a soldier a welcome Christmas gift?" Then it answered its own question: "YOU CAN DO IT just by spending the holidays at home! By *staying* home, you see, you leave more room on trains for soldiers *coming* home" (37).

The purpose of a few Christmas ads was to raise the morale of the home front. In the December 1942 *Ladies Home Journal,* one such ad from Armour and Company probably was designed to console mothers worrying about whether their GI sons would get a nice Christmas dinner. Front and center, the ad showed a well-laden dinner tray and in the upper right a happy-looking sailor eating contentedly; the ad's copy gave the detailed menus for the Army, Navy, and Marines' Christmas dinners — each one a veritable feast — with the whole thing headed "His Christmas dinner will have all the trimmings he loved at home" (2). A Pabst Blue Ribbon beer ad in *Collier's* on December 18, 1943, was written in rhyme too dreadful to bear quoting, but all the right morale-boosting sentiments were there. In the art and in the gist of the four-stanza poem, a home front mother and father mitigate their Christmastime loneliness by reading and rereading letters their overseas son has sent them, implying that this might be a way for other parents of GIs to lighten the mood of the holiday. Textile manufacturer Pacific Mills no doubt thought that once the war was over, servicemen who had returned home could still use a lift at Christmastime when they themselves were once again part of the home front. And Pacific Mills was probably right. To do its part the company placed a lovely ad in *Life* on December 3, 1945, in which the art depicted a soldier relaxing in an easy chair, hands behind his head, his wife in her dressing gown partially hidden by a very welcoming Christmas tree. The copy, headed "Twice-lived Christmas," was brief and to the point: "Last year it was just a dream; this year it's a glorious reality— Christmas at home! We at Pacific Mills want to say to every returning serviceman, including thousands of our own veteran employees, welcome home . . . thanks . . . and the very merriest Christmas ever!" (24). As touching or practical as many holiday ads were, Christmas, as they say, comes but once a year, while helping keep up both GI and civilian morale was one of advertising's year-round challenges for the duration.

Morale for Sale

Can a product actually sustain or lift morale not just in the sense of fleeting pleasure or happiness but in its primary sense of an abiding resolve to see something through against all odds? Some ads for name brand goods seem to have thought so or at least counted on readers believing their claims that they did. Other ads, however, made no such claims, suggesting only that a product was intended to give someone a transitory lift. Both kinds of ads selling goods on their alleged ability to help raise morale were legion in wartime magazines, especially from makers of cigarettes, candy, and soft drinks. Camel Cigarettes alone placed about a hundred such ads, Coca-Cola sixty-five or so, and the manufacturers of Baby Ruth, Milky Way, Nestle's, and Whitman's candies combined for close to fifty "morale products" ads. Some boldly trumpeted their wares' capacity to raise morale, but most were more circumspect, rarely using the word itself, although it's unmistakable that morale was what the ad was referring to.

Some claims of a product's morale-boosting properties were patently preposterous or at least suspect, none more so than those that ballyhooed the miracles a certain toothpaste, soap, or deodorant could work on one's morale—usually by way of a serviceman's new success with a girl or a girl's heightened popularity among GIs. Such ads were pretty silly, but their intention appears to have been earnest, as well as to sell the advertisers' products. Ads by Colgate toothpaste (called Dental Cream then), Lifebuoy soap, and Mum deodorant uniformly told a little story in words and pictures, while the ads for Cashmere Bouquet soap varied only in that they were a dialogue between "The Girl" and "Us," meaning the soap's manufacturer. Typically, the narrative began either with a GI down in the dumps because somebody stole his gal or because she was mysteriously unresponsive to him, or with a girl in the service or on the home front equally miserable because of a shortage of male admirers. Midway through, the protagonist discovers Colgate's miraculous power to destroy bad breath or the soaps' and deodorant's ability to banish body odor. Use of the product apparently solves every problem in each character's love life and they all end up as happy as they were despondent at the start. Colgate was the grand champion of such advertising, publishing well over two dozen such ads over the course of the war, most of them in *Life*. The ads were all similar regardless of their individual "plots," so one each of Colgate's with a female and male protagonist will illustrate the typical details of these dubious morale builders. In *Look* on April 4, 1944, and in *Life* on May 8, in the large first frame a gloomy looking WAVE, head in hands says, "Nobody Writes to ME!" (*Look* 12; *Life* 8). She tells a fellow WAVE how boyfriends and even acquaintances have been drifting away from her in alarming numbers, whereupon her friend advises her, "A visit to your dentist—next time you're home on liberty—might brighten up the male situation more than you think." The next two frames find the WAVE with her dentist, who explains, as does every dentist in the series in exactly the same words, how Colgate not only cleans teeth but gets rid of bad breath as well. In the final frame, captioned "*LATER, THANKS TO COLGATE DENTAL CREAM*," the happy WAVE is poring over a sheaf of letters and remarking to her friend, "Thanks to you—mail-call is male-call these days." In Colgate ads featuring male GIs, the copywriters' tactics knew no bounds. The ad in *Life* on April 12, 1943, was a deliberate spin-off from the enormously popular sentimental ballad of that year, "Johnny Doughboy Found a Rose in Ireland." Colgate's story of an American soldier encamped in Ireland is headed "Johnny Doughboy Met a Thorn in Rosie." His sweet Irish girlfriend can't even bear to look him in the face, suggesting instead that he see a dentist, with the predictable results. The final frame, again captioned "*LATER—THANKS TO COLGATE DENTAL CREAM*," finds Rosie in a wedding dress saying, "Sure and it's the lucky bride I am, Johnny!" and Johnny replying "I'm the one who's shot with luck, Rosie! Johnny Doughboy's found a Rose in Ireland—and a wife!" All thanks to a toothpaste. Amazing!

No less "amazing" were the morale-building powers of the soaps and deodorant. In the same issue of *Life* as the Colgate "Johnny Doughboy" ad, The Girl in a Cashmere Bouquet ad begins by saying, "Out of that whole Army you'd think I could find at least one soldier who'd take me out," launching a dialogue with "Us" about the deodorizing properties and perfumed scent of Cashmere Bouquet as opposed to the "mannish" aroma of other deodorizing soap, a not-so oblique smack at Lifebuoy. Us convinces The Girl to try Cashmere Bouquet; she does and goes to a USO dance. Us remarks, "Looks like the Army has moved in and you seem to have everything under control," prompting The Girl to ask, "Glory be! Does Cashmere Bouquet *guarantee* such popularity?" To which the advertiser, nicely hedging its bets, answers, "It's you who rates the popularity, my dear . . . Cashmere Bouquet just insures the perfection of your daintiness!" (8). Apparently the girl in the Lifebuoy cartoon ad in *Life* on June 15, 1942, wasn't put off by the soap's "mannish" odor since after bathing with it she manages to turn a soldier's first-date avoidance to ardent admiration, he saying in the final frame, "I've got an idea we're going to dance together for a long, long time!" with her thinking, "No foolin' . . . It's Lifebuoy for me from now on" (72). And in *Life* on October 9, 1944, USO hostess Janet says to her friend Elsie that she could "go for" a certain Marine, but that "he acts as if I didn't exist" (13). Elsie tells Janet about Mum deodorant and in the last frame, while she and the Marine are playing ring-toss at a carnival, Janet thinks to herself, "He thinks I'm simply super—thanks to Mum!"

Other ads offering a product to lift morale were more modest in their claims, usually suggesting it would provide a brief respite from one's routine. In *Life* on November 9, 1942, a talking bottle of Royal Crown Cola dropped in on civilians and military on the home front, saying that for a man running a power lathe "it's a pleasure to give him a frosty lift," for a woman making ammunition that Royal Crown was "ready to give her a relaxed moment and a fresh start," and for a sailor just back from PT boat training that it was "glad to help him get a few minutes of glorious, sprawled-out relaxation" (117). Also in *Life*, on January 24, 1944, 7-Up set its morale-building sights realistically with copy beginning "Sure as the day follows night, a smile follows 7-Up. It's a happy, bubbling drink that goes romping over your tongue . . . waking up each taste bud . . . giving your spirits a 'fresh up'" (13). And nearly every Coca-Cola ad included some version of its famous slogan "The pause that refreshes."

Other products-for-morale ads obliquely or implicitly suggested that the kind of morale they alluded to was the positive long-term spirit or attitude needed by both soldier and civilian to make it through the war successfully. These ads never mentioned morale by name. Typical was the ad for Kaywoodie Briar Pipes in *Life* on November 23, 1942: "Always a personal companion of the most trusted sort, always a source of inspiration and confidence, a Kaywoodie is as good in war as in peace — sure, steady, reliable" (10). In *Life* on August 17, 1942, a young woman in a Munsingwear ad forthrightly said, "I want a girdle . . . and a good one. It keeps my pride up as well as my stockings. When you're working hard as I am on this defense job, a girdle makes you feel better!" (83), and she didn't mean just physically better but also attitudinally. A full-page cartoon ad for Pepsi-Cola in *Time* on September 24, 1945, depicted a car on a troop train jam-packed with GIs all drinking the advertiser's product and a sergeant saying to a lieutenant, "Sgt. Thomas reporting. Not a single gripe on this trip, since we put on Pepsi" (33), and an ad by Pepsi's biggest rival in *Life* on June 7, 1943, virtually equated Coke with those things that helped ensure long-term, deep-seated morale in servicemen: "Next to wives, sweethearts and letters from home, among things our soldiers mention most is Coca-Cola" (back cover).

Coca-Cola was also one of the rare advertisers to even occasionally use the word itself in ads claiming a product was good for morale. Of the sixty-plus Coke ads, just four addressed morale directly, the language of the earliest clearly suggesting it was referring to Coca-Cola's benefit to long-term morale during the war. Under a picture of a war worker bowling after work, the copy read, "Simple pleasures build up morale and peace of mind. That's one reason why the enjoyment of ice-cold Coca-Cola has new meaning in wartime" (*Life* 2 Nov. 1942: 34). The copy in *Life* on May 3, 1943, could refer to Coke's benefit to either short- or long-term morale: "Today *the pause that refreshes* with ice-cold Coca-Cola is a standby of men in the Army, Navy, and Marine Corps, and a standby of the great army of men and women war workers. Every time you enjoy a Coke it tells you all over again what it means to morale" (back cover). In a direct reference to morale, Pepsi-Cola could have meant either variety, when the copy in *Time* on April 20, 1942, declared, "Pepsi-Cola lifts morale, keeps the spirit up" (47). And Nestle's clearly was referring to momentary morale lifting when in *Life* on December 6, 1943, it stated that "*Chocolate Bars, Hot Chocolate* and *Chocolate Flavored Drinks* by the millions boost the morale of our Soldiers, Sailors, and Marines at Post Exchanges and Ships Service Stores all over the globe" (68).

If products to drink and eat inspired using the word morale in ads focusing on GIs, for the home front it was articles of clothing that prompted such copywriting. In two different ads in *Life*, one on September 27, the other on November 22, 1943, Munsingwear promoted its girdles and other foundation garments for women by reiterating the apparent fact that "the government now knows that foundations *are* essential to health and morale" (27 Sept. 1942: 52). Similarly, but without invoking government support, Wilson Brothers, a maker of men's wear, had a war worker say in *Life* on April 5, 1943, "And for my own morale on the job and at home, I've got to look *good*" (62), while on September 6, 1943, its ad in *Life* said of another war worker, "Joe keeps his morale hitched high with long-wearing clothes that fit well and look swell" (114). Both ads added that Wilson Brothers' duds were so reasonably priced that these two working stiffs could still pay their taxes and buy War Bonds. Without belaboring the point, ads for Jockey Underwear for men and Walk-Over Shoes for women also emphasized how their products were, in Walk-Over's words, "good-for-the-old-morale" (*Life* 21 Sept. 1942: 140).

A few ads hinted that using the same products as the military would boost civilians' morale, even though it was verboten for the armed forces to officially endorse a product. Yet some admen made it seem they did, as in an ad in the August 1944 *Ladies' Home Journal*. The art showed a stylish woman looking at her well-manicured nails in front of five portraits labeled WAC, Women Marine, WAVE, SPAR, and Navy Nurse. The caption read "These Women—1944's best dressed—choose favorite Cutex Shade" (114), which looks a lot like a service endorsement for the nail polish but actually isn't. In Barbasol's tongue-in-cheek pseudo-endorsement in *Life* on March 27, 1944, a drawing of an attractive WAC, WAVE, Woman Marine, and SPAR walking and saluting in unison was captioned "A MAJOR IS PASSING BY with a handsome Barbasol Face." The copy explained, "Girls in uniform salute more Barbasol Faces than any other kind for the simple reason that more men in uniform shave with Barbasol than any other brand" (129), the logic of which renders service endorsements all but ludicrous.

Then there were the cigarette ads, which, when it came to morale, seem to have obeyed a logic all their own. In the 1940s, claims made in cigarette advertising were not as stringently regulated as they would be in later decades as more and more became known about the deleterious effects of tobacco smoke on human health. Nevertheless, cigarette manufacturers seemed to feel constrained against making grandiose claims about any physical or psychic euphoria that smoking their brand would induce. And, too, like other wartime advertising, cigarette ads had to eschew explicit endorsements from the armed forces—or seemingly so. Yet these strictures on cigarette advertising were, as Hamlet said, more honored in the breach than the observance. Of the three best-selling brands, Lucky Strike alone created no war-themed magazine advertising, but Chesterfield and Camel more than made up for that lack and then some. From the war's beginning until after its end, virtually every ad by these two brands featured men or women in the service, war workers (usually women), or farmers (in Camels ads in *Farm Journal*), singly or in various combinations. In each ad they proclaimed their loyalty to one cigarette or the other because of its mildness, lower nicotine, or better taste, nearly always falling just short of directly saying that the Camel or Chesterfield lifted their morale. While almost no ads contained explicit endorsements from the services, each Camels ad came very close by including a statement similar to this one in *Life* on September 21, 1942: "With men in the Army, Navy, Marines, and the Coast Guard, the favorite cigarette is Camel. (Based on actual sales records in Post Exchanges, Sales Commissaries, Ship's Service Stores, Ship's Stores, and Canteens)" (back cover). All of which sounds a lot like an endorsement.

Chesterfield went Camel one better with what can only be construed as a service endorsement on the back cover of *Time* on October 11, 1943. The picture was of a woman in flying gear, her goggles pushed onto her forehead while she lit a Chesterfield. The copy explained that she was in the WAFS, the Women's Auxiliary Ferrying Squadron created by the Army Air Force in 1942 to fly planes from factories to air bases, clearly making her a member of the armed forces. Under her picture in very large letters was the unmistakable endorsement "With Us It's Chesterfield."

If cigarette advertising mostly skirted the ban on service endorsements, it was equally good at suggesting the morale-lifting power of cigarettes without coming right out and saying the smoker would get a quick nicotine high from the advertiser's product. In the myriad Camel ads, the word "morale" occurred only twice, and then obliquely. Under a photo in one Camel ad was a description of the leisure time of an actual woman named Betty Rice whose unusual war work was designing camouflage: "Morale experts say that it's a good idea for women in the war to be 'just women' once in a while. So here's Betty Rice following that advice . . . complete with king's yellow evening dress, Prince Charming escort [a ranking army officer in dress uniform] and very-much-part-of-the-picture Camels" (*Ladies' Home Journal* Dec. 1942: 46; *Life* 2 Nov. 1942: back cover). Another Camel ad on the back cover of *Life* on May 15, 1944, concluded describing the special duties and heroics of M.D.s at the front with "And doctor that he is . . . doctor of medicine and morale . . . he well knows the comfort and cheer there is in a few moments' relaxation with a good cigarette . . . like Camel."

Other ads for Camels and Chesterfields strongly implied the cigarettes' positive effect on morale without actually saying it: A fighter pilot says that "a good cigarette is mighty comforting to have along . . . and Chesterfields are *on the beam*" (*Life* 28 Sept. 1942: 44; *Time* 14 Sept. 1942: back cover). The tail gunner in a Flying Fortress remarks, "I say that a pack of Camels is a lot of company. Because when I can lean back and light up a Camel, everything's okay" (*Life* 27 Dec. 1943: back cover). Such ads, of course, implied that home front readers should choose that brand for its morale-boosting capacity.

Reach Out and Touch Someone

More than three decades before AT&T began using that slogan in 1979 to encourage long-distance usage, during World War II the Bell Telephone System, AT&T's earlier incarnation, ran numerous ads asking civilians *not* to make long distance calls at certain times of day for the sake of GI morale and the morale of their families at home. In *Life* on July 19, 1943, Bell captioned a photo of a soldier in a phone booth, "GIVE HIM A BREAK! Evening is about his only chance to telephone home. He can get through easier if the wires aren't crowded—and his calls mean so much to him and the home folks. So please don't call Long Distance between 7 p.m. and 10 p.m. unless your calls are really necessary. Many thanks" (3). This was one of many ads asking, sometimes even pleading with the home front to do things costing almost nothing in time, effort, or, especially, money, that would enhance service personnel's morale stateside and abroad. In some ads the advertiser had a particular interest in the message, as was the case with Bell Telephone, but other companies having nothing to do with the product or service involved placed similar messages purely to urge morale-lifting endeavors by the home front. A cartoon ad by the Ethyl Corporation in *Look* on October 19, 1943, included a WAC hopping mad about a love-struck civilian monopolizing a phone booth, followed by "Give the service men a break—Help keep Long Distance lines clear for them between 7 and 10 p.m." (10).

Just as Bell Telephone frequently encouraged telecommunication courtesy for the sake of GIs' morale, Greyhound and Pullman did the same for public transportation. From Greyhound in *Life* on November 30, 1942: *If possible, postpone your usual year-end trip, so that there will be more seat space for men in uniform—at a time when leaves or furloughs spent with friends and loved ones mean so much to them"* (141). And, among several of its kind, one sure-fire guilt-inducing ad by Pullman captioned a large picture of two more than disheartened GIs in a train station with "***Have a Heart, Pal!***" (*Life* 29 May 1944: 77; *Time* 3 July 1944: 36; *Post* 8 July 1944: 43; see fig. 35). The modes of civilian behavior recommended in advertisements like these by Bell, Greyhound, and Pullman were for the benefit of each and every GI, most of them total strangers to the people who modified their telephone and travel habits for the sake of servicemen. A few ads went so far as to recommend inviting some of them into one's home as a way of lifting their morale, whether for a special occasion like a holiday or just as something to do once a week or once a month. Such ads, of course, had to have been aimed at readers within reasonable striking distance of a stateside army camp or naval base. Hart Schaffner & Marx, a company with no connection at all to food, drink, or other aspects of entertaining, in the December 1944 *Esquire* made an emotionally charged appeal to invite for Thanksgiving one or more GIs unable to travel to their own home: "So you're not sentimental, huh? . . . So Thanksgiving is just another day. Well, just try wandering around a strange town for a few days where you don't know a soul . . . eat in diners where the man next to you is just another elbow in your side. *Then* you'll know what 'home' and 'welcome' mean to a lonely soldier. Put yourself in *his* place . . . then see if you can eat that turkey without inviting at least one serviceman to *your* home this Thanksgiving!" (43). (Lest December 1944 seems rather late for *Esquire* to have published this urging, monthly magazines came out weeks

"Have a Heart, Pal!"

"SURE, YOU NEED A VACATION. You deserve one, too!

"But have a heart, will you? Go easy on the traveling and leave *some* room on trains for us.

"We'd appreciate that—'cause we'd *like* to get home as fast as we can to make the most of our furloughs.

"And we *have* to be back in camp on time—ready to shove off and do that job you're counting on us to do!"

PULLMAN

● For more than 80 years, the greatest name in passenger transportation—now carrying out mass troop movements with *half* its fleet of sleeping cars and carrying more passengers in the *other* half than the *whole* fleet carried in peacetime!

BUY an EXTRA WAR BOND with what your trip would cost!

77

FIGURE 35

before their cover dates.) More informally, in the May 1943 *Ladies' Home Journal*, Coca-Cola invited readers to invite GIs into their homes for no particular reason except lifting their morale (and, of course, serving them Coke): "Put out the welcome mat for the soldiers. Let them take over your house and kitchen on Sunday evenings. Their efficiency will probably shame you into taking that cooking course you've heard about. [. . .] You can vary the menu from week to week, but don't attempt to change the refreshment. There just isn't any substitute for the taste and refreshment of Coke to the boys of the fighting forces" (102).

Despite these kinds of ads, the majority urging the home front to help lift GIs' morale focused on personally touching one's own family members, close friends, or casual acquaintances in the service. In ascending order of their frequency (and, arguably, of their importance as well) were ads promoting making phonograph records, taking snapshots, and, most prevalent of all, writing letters. What these ads had in common was that selling was kept to a minimum, although most were by commercial advertisers,

Long before the war the Wilcox-Gay Corporation of Charlotte, Michigan, was building and marketing a device called a Recordio. Coin-operated versions were often found in amusement parks, penny arcades, seaside resorts, and other venues from which a person might want to record a message on a standard 78 rpm phonograph disk and mail it to the folks back home. The Recordio for home use was essentially the same except that the user didn't have to feed it with nickels. If the ads in *Life* can be believed, by 1942 there were hundreds of thousands of these gadgets in homes across the country. Of course once the war began, Wilcox-Gay, like most manufacturers, was engaged in war work, and no Recordios were being built. With no machines to sell, Recordio's ads on November 16, November 30, and December 14, 1942, were essentially public service announcements asking owners of one to share its use with friends and neighbors to make home-made records for their loved ones in the service since "recorded messages have become one of the great morale-building ideas of this war. They carry a cheerful note straight from the hearts of those who are back home" (14 Nov. 1942: 48). Recordio disks, which could still be purchased, came with a convenient mailing envelope.

Recordio's few GI morale ads were confined to the closing months of 1942 when very large numbers of servicemen were still in camps and bases stateside, making it comparatively easy for them to find a phonograph on which to play records from home. But since photographs needed no special equipment to view them, the more than twenty-five ads placed by Kodak in its "Visit him this week in SNAPSHOTS" series ran from June 1942, through December 1945, most often with a different ad in each weekly issue of *Life*, *Collier's*, or the *Post*. Although the series was so extensive, three elements of all the ads were so similar that little need be said about the individual ads in particular. First, in one way or another they all conveyed the benefit of snapshots for GIs' morale: "Wherever they may pause . . . on the long, tough road that stretches on ahead . . . it's up to us to be on hand . . . We can do it, if we send 'snapshots from home'" (*Life* 25 Oct. 1943: 59). Second, nearly all the ads made reference to Kodak products, but differently. During the early going in 1942 the copy contained a strong sales pitch for Kodak Verichrome Film. By 1943 the ads were saying, "Of course, there isn't as much film for you as in normal times—Kodak Film is now rationed to dealers because the Army and Navy need so much" (*Life* 24 May 1943: 43). And by 1944, the brand name disappeared from the copy: "Film is still scarce, the Army and Navy need so much. So make the most of every roll you can get" (*Life* 3 Apr. 1944: 63). Such copy seems to be referring not just to Kodak, but to all brands of film—and there were others, such as Ansco. The third most noticeable thing about the Kodak ads is that although their message was essentially the same, the copywriters continually varied the approach over the four years of the war. There's a world of difference, say, between the breezy opening of an ad in *Collier's* on August 8, 1942: "Keep him happy by slipping a few snapshots into your letter every time you write" (29), and the beginning of another *Collier's* ad on August 11, 1945, that managed to pack the tedium and weariness of four years of soldiering into just a few lines of copy: "If the time seems long to you—think how it seems to them. Bring home close to them in snapshots . . . Yes, it's real—the snapshots say so. Home is real, and pretty girls, and happy children. America is real. And some day they'll be there" (53). Being Kodak, the art in these ads—always photographs, never illustrations—was of superior quality, featuring soldiers, sailors, fliers, and even an occasional WAC, in the mess hall, on an airstrip, in barracks, on maneuvers, or taking a breather during combat to show snapshots from home to their buddies.

Recordio and Kodak made cogent pitches for records and snapshots from home to boost GI morale. But, like most GIs and civilians alike,

America's advertisers and ad agencies knew that letters gave the biggest, most meaningful lift to the morale of servicemen overseas. Accordingly, in just the ten leading national magazines more than a hundred war ads used every tactic from cajoling and prodding to shaming and browbeating in stressing the urgency of writing to servicemen and women on a regular and frequent basis. Predictably, Parker, Esterbrook, Shaeffer's, Waterman's and other brands of pens and pencils placed quite a few letters-for-morale ads, and, equally predictably, these advertisers often devoted as much or more of the copy to promoting their products as to encouraging writing letters to GIs. Far less predictably, the overwhelming majority of letter-writing ads were sponsored by products and companies having nothing to do with writing or mailing letters, some of them fairly obscure to average civilians, like the Tobe Deutschmann Corp., but most of them nationally familiar names like Fred Harvey Restaurants, Sanka, Pontiac, Dole, Windex, Westinghouse, Borden's, and Gaines Dog Meal. Some of these advertisers also did a fair bit of selling along with their letter-writing appeals, but the emphasis—if not the entirety—of their ads was on boosting GI morale through letters from home.

Such ads began almost as soon as the war began for American forces. On April 4, 1942, in the *Post*, the Parker Pen Company began an ad, most of which sold pens, with "Mail time is the high spot in the day of every soldier or sailor—the time when he feels either close to home, or unremembered and alone" (inside front cover). Throughout 1942 nearly all the messages were just about as brief and straightforward: from Esterbrook Pens in *Collier's* on October 10, 1942, "If you could be there when the mail is passed around . . . you'd get a real idea of how much a letter means" (57); and, also in *Collier's*, from Sheaffer's on October 24, 1942: "If he's in Uncle Sam's forces, he's fighting for all of us. Let him know we're with him wherever he is. A letter takes only a few minutes to write—we can load it full of doings and love. A 3c stamp takes us right into camp" (inside front). By 1943, much of the copy took on a sentimental tone as, again from Sheaffer's, in the September issue of *Esquire*: "While he reads—and re-reads your letters—it is like a moment by the fireside . . . an evening at home. You are at his side—giving him courage—helping him to look forward to the wonderful days to come . . . two hearts in Wartime . . . a pause in the fulfillment of dreams and plans because of bigger things that must be done. But—planning, dreaming . . . and love go on . . . kept alive by letters. Your letters and his—become parts of your lives . . . something more on which to build a glorious future. Write him another letter today" (inside front cover). By 1944 nostalgia became a key ingredient in persuading civilians to write to servicemen abroad, as seen in *Life* on November 20, 1944, in an ad sponsored by the Cavalier Corporation, a furniture manufacturer: "To him . . . wherever he is . . . a letter from *home* is still more important than anything else [. . .] He wants news of little things, too; even the rooms he lived in have become so fond a memory to a man in service that every small detail you report conjures up visions of home to him . . . the home he's fighting for. Main Street, Court House Square, the high school gang at the drug store . . . they're all important. But most precious of all is the place where he lived, with his Mom, his Dad, and Sis. It's little enough . . . write that letter today" (69). In letter-writing ads through-out the war, the most emotionally charged word was invariably "home."

Even as emotional content in letter-writing ads ramped up over the course of the war, another kind of ad occasionally appeared, sometimes humorous, sometimes serious and tinged with emotion. These ads didn't tell people to write, but instead told them *what and what not to write to GIs.* One of the earliest was in the December 1942 *Ladies' Home Journal.* Captioning a picture of a woman saying good-bye to a soldier "When someone you love goes to war—" Westinghouse laid out basic rules for the right kinds of letters: Keep them simple, and leave out anything gloomy, troublesome, or problematic: "Make your letters cheerful and encouraging. Leave out the news about the rainy weather and Junior's siege of the grippe and the trouble with the hot-water system. Tell him, instead, the things he wants to hear . . . That you're well, and that things at home are fine. That the baby has a tooth, or you got a raise [. . .] The *good* news. The news that makes it easier for *him.* Send it to him *often*" (53). Then Westinghouse asked and answered a question: "Why is an *electrical manufacturer* asking you to do this? We don't make fountain pens or stationery, or anything connected with letter writing. We proba-bly never shall. [. . .] But we believe that *the morale of our fighting men* is a bigger and more important Victory weapon than anything we have ever made, or shall ever make. That's where *you* can help out. That's *your* job. *Good news*—often." Altogether an unusual and impressive ad. Later in the war, Sanka took the comic approach to the proper content of let-ters to GIs in a cartoon ad again featuring snoopy and strident War Con-science chastising an overcaffeinated woman for writing cranky things like "'Rationing's such trouble,' . . . 'can't find a maid anywhere' . . . ! Don't you know you ought to be building up his morale? Write cheerful stuff and keep complaints to yourself. You ought to be ashamed!" (*Life* 9 Oct. 1944: 42). And, without going into detail, it's enough to know that in *Ladies' Home Journal* for the following month, a six-frame, *rhymed* cartoon ad by Windex managed to sell the glass cleaner and advise the proper content for letters simultaneously, the entire silliness ending with "Get WINDEX—the 20-ounce bottle's a buy! / (P. S. *Do* be cheerful when writing your guy!)" (70).

In mid-1943, a new kind of letter-writing ad began to appear, at first in a barely perceptible trickle, but in 1944 and the first half of 1945 swelling into a veritable deluge. These ads went beyond asking the folks at home to write GIs by specifically urging them to use V-Mail when they did. Briefly, V-Mail was developed by Kodak and the British and American governments. A person wrote a letter on specially sized self-addressable stationary and mailed it with a regular 3¢ stamp to an APO address. The letter, along with millions more like it, was then microfilmed and the film flown overseas where it was blown-up to readable-size paper copy and delivered to its recipient. GIs in turn wrote V-Mails home with the process going in reverse back to the states. This system was not only much faster than paper letters traveling by ship, which sometimes took months to arrive; it also freed up considerable cargo space on both ships and planes. The only mystery about ads encouraging V-Mail is why they began so late. According to *Business Week* on February 17, 1945, V-Mail was in use by the home front to the troops and vice versa since July 1942, although with only three and seven million letters sent in each of the last two quarters of the year. By 1943, the numbers skyrocketed, with over sixteen million V-Mails sent from the United States alone from January through March, leaping to almost fifty-seven million during October through December. In 1944 they rose even higher, except for a slight tailing off in the fourth quarter (40). Although GIs claimed not to like V-Mails—"I can't read 'em"; "They aren't long enough to tell me the news from home"—they wrote and received them in staggering numbers, as did the home front. Two V-Mail ads by Sheaffer's in May were the only ones in 1943, but then with so many people using V-Mail in 1944, the sudden torrent of ads seems almost a case of preaching to the choir.

But preach they did, sometimes with more raw emotion than any earlier ads about writing. Other ads remained upbeat, such as one with a nearly full-page portrait of General A. A. Vandegrift, Commandant of the United States Marine Corps, and a signed message from him: "Mail is morale. Ask any man overseas. He'll tell you that a bright cheerful letter from home is like a five minute furlough. So write cheerfully and write often. Frequent letters—even though short, are best. And V-Mail is ideal for this purpose" (Big Ben Westclox, *Post* 9 June 1945: 1). But most V-Mail ads were heavy hitters, few more so than those by the Pitney-Bowes Postage Meter Company; two excerpts will give a clear picture of this: In *Time* on May 29, 1944, a GI says, "*'Don't know if I can take it!* . . . *Last letter a month before we went in.* . . . *three weeks' of shells, bein' shot at, no sleep* . . . *Back today, everybody's got mail but me* . . . *What's the matter at home?'* If people would only—Use V-MAIL" (102); and also from *Time* on January 24, 1944: "Letters can come too late! Men go into battle, and don't come back . . . Yet for weeks afterward, letters keep coming for them . . . letters they waited, hoped and hungered for, worried about . . . *letters that V-Mail could have brought in time*! Use V-MAIL" (6).

Not that emotional appeals were the private province of V-Mail ads, nor were they all contained in such brief "sound-bites" as the two excerpts above. Some took up nearly all the very long copy in full page ads, as when, in one by Nash-Kelvinator on June 14, 1943, a GI in a Japanese prison camp reacted to how much a letter from his wife meant to him, or when a soldier in a fox hole preached a strongly worded sermon (as he called it) on how much letters meant to men in combat, saying, "Neither heroes nor brave fighters step from the ranks of men made lonely by a hunger in their hearts for news from home" (Gartner & Bender [a greeting card company], *Collier's* 3 Apr. 1943: 81). But perhaps the most affecting emotional copy was the largely narrative text of a Parker Pen Company ad in *Life* on July 20, 1942, titled "The SOLDIER Whose LETTER Never Comes" (20; see fig. 36 for the full ad). Very likely it was this ad that the father of my friend Elva Mathiesen, Lt. Benjamin R. Jordan of the 4th Infantry, had in mind when he wrote his parents from Nome, Alaska, on October 10, 1942: "It has been quite some time since anyone has gotten any letters up here [. . .] These ads in the magazines put out by the Parker Pen Company and such like are the first ads I have seen that do not exaggerate the way a soldier feels about getting mail"— clear testimony to the impact of letters, and ads about them, on GIs.

The emotion and sentiment in letter-writing ads are second in intensity only to those qualities in War Bond ads. If they seem excessive more

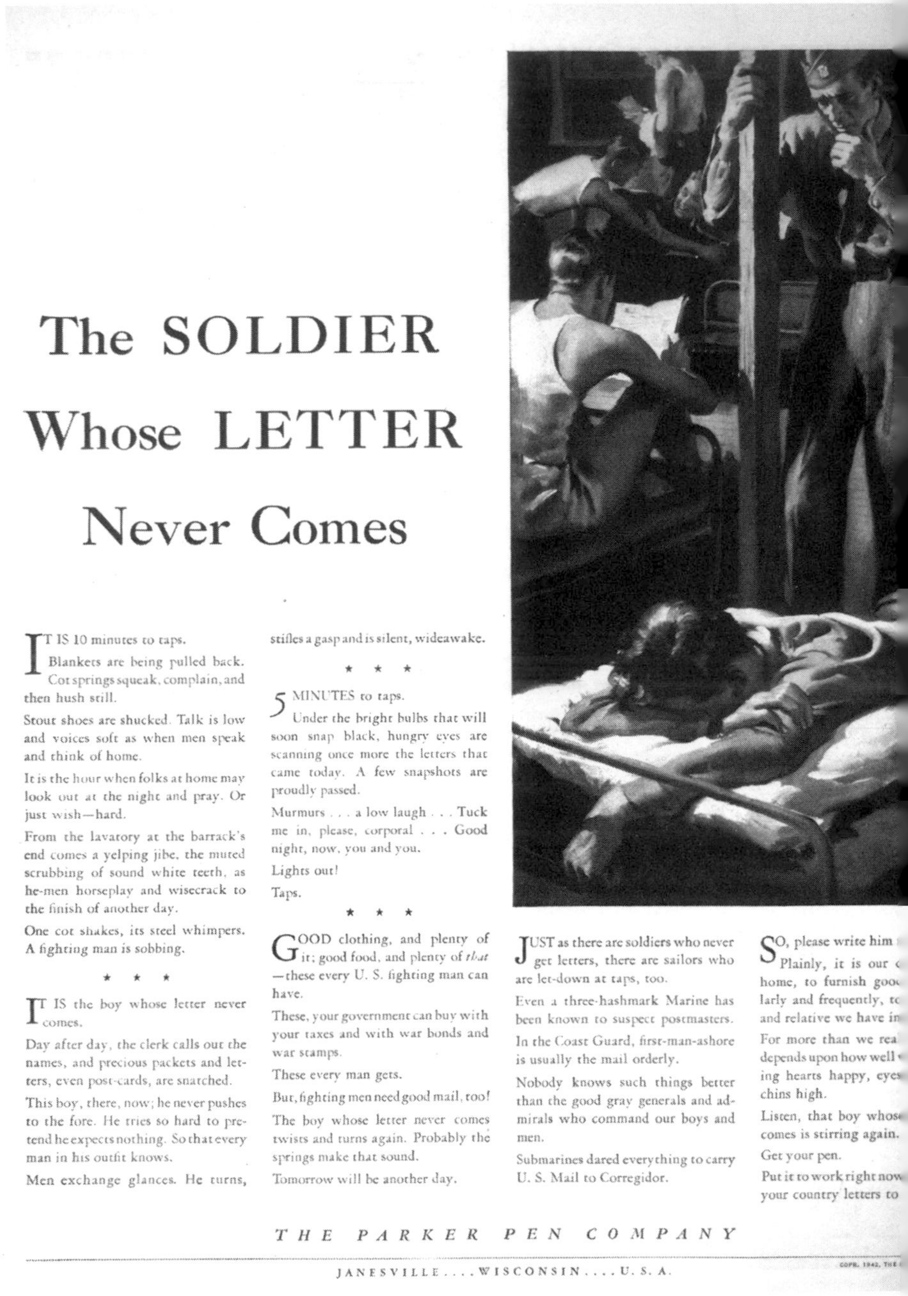

The SOLDIER Whose LETTER Never Comes

IT IS 10 minutes to taps.

Blankets are being pulled back. Cot springs squeak, complain, and then hush still.

Stout shoes are shucked. Talk is low and voices soft as when men speak and think of home.

It is the hour when folks at home may look out at the night and pray. Or just wish—hard.

From the lavatory at the barrack's end comes a yelping jibe, the muted scrubbing of sound white teeth, as he-men horseplay and wisecrack to the finish of another day.

One cot shakes, its steel whimpers. A fighting man is sobbing.

* * *

IT IS the boy whose letter never comes.

Day after day, the clerk calls out the names, and precious packets and letters, even post-cards, are snatched.

This boy, there, now; he never pushes to the fore. He tries so hard to pretend he expects nothing. So that every man in his outfit knows.

Men exchange glances. He turns, stifles a gasp and is silent, wideawake.

* * *

5 MINUTES to taps.

Under the bright bulbs that will soon snap black, hungry eyes are scanning once more the letters that came today. A few snapshots are proudly passed.

Murmurs . . . a low laugh . . . Tuck me in, please, corporal . . . Good night, now, you and you.

Lights out!

Taps.

* * *

GOOD clothing, and plenty of it; good food, and plenty of *that* —these every U. S. fighting man can have.

These, your government can buy with your taxes and with war bonds and war stamps.

These every man gets.

But, fighting men need good mail, too!

The boy whose letter never comes twists and turns again. Probably the springs make that sound.

Tomorrow will be another day.

JUST as there are soldiers who never get letters, there are sailors who are let-down at taps, too.

Even a three-hashmark Marine has been known to suspect postmasters.

In the Coast Guard, first-man-ashore is usually the mail orderly.

Nobody knows such things better than the good gray generals and admirals who command our boys and men.

Submarines dared everything to carry U. S. Mail to Corregidor.

SO, please write him Plainly, it is our c home, to furnish goo larly and frequently, to and relative we have in

For more than we rea depends upon how well ing hearts happy, eyes chins high.

Listen, that boy whose comes is stirring again.

Get your pen.

Put it to work right now your country letters to

THE PARKER PEN COMPANY

JANESVILLE....WISCONSIN....U. S. A.

FIGURE 36

than six decades later, we should not lay the blame on the creators of the ads but on the twenty-first-century sensibilities of readers reacting to them now, sensibilities worlds apart from those of most Americans during World War II. For many people, the romance, charm, and gallantry that still flourished then are dead or dying now, largely displaced by apathy, coarseness, and cynicism. While emotion, sentiment, and nostalgia were thought of positively during the war, for many today they belong only in the most maudlin of greeting cards. The result is that many of us, and especially younger Americans, are ill-equipped to fairly evaluate the expression of emotion and sentiment in war ads. To understand and appreciate the value Americans in the war years placed upon these qualities in advertising one must consider how they viewed them elsewhere in the culture of the time. Sentimental and emotional songs and movies were enormously successful during the war. The popularity of the songs can be measured by their rankings on the charts of sheet music and phonograph record sales in *Billboard* and *Variety*, just as the charts of box office receipts can track the popularity of sentimental films. In the absence of such yardsticks to measure the home front's response to sentiment or emotion in advertising, we can at least extrapolate from the data about their reception in media that *were* measurable. And since the data show the home front enjoyed sentimental and emotional movies and popular songs, it stands to reason that it accepted these qualities in advertising as well.

Speaking of music, a Birds Eye Frosted Foods ad in *Life* on November 20, 1944, had popular singer Dinah Shore saying, "After singing to our boys abroad [. . .] I know that no song is half so sweet to them as the latest letter from home!" (38), which is fine for a message promoting using V-Mail. But as a singer who frequently entertained troops overseas and occasionally spoke or wrote on the effect of music on morale, in the ad Shore seems to be selling music short as a morale builder. In fact, the positive effect of music on morale was widely recognized during the war, as was music's veritable healing power in helping GIs come out of shell shock or battle fatigue—what today we call posttraumatic stress disorder. An ad by Stromberg-Carlson in *Life* on June 12, 1944, focused entirely on this healing power of music. The many-faceted relationships between music and morale are beyond the scope of an account of advertising but are treated more extensively in *The Songs That Fought the War* (see Jones 25–31 and *passim*). Music's relevance here is that a number of war ads neither selling products nor urging morale-lifting actions by civilians simply spread the word about the value of music in building morale both among GIs overseas and civilians at home. Most such ads were by companies connected with the music industry—RCA, Wurlitzer, Stromberg-Carlson, Westinghouse—but, with the exception of RCA Victor, which was still making and selling records, none of the firms had radios, phonographs, or jukeboxes to sell since they were engaged entirely in war work. All the ads about music for GI morale emphasized its ability to lift spirits and let minds reflect on home, as in the Stromberg-Carlson ad in *Life* on October 16, 1944. A Flying Fortress is heading back to base after a bombing mission: "Inside, ten tired men begged their minds to forget the hell they had lived through. Then, like the singing of angels, music came through the intercom. The Brooklyn kid at the radio had tuned in a broadcasting station. And each man was at peace and home again . . . remembering through music all the little, wonderful things of the wonderful free life he had lived . . . and was fighting to protect. You CANNOT DESCRIBE MUSIC any more than you can describe love. It's just . . . music. And it's sometimes the most important thing in the world" (7).

RCA Victor and Bluebird Records' cheerful two-page ad in *Life* on December 6, 1943, featured full-color illustrations of popular singers and band leaders Lena Horne, Vaughn Monroe, Artie Shaw, Fats Waller, Spike Jones, and Hal McIntyre. Headed "From Main Street to War Plant to Guadalcanal / their Records help keep up our Nation's Morale," the ad showed how music helped just about everybody's. Along with the portraits and blurbs about each recording artist were inset photos of home front, war plant, and military life, with a statement of specific ways that music contributed to the morale of each (66–67). For the morale needs of individuals on the home front, Stromberg-Carlson fashioned an ad in *Newsweek* on July 3, 1944, in which a woman has had no letter from her soldier husband for three weeks and tries to comfort herself by rationalizing, "He must be all right . . . or I'd have heard something. They let you know . . . they always let you know . . . But you get to thinking, especially at night. [. . .] Then you turn on some music . . . some old familiar song . . . and for a while you're back again in a safe and better world!" (15). An especially engaging and uplifting music for morale ad came from a company not associated with music in any way, Caterpillar Tractor, and appeared in the *Post* on May 6, 1944. The large illustration was by Amos Sewell, a gifted *Post* illustrator nearly as prolific if not as well remembered as Norman Rockwell; it depicted children of various ages standing in a one-room schoolhouse in Kansas, mouths open wide in song. The copy devoted itself entirely to how singing, especially by children, lifts the morale and national unity of all Americans (71; see fig. 37). It didn't ask people to write letters or stay off long-distance lines, but the ad was still a kind of outreach for morale.

When Johnny Comes Marching Home

Outreach lay at the heart of a new kind of morale advertising starting occasionally in the spring and summer of 1944 and continuing with more frequency that fall and winter and throughout 1945, even beyond the end of the war. These ads addressed how private citizens, the business and industrial community, and social service organizations could help returning servicemen readjust to civilian life. The earliest such ad was also the most unusual. In the *Post* on May 20, 1944, the Cunningham Drug Store chain of 150 pharmacies in Michigan, Ohio, and Pennsylvania offered qualified veterans free scholarships to pharmacy school, and "an opportunity to earn while attending college will be provided suc cessful candidates." The ad gave an address to write to for more information and application forms (1).

Most ads on helping the morale of returned GIs dealt with their finding jobs. Such ads were about equally divided between those by companies such as Greyhound, Bell Telephone, and Republic Steel inviting their own veterans to return to work, either at the same job or a better one, and ads by other companies and organizations that more generally urged business and industry to hire veterans. The ads welcoming veterans back to their former place of employment began in the summer of 1944. Most are quite similar, welcoming GIs already home and those yet to arrive, and then echoing the common theme of what GIs want when they return home, first expressed by the Monsanto Chemical Company in *Time* on July 24, 1944, and the *Post* on August 5: "Next to seeing the folks, they're looking ahead to their return to The Job. At wages, not 'benefits.' Paying off not only in money but also in self reliance and self respect. A heads-up future . . . not a hands-out existence" (*Time* 12; *Post* inside back cover). Other ads addressed the special steps necessary for employing disabled veterans: "REVERE COPPER AND BRASS INCORPO-RATED is working now to analyze every job which men with physical dis-

Let Freedom Ring

It is singing time in schools across the nation —

In a village in Kansas the prairie stretches right up to the schoolhouse door. And through the frame walls —

> O beautiful for spacious skies,
> For amber waves of grain —

On the rocky shoulder of Maine, a small building looks over the Atlantic. And in the early morning —

> Land where my fathers died,
> Land of the Pilgrims' pride —

In a foreign quarter of New York City —

> O'er the land of the free
> and the home of the brave —

Children — all over America — well fed, sent happily to school! And singing!

Singing — perhaps unconscious of the words — of America's woods and hills, her rivers and grass lands!

Singing of America's heritage, hard won through early Colonial winter, through wagon trail privation, through pain of growth and pain of war.

Children — innocent of fear — singing happily of their birthright of freedom in a blessed land!

FOR YOUR TOMORROW — FOR YOUR CHILDREN'S INSURED FUTURE — BUY MORE WAR BONDS TODAY!

CONTRIBUTED TO THE WAR EFFORT BY
CATERPILLAR TRACTOR CO., PEORIA, ILL.

FIGURE 37

abilities could perform, so that these jobs can be made available first to returning wounded service men" (*Life* 6 Nov. 1944: 7). A singular ad by Bethlehem Steel in *Newsweek* on May 21, 1945, went beyond inviting its old employees back, to inviting other veterans to apply for jobs there or just take advantage of the expertise of a trained "Veterans' Counsellor [sic]" at each Bethlehem plant and shipyard (21).

The ads by businesses to businesses encouraging them to hire veterans also shared a common theme, and that was precisely it, even though some ads, including a few prepared by the War Advertising Council, took nearly a full page of fairly uninspired copy to say it. Far more effective was succinct, powerful copy such as Young & Rubicam's in *Newsweek* on September 17, 1945. Beneath a picture of wounded, possibly disabled, soldiers in beds and wheelchairs in a hospital ward, the entirety of the copy read, "It was their job to win the war. They discharged their responsibility gallantly and successfully. It is the responsibility of business to put them gainfully to work as fast as they are discharged. We must not fail them" (9). Even more succinct was the one sentence on a sheet of paper coming out of a duplicating machine in Mimeograph's ad in *Time* on October 2, 1944, and *Newsweek* on October 16: "Now is the time for good businesses to plan good jobs for good fighters" (*Time* 76; *Newsweek* 1). A few ads, notably two by the insurance companies New England Mutual in *Time* on August 13, 1945, and *Life* on August 27, and Metropolitan Life in the *Post* on September 29, 1945, and the October *Ladies' Home Journal*, acknowledged the importance of returned GIs finding gainful and meaningful employment but also stressed the urgency of assuring veterans' medical and psychological well-being and their having access to legal, educational, and domestic affairs counsel. Each insurer urged every city and town great and small to establish veterans' centers to provide such counseling and guidance. Both New England Mutual and Metropolitan offered free booklets on how municipalities could set up and run such centers.

Ads asking private citizens to help GIs make a smooth transition back to civilian life began only in March 1945. All four such ads were filled with sardonic, grim humor to illustrate what and what *not* to say to returned GIs. One ad concentrated on those with disabilities, the others on any and all GIs. The ad sponsored by Lambert Pharmacal Company (Listerine) in *Collier's* on October 20, 1945, is representative (see fig. 38). The crisp, brief, to-the-point copy here, as in the other three ads, was

Motor Martyr. Okinawa may have been tough all right, but wait'll you hear this civilian on the rigors of rationed driving.

Lady with the needle nose. "Tell me how it feels to be wounded, Ensign. Did you bleed much?"

The Tsk-Tsk Sister. Just can't take her eyes off a disabled soldier. Thinks it's awful, and what's more, lets him know it.

Norman Rockwell asks:

"Would a Veteran find <u>You</u> here?"

The no-nonsense type. "You've been home a whole week, son. Isn't it time to look for a job? Can't pamper ourselves, you know."

Yankee Doodle boy. "Drop in and see me anytime—after you get a job, that is."

Americans, first-class. "Welcome home, soldier!" *Here's* where a veteran would probably find *you*, glad to see him and eager to help. Because the great majority of Americans are too grateful to these veterans to make the mistakes shown here.

Good Americans don't prod the veteran with questions if he doesn't want to talk. They don't act sorry for him. Nor tell him life has been hard here. (He's been where it *is* hard.) And they don't stare at any disability he may have.

Above all, they remember that his experiences have made him an even more resourceful, capable citizen. They make it their job to help him get back into normal civilian life. Let's *all* be like them!

Prepared by the War Advertising Council, Inc., in Cooperation with the Office of War Information and the Retraining and Reemployment Administration.

FIGURE 38. LISTERINE® is a registered trademark of Johnson & Johnson. Used with permission.

"Prepared by the War Advertising Council, Inc., in Cooperation with the Office of War Information and the Retraining and Reemployment Administration" (3). Its brevity is a far cry from some of the Ad Council's rambling, prolix verbiage in ads urging employment of veterans. The Listerine ad is also notable for its six little drawings by Norman Rockwell, one of his rare excursions into war advertising.

Take It Easy

The few ads focusing on just home front morale scattered throughout this chapter may make it seem that the ad industry neglected or took scant notice of the need to sustain morale at home. But in fact home front morale ads were so concentrated on helping people cope specifically with shortages and rationing that they form the topic of the entire next chapter. This leaves only one small, but not insignificant, aspect of home front morale to be looked at here—the value of recreation and relaxation.

Only a few advertisers placed ads explicitly advocating what Beautyrest called "the gentle art of relaxing in Wartime" on page 95 of *Life* on March 8, 1943. With no mattresses to sell because of war production, Beautyrest could afford to place an entire ad explaining how relaxation improved morale and worker productivity. The ad recommended recreational activities from softball to—for the mechanically minded—tinkering around with one's car or repairing household appliances. But that was just a single ad. In a series of about fifteen ads between late July 1942 and early November 1943 the United States Playing Card Company virtually made the cause of home recreation its own without directly selling its products. The series is striking for warm and welcoming artwork of neighbors entertaining neighbors, only occasionally playing cards. But the copy in all the ads is almost identical; United's ad agency seems to have had more imaginative artists than copywriters. The gist of the series is that recreation helps melt away daily work- and war-related stress and recharges the mind and body for the next day's activities. While the ads invariably mentioned that "Over four-fifths of your fellow Americans now play cards" (*Collier's* 5 Sept. 1942: 7), United never encouraged purchasing its Bicycle and Congress brands.

During the war, ads for radio programs and Hollywood movies were nearly as common in national magazines as they were in local newspapers. While beyond the present concern with war ads, they implicitly advocated forms of recreation to recharge home front morale. Obviously, movie ads were also designed to sell tickets and make money, but since movie tickets were still cheap, going to a film was inexpensive recreation. And radio of course was free. Americans listened to the radio an average of four and a half hours a day (Lingeman 224), suggesting that, news broadcasts aside, the comedy, variety, drama, and music programming was indeed a preferred form of recreation to boost home front morale.

7

"PRODUCE, CONSERVE, SHARE, AND PLAY SQUARE" COPING WITH SHORTAGES AND RATIONING

This chapter is as much about morale as it is about meatloaf. When shortages and rationing became facts of life for the home front, the ad industry found itself with two roles to play. The easiest was simply keeping the public informed about which products faced a shortage, which were totally unavailable, and which would be rationed. Advertising's far more difficult task was finding ways to help the home front cope with shortages and rationing and accept them as cheerfully as possible. These were no small parts for advertising to play, since nothing on the home front touched the lives of Americans more personally and materially than shortages and rationing, especially of food. People asked why they had to scale back on what and how much they ate, considering the country's tremendous prosperity during the war years. Answering this and similar questions was a war-long challenge for the ad industry, but overall admen and the advertisers they represented met the challenge very well.

The majority of all war ads turned from advertising's traditional business of selling products and services to something more closely resembling public relations. This is most apparent in institutional ads designed in part to keep brand and company names before the public while their manufacturers had little or nothing to sell. But the single greatest public relations job facing commercial advertising was to help the public understand, accept, and cope with shortages and rationing. This variety of public relations had little to do with sustaining brand consciousness. Shortage and rationing ads weren't even public relations pieces that encouraged people to get actively behind the war effort. To the contrary, this special breed of advertising aimed to lift home front morale, for example, by showing people how their proper use of ration points wasn't just good for the country and the war, but also how it helped them sustain as comfortable a lifestyle as possible for *themselves*. Just as the exigencies of shortages and rationing most personally touched American consumers, the ads suggesting ways for them to deal with these matters touched them perhaps most personally of all forms of war ads.

The Question of Sacrifice

During the war years the question persisted whether the home front's having to make do with less or do without altogether fairly constituted a "sacrifice." One arena in which the question was played out was magazine advertising. This is not to say there was a running debate among advertisers as to whether or not home front deprivations could be considered actual sacrifices. Rather, some war ads argued that the term should be reserved for the death or permanent disability of combat troops, whereas others saw sacrifice as a perfectly acceptable word for what home front civilians had to endure as well.

Those war ads maintaining that the concept of sacrifice should be reserved for battle deaths and disabilities argued implicitly, and some explicitly, that to do otherwise—to label as sacrifices the temporary deprivations and inconveniences of the home front—trivialized the far greater price paid by American GIs. "And nothing we're asked to do to help [our troops] win," declared a Stewart-Warner ad in the *Post* on February 20, 1943, "can be called a sacrifice . . . Using some foods sparingly—but never lacking food. Walking a few peaceful blocks—while they crawl thru slime and muck. *Loaning* dollars—every dollar we can find—in War Bonds we can spend again" (81). That sentiment was more than echoed in an ad prepared for the Drug, Cosmetic and Allied Industries that appeared in *Look* on December 15, 1942, sponsored by Castoria, and in the February 1943 *Ladies' Home Journal* sponsored by Fresh Underarm Deodorant Cream: " . . . and YOU talk of 'sacrifices'! Maybe you've heard some of them . . . The people who complain because they can't always get their brand of coffee—or because the right cut of meat is scarce. The man who 'sacrifices' an extra week's vacation to buy a War Bond or two, and the woman who 'gives up' a new hat to put the money into a War Bond. Next time you hear such talk, answer like this . . . '*Sacrifice*? Is there *anything* you can do to match the bravery of our fighting men? Is there any 'sacrifice' you can make to equal that of a man who gives his *life*?' [. . .] So don't let anybody talk to you about 'sacrifices'!" (*Look* 49; *LHJ* 54).

On the other side, there's much to be said for ads telling readers that sacrifice was the legitimate name for what they were doing—or doing without—as patriotic home front Americans. Those advertising copywriters who decided to describe what people gave up during the war as "sacrifices" created a masterful public relations campaign vis-à-vis home front morale. When Mr. and Mrs. Home Front saw their making do with less sugar, gasoline, or meat described as sacrifices, not to mention their totally doing without new appliances, cars, and tires, it had to have made them feel like home front heroes in some small way, working in tandem with our fighting forces for Victory. If there ever was a real morale booster for civilians at home, it was seeing themselves heroically making sacrifices.

Ads let them see themselves that way from the very first year of the war, thanks to United States Rubber's two-page spread in the *Post* on November 21, 1942. The first page is a large illustration of a grim-faced man standing up in his family pew at church, his wife looking straight ahead stoically, his young daughter staring up at him with mixed horror and embarrassment, when the man says, "I want to preach a sermon . . . " (54). On the facing page he does, a long one about what people did in the past and what we must do now for America, concluding with lines that fairly shout: "If we need sugar to win this war, take it. If we need rubber to win this war, take it. If we need steel to win this war take it. [. . .] Take everything we've got to win this war, and welcome! [. . .] And we'll like it fine!" (55). As a word, "sacrifice" appears nowhere in the ad, but as an action it resonates in every line. In *Life* on January 11, 1943, a two-page ad by Sparton, an electrical products company, showed an earnest little boy, arms loaded with the tracks and train cars of an electric train set, looking up at a man with an "Official Scrap Collector" armband and saying, "How many bullets will this make, mister?" (16–17). The copy explains, "Sacrifice isn't a thing you can weigh in pounds or count in dollars. It is measured in the brave little gifts of children. In the heartbreaks of women. In the suffering of men. But remember—you boys who toss your precious toys on the salvage heap—They'll be coming back, all gay and new. And you grown-ups who are giving up so many American comforts and conveniences—These will be back, too."

Among the many other ads about home front sacrifice, in *Collier's* on July 24, 1943, an Aircraft Accessories Corporation ad featured a drawing of a pretty little girl in a dress and pinafore looking skyward. The copy rewrote the nursery rhyme "What Are Little Girls Made Of?" into "Sugar and spice . . . and everything nice . . . That's What Bombers Are Made Of": "The sweets your little girl won't eat as often as she used to. Your extra cup of coffee. Those Sunday drives with the kids. [. . .] That new car you're not going to get and tires you won't have to drive on [. . .] AND THAT'S WHAT BOMBERS ARE MADE OF" (29). Overall, since more ads took the position that what the home front endured could be called sacrifices than those maintaining the word should be reserved for battle casualties, the former view apparently prevailed in advertising and perhaps among the public at large.

To Buy or Not To Buy, That Was the Question

War ads answered pretty uniformly "Not to buy" despite (or because of) wartime prosperity putting more money into the pockets of most Americans than they knew what to do with (see Blum 90–116; Lingeman 271–322). Ads came down hard on extravagant and unnecessary spending as running counter to curbing inflation, fighting the Black Market, respecting ceiling prices (the government's top price a product could sell for), and engaging in "thoughtful buying" (buying only what one needed). Despite the shortage of some goods and the rationing of others, there was still plenty that the home front could and did buy, from luxury items like jewelry and furs down to nonessential but entertaining things like comic books, sheet music, and phonograph records. And entertainment itself wasn't rationed. In New York and elsewhere theatres and nightclubs reveled in their highest gross receipts ever; nationwide, movie theatres were packed; and the faithful still filled major league baseball stadiums even though over 4,000 of the roughly 5,700 professional ballplayers were in the service (Lingeman 312).

The federal government mounted its own anti-inflation ad campaign orchestrated by the War Advertising Council, but numerous commercial advertisers on their own also treated not just inflation per se but the several components that cause it. Most commercial advertisers' ads about inflation, the Black Market, and/or ceiling prices were to a greater or lesser degree "teaching tools" designed to educate a public presumed to be basically unfamiliar with such matters. The ads were written in language that virtually any reader of national magazines could grasp with relative ease. Any two or more of the related issues of ceiling prices, inflation, the Black Market, and thoughtful buying might appear in a single ad. Only thoughtful buying also had a stand-alone life of its own and that only because a single advertiser mounted a crystal clear campaign about it that spanned virtually all of the war years.

But before turning to any of these cautionary ads, the story should begin with a perplexing anomaly—one advertiser's series of ads that seemed to go against the tide by promoting business—and buying—as usual. Although war ads about ceiling prices, the Black Market, and inflation argued for restrained, judicious spending (and, by implication or directly, investing the rest of one's disposable income in War Bonds), one prominent national company openly advocated freewheeling consumer spending at its stores, not just once but in a number of national magazine ads every year of the war. The Firestone Tire & Rubber Company of Akron, Ohio, not only was a major manufacturer and purveyor of automobile tires but also had a vast network of nationwide retail outlets it variously called Firestone Dealers and Firestone Stores that sold far more than tires and other automotive products. (The distinction between Firestone's Stores and Dealers is not made apparent in the ads.) According to its ad in *Life* on May 24, 1943, Firestone retailers had departments for "radios, music, home appliances, housewares, hardware, lawn and garden, wheel goods [i.e. bicycles, scooters, tricycles, etc.], recreation supplies [i.e. sporting goods], toys, games, books, paints, wallpaper, clothing for work and recreation, leather goods" and more (49). Even during the war years, these departments were up and running.

The Firestone ads, which ran in *Life*, *Farm Journal*, *Collier's*, and the *Post*, were short on copy and long on art, the copy occasionally throwing a small sop to conservation by telling people they could save gas and tire wear by doing all their shopping in one place. But mostly the brief text enticed people to look at the art, which consisted of drawings of between thirty and fifty or more products sold by Firestone Dealers and Stores. In turn, the illustrations enticed people to see the actual merchandise: "Look at the wide variety of products here, then see them at your nearby Firestone Dealer or Firestone Store. Who can say when you will again be able to get such high quality products at such low prices" (*Farm Journal* Sept. 1942: 36). While such Firestone ads appeared periodically in spring and fall, they rolled out the heavy artillery in their Christmas advertising: "Toyland is open today at your nearby Firestone Dealer or Firestone Store! And what an exciting array of toys for children of all ages—trains and planes, dolls and games, paint sets and musical instruments, kiddie cars and skates . . . Bring the children to see this fascinating display. And take this opportunity to do your own Christmas shopping leisurely and economically" (*Life* 30 Nov. 1942: 54). Another Christmas ad in *Life* on November 13, 1944, paraphrased "'Twas the night before Christmas." But in verse or prose, what the ads really meant was "Spend, spend, spend—and do so at your Firestone Dealer or Store." And unlike other advertisers of still-available products, not once did Firestone also encourage people to buy War Bonds.

What's most peculiar about the Firestone ads is what they had for sale during the war. To cite just a few examples, an ad as late as May 24, 1943, depicted golf clubs despite the fact that the government effectively put a stop to their manufacture as of June 1, 1942. Similarly, the production of fishing tackle came to a halt on May 31, 1942, as did that of electric heating pads on June 30, but both appeared prominently in Firestone ads long after that. The further production of electric ranges ceased on May 31, 1942, and the sale of existing stock to civilians was prohibited, but Firestone was still advertising them on November 30. And as early as April 1942, by government order the "sale, shipment, and delivery" of bicycles were "frozen pending rationing," yet bicycles were never absent from Firestone ads all the way to December 4, 1944 (all production information taken from the *Business Week* lists between April 11 and August 8, 1942). While many more examples could be cited, these are enough to raise the question, where and how did Firestone get products to sell whose manufacture had been cut off completely or at least greatly curtailed by order of the federal government? For me at least, only two answers come to mind. The first is that Firestone had stockpiled huge inventories of such goods before the orders came down for their cessation or curtailment. This is certainly possible, although the orders usually preceded the actual stop dates by no more than a month. The second is that Firestone had connections to illicit, or, if you will, Black Market sources of supply for these verboten goods.

★ ★ ★ Opposite Firestone's advocacy of freehanded consumer spending on the economic spectrum was the simple yet fundamental doctrine of thoughtful buying. Its basic principles began to show up in magazine ads as early as January 1942, although the name that embraced those principles wasn't coined until an Exide Batteries ad in *Time* on November 30 of that year. Exide's ads before then simply described its components while some adman seemed to be groping for a name for them. But even before Exide's ad agency came up with the "thoughtful buying" name, Exide became the primary proponent of the concept and remained so throughout the war. Although other advertisers articulated one or two of the principles of thoughtful buying in just one ad, Exide placed no fewer than thirteen ads advocating it between February 9, 1942, and February 21, 1944, in *Life*, *Collier's*, the *Post*, *Time*, and *Farm Journal*. The earliest ads promoting thoughtful buying linked it primarily to conservation, and while that association never let go, as time went on its implications for fighting inflation and the Black Market became stronger and stronger. The earliest ad that articulated any of the principles of thoughtful buying was the Federal-Mogul Corporation's in *Collier's* on January 10, 1942, just weeks after the United States entered the war. The ad proclaimed simply, "Buy only what you need, and *DON'T WASTE WHAT YOU'VE GOT!*" (41). Exide entered the field a month later on February 9 in *Life*, presenting another of the precepts of thoughtful buying: "From now 'til victory comes, patriotic buying must be the rule. It will help mightily toward winning the war if, for instance, we all buy *longer-lasting* things—when we must buy at all," on the assumption that the longer things last, the less they will have to be replaced, thus conserving money, materials, and the man hours needed for manufacturing (111).

Other companies that jumped into the campaign over time were rather diverse. A woman speaking for Lady Pepperell Sheets and Blankets in the March 1943 *Ladies' Home Journal* put it this way: "We buy only what we really need, and only *quality* merchandise . . . merchandise that will *last*" (11), and in *Esquire* for October 1943 an ad for Paris (men's) Garters and Suspenders spelled it all out very logically: "You help the war effort when you buy only what you need, when you need it—by taking care of what you buy you prolong its life" (104). And as late as September 11, 1944, in *Life* a housewife in an ad for Cannon Percale Sheets exclaims, "If we *want* to get our men back quicker (*do* we!) we'll clutch our purses tighter and get along with things we already have" (5).

But with its thirteen ads over more than two years, Exide was the standard bearer for thoughtful buying, even before its ad agency figured out what to call it. It came close in the headline for the ad in the *Post* on July 25, 1942, and in *Life* on August 10: "LET'S CALL A HALT ON THOUGHTLESS BUYING" (53), the copy presenting a clear rationale for the concept: "Buy only when you must, and then buy *longer-lasting* things! Don't waste your country's material, manpower, machine time on things that will need to be replaced too soon. Buy only for long, hard service and you conserve for Uncle Sam." Subsequent Exide ads repeated these ideas more or less briefly until in *Time* on November 30, 1942, the headline read "Thoughtful buying helps 'keep 'em flying,'" after which "thoughtful buying" appeared somewhere in every Exide ad (87). Throughout most of them, Exide cited just two components of thoughtful buying—buying only what you need, and buying the best, longest-lasting products available—but late in its campaign Exide expanded the essentials of thoughtful buying to three: "1. Don't buy *anything* you can do without. 2. If you MUST buy, insist on dependable, long-lasting merchandise. 3. Take care of the things you have. *Make them last*" (*Life* 2 Feb. 1944: 128). And almost no Exide ads included selling the company's automobile batteries, no matter how long they lasted!

★ ★ ★ Never paying more than government-imposed ceiling prices, eschewing the Black Market, and helping to fight inflation were so intertwined that most ads emphasizing any of these concerns also said something about one or both of the others. And with good reason; they were linked in a causal relationship: By never paying more than ceiling prices and never patronizing the Black Market, consumers could help keep inflation in check. The federal government's Office of Price Administration (OPA) began freezing prices on consumer goods so early in the war that by its issue for May 9, 1942, *Business Week* could publish a list of over 165 consumer commodities that had ceiling prices, ranging from rump roast and radios to light bulbs and linoleum (30). Then and later OPA also imposed ceiling prices on raw materials for industry, cattle and hogs bound for slaughter, and similar items, but since these ceiling prices did not directly touch the consumer no national advertising dealt with them. In fact, war ads about ceiling prices didn't begin to appear until much later in 1942. In one of the earliest the ubiquitous Black & White Scotch dogs are looking in a butcher shop window at a sign depicting a bone and reading "Our ceiling price 4¢" (*Time* 21 Dec. 1942: 48). Blackie asks, "What is this ceiling price business, Whitey?" to which Whitey replies, "That's Uncle Sam's way of keeping down the cost of living for all of us, Blackie." The copy continues, "America will have no run-away prices during this war. To prevent inflation—your Government has frozen prices, curtailed the manufacture of unessential goods, and has instituted rationing" (48). Not a bad explanation of ceiling prices, and more followed throughout the war. One of the clearest came in an ad by

Dr. Pepper in the November 1943 issue of *Ladies' Home Journal*: "Ceiling prices—ration stamps—OPA rules . . . all are designed to curb inflation . . . and thus make YOUR dollars go farther. Unbridled inflation can bring disastrous times. We should all 'observe the rules' . . . for it is in our own individual interest to do so" (99). In *Life* on March 6, 1944, an ad by Armour and Company gave equal space to three long paragraphs on ways to fight inflation headed "Don't pay more than ceiling prices," "Avoid black markets," and "Buy only what you need" (22). Even as late as July 21, 1944, in the *Post*, Canada Dry sponsored an ad featuring a photo of a woman giving ration coupons to her grocer, captioned, "She will not buy above ceiling prices. She knows that as prices go up the value of a dollar goes down, drains the value of real property, threatens the future of our country"—another brief lesson on the damaging effects of inflation (42).

Ads dealing just with inflation were about equally split between those explaining it and those telling people what they could do to combat it. An all-copy ad by Warner & Swasey in *Business Week* on August 21, 1943, began with "Inflation is easy to understand. When prices soar that's inflation. Two things cause it: 1—When there are not enough things to go around, people bid against each other, and up go prices. . . . 2—When the cost of anything goes up (because of higher wages, higher salaries, higher taxes) its price has to go up" (inside front cover). In two ads a year apart in *Life* on April 3, 1944, and April 16, 1945, the Borden cow and bull, Elsie and Elmer, bantered about the meaning of inflation, with Elsie, as usual, getting the last word: "Now everytime [sic] you *or anyone* buys anything you don't actually need, you help shoot prices up. You help bring on inflation and undermine the country" (16 Apr. 1945: 16). The Aetna Insurance Group gave practical advice on curbing inflation in an ad in *Time* on May 1, 1944: "Patch and repair what you have instead of buying new. Put your money in War Bonds instead of buying articles you can get along without. Pay off old debts instead of contracting new ones. Patronize only legitimate merchants who sell at ceiling prices. *SHUN* the Black Market" (3).

Today most of us tend to visualize the Black Market as an unsavory-looking character in a slouch hat hanging out in an alley, the lining of his trench coat stuffed with contraband cigarettes or T-bone steaks. And, truth to tell, that's how many people on the home front pictured it as

THIS VULTURE IS AFTER BLOOD — *Yours!*

Not a very savory creature, this man, is he?

Yet thousands of foolish Americans—men and women —place their trust in him to the extent of letting him supply the meat that is consumed by their families.

Imagine—if you can!—serving meat that has been slaughtered in a filth-fouled barn—without adequate refrigeration—to your curly-haired son or daughter...

Sure, the meat is stamped "Government Inspected"—but when it's bought in a black market, the chances are ten to one the seal is counterfeit. So that's no protection.

But there is a very simple way to get full and positive protection:

Don't buy meat—or anything else—at over ceiling prices.

Don't buy meat—or other rationed goods—at stores that do not insist upon receiving stamps or coupons.

And by so doing you'll put a brake on the rising cost of living as well... because refusing to patronize black markets is refusing to give thugs and racketeers the money they need to finance their illegal operations... which channel all manner of scarce goods into crook-run stores... force prices skyhigh—beyond the pocketbooks of most of us.

Refusing to deal with such vultures is the way to stop inflation. It's the only way to assure that people who live on fixed incomes — and most Americans do— will be able to buy life's necessities and safeguard their investments in insurance, savings, their homes and their jobs.

Remember, most shops are operated by respectable, law-abiding citizens—doing an important, almost super-human job in the face of serious wartime shortages. These men and women deserve—and have earned— your respect and thanks.

And there are some who flout ceiling prices and deal in black market goods. They deserve—and have earned —your scorn and your hate.

Where will YOU shop today?

FIGURE 39

well. In its ad in *Business Week* on September 9, 1944, featuring a typically grotesque Arthur Szyk illustration (see fig. 39), the Rogers Diesel
and Aircraft Corporation cautioned, "Imagine—if you can!—serving
meat that has been slaughtered in a filth-fouled barn—without adequate refrigeration—to your curly-haired son or daughter . . . Don't buy
meat—or anything else—at over ceiling prices. [. . .] refusing to patronize black markets is refusing to give thugs and racketeers the money
they need to finance their illegal operations . . . which channel all manner of scarce goods into crook-run stores . . . force prices skyhigh" (50).

While there's no denying that organized crime and other unscrupu-
lous types were behind some of the wartime Black Market, most of it was
far more insidious, although seemingly innocent, since its participants
were respectable shopkeepers and their equally respectable customers.
When a friendly corner druggist or grocer stooped beneath the counter
to get a regular customer a pack of "Stoopies," the name for scarce pop-
ular-brand cigarettes sold above ceiling prices, that was the Black Market. When a housewife offered to pay the butcher a cash premium for a
certain cut of meat instead of turning in ration coupons she could use for
other things, that was the Black Market, too. Or, as Elsie the Borden cow
explained to her blustering husband who wanted to blast away the Black
Market with a shotgun, "You see, a big Black Market is hundreds of little
things. It's every housewife who doesn't take the trouble to check the
ceiling price of everything she buys. It's all the people who count it a bar-
gain when the butcher gives them a 12-point cut of meat for 8 points. It's
the butcher who doesn't play by the rules" (*Life* 23 Oct. 1944: 6). While
most ads just described the Black Market, a few told consumers what
they could do to help fight it: "There's tremendous power in those little
coupons in your War Ration Books. They're the average civilian's chief
defense against a savage, criminal menace . . . the Black Markets" (SKF
Ball and Roller Bearings, *Newsweek* 20 Sept. 1943: 76); "Always to use
Ration Coupons / And never to pay over ceiling prices / Is one of those
Little Things / That's as Big as fair play and victory" (Tobe Deutschmann
Corporation, *Time* 3 Jan. 1944: 87). Despite such advice, the Black Market proved nearly impossible to crack. The primary reason is that it
wasn't a way for people to get things on the cheap; no, it was a way for
them to buy hard-to-get goods for *more* money than ceiling prices and
rationing allowed, and *that* didn't much bother the affluent home front
during wartime prosperity.

"You Can't Get That No More"

Louis Jordan's 1944 recording of that title was almost as accurate as it was humorous: "Mary went out shopping but she came home all tired out, / No matter where Mary went she'd always hear them shout: YOU CAN'T GET THAT NO MORE, YOU CAN'T GET THAT NO MORE, / The store keeper said 'I'm sorry miss, I'm all out of that and I ain't got this, / YOU CAN'T GET THAT NO MORE." Thanks to war production and the numerous needs of the ever-growing armed forces, shortages of goods for civilian consumption extended wide and deep. Essential foodstuffs are what normally first come to mind in this connection, but the titles alone of some *Business Week* articles paint a picture of just how wide and deep shortages went at various times during the war: "Razor Blade Panic" (11 April 1942), "Candy Gets Tight" (12 Dec. 1942), "Battle for Girdles" (19 June 1943), "Kraut [i.e. sauerkraut] Is Out" (23 Oct. 1943), "Shoes Stretched" (23 Oct. 1943), "Gum's Still Tight" (15 Jan. 1944), "Rug Stocks Ebb" (3 June 1944), "Toys Are Scarce" (7 Oct. 1944), "Cigarette Famine" (14 Oct. 1944), "Stockings Scarce" (3 March 1945), "Ball and Bat Crisis" (2 June 1945) — all these *in addition to* articles about shortages of meat, produce, canned goods, and dairy products.

In the face of so many shortages and the public's worry and even occasional panic about them, commercial advertising assumed the role of morale officer for the home front, charged with the task of bucking up civilians' spirits about such things, as advertising also did vis-à-vis the home front's concerns about rationing. Most ads about shortages explained the reasons for the shortage or unavailability of a certain product or kinds of products. Others gave housewives pragmatic tips on how to conserve food. Since food conservation ads are so closely allied with those helping people cope with rationing, they are taken up in the next section, leaving just the ads explaining shortages to be dealt with here.

The largest number of ads dealing with shortages—about 155—explained the reasons for them, This large figure suggests that advertisers believed the best way for people to come to terms with shortages was to grasp why they occurred; the more that people understood about *why* they couldn't buy certain merchandise, the less they would grumble about it. A frequent tag line to many explanatory ads was a phrase to the effect of "don't blame the grocer," in order to benefit grocers' (and other merchants' or store clerks') morale as well as shoppers'. Virtually all these educational ads gave one of three general reasons for a shortage or product unavailability: The manufacturer had converted entirely to war production, the necessary materials for making the product had been diverted to military purposes, or, most frequently, the armed forces were receiving so much of the product that far less of it (if any) was available for civilians. The explanations in the ads ranged from perfunctory to elaborate.

The number of ads about the complete unavailability of a product was miniscule compared to those about product shortages, mostly because far more products suffered a shortage for home front consumption than, like automobiles, became totally unavailable. The explanations in most product unavailability ads were of the perfunctory type. The makers of the two most popular brands of cigarette lighters, Ronson and Zippo, both just stated that by government regulation all the lighters they made were consigned directly to the armed forces. Similarly, in *Time* on May 15, 1944, Smith-Corona corrected an erroneous press release by informing readers that its portable typewriters were *not* available to the public but were still being made for the military. Gorham Silver stated succinctly that it was making no more of its sterling silver pieces since all of the company's metal workers were making "parts for tanks, torpedoes, submarines, parachutes" (*Ladies' Home Journal* Nov. 1942: 85); and United States Rubber explained why Keds and Kedettes were not being made by simply stating, "We are making rubber-soled fabric shoes for the armed forces only" (*Ladies' Home Journal* May 1943: 77). By contrast, the Hood Rubber division of B. F. Goodrich went into considerable detail as to why people couldn't buy its own brand of what we'd call sneakers: "Over 3,000,000 life vests—or over 100,000 four man life rafts—or over 60,000 bullet-proof gas tanks for our planes can be made from the rubber *not* being used in canvas shoes for millions of boys and girls. That is why America's sportsmen—young and old—are gladly taking this small sacrifice in stride" (*Life* 26 Apr. 1943: 4).

Generally speaking, ads explaining shortages were less perfunctory than those explaining product unavailability, and the ad copy displays great variety and, in some cases, genuine imagination. Other than an interesting handful of ads that can't be categorized at all, the fewest ads explaining shortages discussed how manufacturers had turned almost exclusively to war production. Elgin Watches was making "timing devices and precision instruments needed by our fighting forces" (*Life* 16

Oct. 1944: 76). As the company that made the telephones, switchboards, and cable for Bell Telephone, Western Electric's "manpower and manufacturing facilities are devoted to meeting our fighters' increased need" for communications equipment (*Look* 15 May 1945: 15). Even "the makers of Red Heart Dehydrated [Dog Food] have their hands full turning out many items vital to the war effort" (*Life* 21 June 1943: 18). Almost by definition most explanatory ads were pretty matter-of-fact, but Roadmaster bicycles' ad in *Life* on 21 December 1942, shows how creative copywriters and artists could turn out an emotional ad even about a switch to war production. The art is a drawing of Santa Claus's face, one hand around the shoulder of a young boy whose tears course down his cheek; Santa says, "I'm Sorry Son— . . . This year I just couldn't give you that ROADMASTER Bicycle you had your heart set on. You see, son, it's like this: The people who made ROADMASTERS are now making war materials for your big brother and the millions of other American soldiers fighting for victory. That's why they can't make bicycles. This Christmas your dad's bought you a Victory bond and that's the best kind of a Christmas present" (133).

There's nothing particularly noteworthy about the ads informing the public that insufficiency of materials was the primary cause of the shortage of certain products. Still, the range of companies that placed such ads provides insight into what materials the government diverted for war production: The shortage of wool cut down the number of Hart Schaffner & Marx men's suits and Kenwood blankets, while the need for cotton by the military greatly reduced the number and kinds of civilian textiles made by Bibb Manufacturing, and shortages of metals such as nickel, copper, iron, and steel caused the scarcity of everything from Parker Pens and long-distance wire for Bell Telephone to toys in Fred Harvey Restaurants gift shops. Some shortages came about because one or more components of a product were needed for other uses. As Elsie the cow patiently explained to Elmer the bull when he became irate that he couldn't get a dish of ice cream at a soda fountain in the Borden ad in *Life* on July 5, 1943, it wasn't because of a shortage of ice cream per se, but because most cream was being made into butter for our GIs and most milk into cheese, evaporated milk, and powdered milk for our armed forces and Allies (76). Similarly, in *Life* on May 7, 1945, when there was still a tire crisis despite synthetic rubber being used for civilian purposes, B. F. Goodrich took pains to explain that other shortages were crimping tire production: carbon black, used to make tires wear longer, steel wire, 125 feet of which formed each tire's "backbone, or bead," and cotton, rayon, and nylon cord, all used in making tires (1).

The roughly 125 ads in the largest group explaining shortages have a predictable sameness about them. No matter what the length or general content of the copy, each ad finally gives the same reason for the shortage of certain products: The military's need for them has reduced their availability for home front consumers. In descending order, most of these ads are about foods, followed by textile products, petroleum products, and a small, miscellaneous group of consumer goods. The largest number of ads about home front food shortages due to the ever-increasing needs of our fighting forces and our Allies were those about meat, and of those, all but one were sponsored by one or the other of the two largest meat packers, Armour and Company and Swift & Company. The ads of these rival companies are so similar in their essentials that they all could have been written by the same ad agency. Even the one ad explaining meat shortages *not* by Armour or Swift but by the A&P Super Markets echoed precisely the meat packers' theme. An Air Force major is chatting with his wife after dinner: "That roast you didn't serve is seeing action with our troops. And since we have a war to win, civilian supplies of meat *must* be less than usual" (*Ladies' Home Journal* Feb. 1943: 123). The frequent repetitions of this litany by Swift and Armour ran something like this: from Swift in *Life* on July 24, 1944, "Military needs come first . . . for meat proteins are vitally necessary to give fighting men strength, vitality, stamina" (40); and from Armour in the *Post* on April 24, 1943, "That's why civilians must get along on less meat . . . why every loyal American will seek only his fair share. By limiting the amount of meat you eat, you'll be doing your part to help keep our fighters better fed" (inside front cover). If any of these ads are more interesting or eye-catching than the rest, it's those of Armour's that gave detailed menus of what soldiers, sailors, or marines ate in camp, in the field, in tank crews, on board ships and submarines, and elsewhere, each menu ad lavishly illustrated with pictures of the meals (see fig. 40 for a week of army meals from *Life* 28 Sept. 1942: 49). Armour continued this theme in some of its ads about rationing.

Borden's was in the vanguard of ads explaining that large quantities of dairy products that once stayed at home were being shipped overseas for our troops and those of our Allies. Not only did "the men in our

Meet the best fed fighters

in the world—

the U. S. Soldier, Sailor and Marine!

Not one man in ten ate as nourishing, well balanced meals at home as he does in the U. S. Armed Forces today.

You could be proud to serve meals like these on company occasions — but the Army gets them for dinner every day. They show what care Uncle Sam takes of a son, husband or friend in the service today.

Because meat is as important as fighting weapons to a soldier's stamina and morale, the U. S. Quartermaster Corps sees that every man gets a pound of muscle-building meat every day.

That means Armour and Company

and other packers are shipping millions of pounds of meat *every day* to the Army alone! Besides Armour is supplying tons of meat and dairy products daily for our allies through lend-lease.

That's why you may find temporary shortages in certain meats at home — but our boys in service haven't felt any delays or shortages. The 3 billion dollar plants of the meat industry went to work for Uncle Sam the day war struck. We are glad that Armour and Company, manufacturers of Star Meats and Cloverbloom dairy products, is big enough to help this vital program in an important way.

Typical dinners served the Army, week of Oct. 4th ...and our Sailors and Marines fared equally well.

SUNDAY	MONDAY	TUESDAY	WEDNESDAY

ROAST CHICKEN with brown gravy for Sunday dinner! Served with noodle soup, candied sweet potatoes, broccoli and raw carrot strips. Buttered Parker House Rolls. Ice cream for dessert. Cocoa. Each soldier's portion averaged a full pound of roast chicken.

FRANKFURTERS with Spanish Sauce. A ½ pound portion served each man, with potato cakes and buttered string beans. Orange-grapefruit salad. Bread, butter and coffee. Rice raisin pudding for dessert. The Army's menus are balanced by expert dietitians.

BARBECUED SPARERIBS and sauerkraut. ½ pound of spareribs for each soldier, topped off with mashed potatoes. Mixed vegetable salad. Bread, butter and tea. Butterscotch meringue pie. Armour supplies a big share of the Army's prime quality pork.

BAKED CORNED BEEF with horseradish sauce — a generous ½ pound portion for each man. Also potatoes au gratin, buttered peas, celery. Bread, butter and coffee. Peach cobbler. Soldiers can have second helpings of everything in these Army menus.

THURSDAY	FRIDAY	SATURDAY	

Armour and Company

SWISS STEAK with gravy—and each soldier's portion averaged .3 5 of a pound. Baked browned potatoes, buttered carrots, pepper hash. Bread, butter and cocoa. For dessert, apple turnovers with sweet sauce! Steak is a big favorite with men in the Army.

BAKED FISH with tartar sauce — a generous ½ pound serving for each soldier. Balance of dinner includes parsley potatoes, buttered peas, cole slaw. Bread, butter and tea. And chocolate layer cake for dessert. Pastries are "home-made" by Army cooks.

ROAST BEEF with brown gravy. Also split pea soup, parsley potatoes, stewed tomatoes. String bean salad. Pumpkin pie, coffee. For this war the Quartermaster Corps and packers have developed a new *boneless* beef that is easier to handle and keep.

FREE ILLUSTRATED BOOKLET, "Food for Freedom"—shows why our fighting forces are the best fed, best equipped fighting men in the world. Send today for your copy free. Write Armour and Company, Department S, Chicago, Illinois.

FIGURE 40. Armour® is a federally registered trademark of Jonmor Investments, Inc., used with permission, All Rights Reserved.

armed forces drink more milk than they ever did as civilians" (*Life* 5 Apr. 1943: 41) but they were also eating more butter, cheese, and ice cream. The Borden ads also informed the public of a lesser known reason for the milk shortage: "[. . .] there are just so many cows in the country and thousands of dairy hands have gone to war and into war plants. So it's hard to increase milk production and we have a shortage" (*Life* 16 Aug. 1943: 18). The Kraft Food Company chimed in about cheese nearly two months after the war when there was still a shortage and what there was commanded "a heavy [ration] point value": "Well, cheddar cheese is a highly concentrated form of milk that can be shipped overseas. So the Government took some 380 million pounds [of the 800 million pounds produced in 1944] for our armed forces and our Allies. All the rest was allotted to civilians" (*Collier's* 6 Oct. 1945: 70).

With producers of meat and dairy foods explaining shortages of their own kinds of products by their diversion to the military, the packers of canned goods placed ads about why they too were getting scarce on the grocer's shelf. Green Giant told the public that although the government requisitioned 25% of the peas from all of America's 300 pea canners in 1942, "In the 1943 season it will be at least 50 per cent. More and more peas are needed to help feed the men behind the guns" (*Life* 26 Apr. 1943: 54). In several different ads, the Campbell Soup Company explained the shortage of its condensed soups by letting the home front know that along with some of the soup going to the military, a primary wartime endeavor of Campbell's was the creation and canning of field rations. Also, in *Life* on February 5, 1945, Campbell's placed a full-page ad to explain the severe domestic shortage of its tomato juice since the armed forces were getting almost all of it (35). There's nothing remarkable about this ad except that on page 81 of the same issue of *Life* Libby's ran a full-page color ad extolling the virtues of its own tomato juice with nary a word about a shortage. The only explanation for this I can come up with is that Campbell's got the government contract for tomato juice and Libby's didn't. (This may explain why I remember my family and myself drinking a lot of Libby's tomato juice during the war and later.) Dromedary and Sunsweet, between them packers of such dried fruits as dates, peaches, apricots, raisins, and prunes, placed ads to explain that their shortage would be severe in light of the armed forces needing fruits that would travel well and not be as perishable as fresh ones. And because of the quick-fix energy power of chocolate, both Nestle's and Curtiss Candies (makers of Baby Ruth and Butterfinger candy bars) ran numerous ads explaining that for this reason the army and navy needed them first, with greatly reduced supplies for the home front, mostly affecting America's kids and kids-at-heart.

More offbeat was the reason for the home front scarcity of canned and frozen fish. It had nothing to with canneries switching to war production, nothing to do with the shortage of materials—there were still plenty of fish in the sea, as the singing and frolicking fish pictured in the Birds Eye ads gleefully pointed out—and nothing to do with military needs depleting civilian supply. The shortage came down to just one thing—boats, or, more precisely, the lack of them. As the happy Birds Eye fish explained, "You see, under wartime conditions, trawler fleets have mostly gone to the government" (*Life* 29 May 1944: 46), and about the same time, Van Camp Sea Food, packer of Chicken of the Sea and White Star canned tuna, elaborated, "We're proud our tuna clippers are helping to carry out MacArthur's promise, 'I'm going back to Manila.' Until that job is accomplished, we have only smaller boats for 'off-shore' fishing" (*Ladies' Home Journal* June 1944: 89).

Like the explanations of food shortages, ads explaining diminished stocks of bed sheets, bath towels, shirts, and other textile products by such makers as Martex, Cannon, Pepperell, and Utica Mills said in effect, "We're sorry if you can't find the goods you want at your favorite department or dry goods store, but nearly all we make go to our boys overseas." There were a few interesting exceptions. One Pepperell ad packed some emotion into its sheet shortage explanation. The art in the ad in *Life* on September 21, 1942, depicted a bed in a makeshift army hospital, a man lying in it, what appears to be a ranking officer, his back to us, sitting beside it, and a nurse in a crisp white uniform checking the wounded soldier's pulse. The copy proclaimed, "<u>YOUR</u> SHEETS CAN WAIT—Somewhere there's a bed like this that needs them. It must have them before you get yours. Nothing else matters so much today to you or to us. Maybe a Maine or Alabama or Georgia or Massachusetts boy, enlisted from one of our mills, will get well in those sheets. Or maybe he's a boy from your own home town" (20).

If the Pepperell ad is noteworthy for its emotional charge, an ad about where all the Jockey men's underwear went is equally singular for its specificity: "The Marines have first call on our production of Jockey Midways until they have all they need. That's why Midways especially are hard to get . . . that's why other mills are helping to fill Marine Corps orders, by making Y-front garments under our patents . . . the Marines need millions and they naturally come first. Not enough Jockeys of any style are available, because many machines that normally make them are turning out huge quantities of other types of garments for the armed forces" (*Life* 2 Apr. 1945: 51).

Petroleum ads telling home front civilians that the military needs what you want swung between some that were brusquely matter-of-fact and others displaying tremendous ingenuity in their art and copy. On the blunt end was an ad by the National Carbon Company unit of Union Carbide, maker of Prestone antifreeze, simply stating flat out, "All branches of our fighting forces and our Allies must receive 'Prestone' anti-freeze in sufficient quantities before the civilian is served. It takes millions of gallons of 'Prestone' anti-freeze to fill these needs. Civilians as a result, are drawing their supply of 'Prestone' anti-freeze this fall from a curtailed supply" (*Look* 31 Oct. 1944: 53). At least the essential information is there, however inelegantly. Quite the opposite were the nearly fifty varied and clever war ads produced on behalf of the Ethyl Corporation, close to two dozen of which were specifically designed to explain civilian shortages of so-called "hi-test" or premium grades of gasoline containing Ethyl antiknock fluid since it was needed to produce specialized, high-octane gasolines needed in tanks, trucks, jeeps, and, most critically, airplanes, from transports to bombers. Not that Ethyl itself is something a consumer would ever buy, but during and after the war the trademarked name became synonymous to the public for the highest grade of gasoline. I can still hear my mother pulling up to the pump at our local Pure Oil station and saying to the attendant (no self-service then), "Fill it with Ethyl, please." What's striking about Ethyl's ads explaining its home front shortage is that the art is always fun to look at, as is some of the copy too. Some illustrations are amusing cartoons, others a patriotic display, and yet more decorate "interactive ads" inviting readers to take a quiz about Ethyl at home and at war. Some art was even wistfully sentimental, as on the inside front cover of *Life* for August 28, 1944 (fig. 41).

A few products not in any of the above categories also explained their home front shortages in terms of their use by the military. Burgess Batteries ran several ads in *Farm Journal* telling why its flashlight batteries weren't available because the army needed them for hand-held, port-

He *must* have gasoline to fight.

What's more, the gasoline needed to power a plane, tank, truck or jeep must be top-quality gasoline. That's why the antiknock quality of nearly every gallon of fighting gasoline—aviation and motor—is improved with Ethyl fluid. And that's why government agencies have placed limits on the quantity and quality of gasoline for civilian use.

Remember—"Gasoline powers the attack —don't waste a drop!"

ETHYL CORPORATION
Chrysler Building, New York, N. Y.

FIGURE 41. Reprinted by permission of the Ethyl Corporation.

able equipment like the mine detector in the Burgess ad in the issue for May 1945. Pepsodent explained the shortage of its toothpaste and tooth powder by telling readers that one-fourth of what the company made went directly to "men in uniform," followed by a six-point lesson on how not to waste these products (*Life* 15 Feb. 1943: 15). But first place for the most unusual ad explaining the home front shortage of a common household product because of the military goes to a scouring pad. In the September 1943 *Ladies' Home Journal*, a fictional soldier writes his mother about a very real situation: "Dear Mom: I know where your BRILLO went . . . Maybe your pots and pans are black and burned but *we* are bright and protected because they are using Brillo for camouflage in the Army—*bales* of it—painted green like grass!" (151).

"Ration Blues"

"Baby, Baby, Baby, what's wrong with Uncle Sam? / He's cut down on my sugar, now he's messin' with my ham," lamented Louis Jordan in his comically mournful "Ration Blues," written and recorded after meat rationing began at the end of March 1943. One really *must* wonder what was wrong with Uncle Sam that year, since only in mid-August—five months after all rationing programs were in place—did Washington finally begin an educational ad campaign to end food waste organized by the War Advertising Council under the banner "Food Fights for Freedom." The Council first targeted "150 trade papers" to carry "a series of twelve monthly advertisements." Then, "as the trade press begins handing the drive down to food processors, distributors, and retailers, the council will start laying down an educational barrage on consumers through radio, newspapers, and posters," under the slogan "Produce, Conserve, Share, and Play Square" (*Business Week* 14 Aug. 1943: 98, 99). In other words, those who needed the information most—home front civilians, and especially housewives—would get it last, with the "campaign scheduled to reach top-speed in mid-November." Yet the public *had* come first to a degree. Commercial advertisers were independently placing magazine ads advocating food conservation and offering practical ways to do it almost since the war began, anticipating and recognizing the need for food waste advertising over a year and a half before the government's campaign even got started.

And the commercial advertisers did it very well, even if some sold a product of theirs in the process, which in this circumstance seems perfectly justifiable since these products genuinely helped prevent food waste. On May 5, 1942, the first rationing program—for sugar—went into effect, and just six days later in the issue of *Life* for May 11 the first food conservation ad in a leading national magazine appeared. The ad was for Du Pont's processed cellulose film product Cellophane (no, Cellophane isn't plastic like Saran), even though Cellophane couldn't be purchased for home use during the war. Instead, the ad encouraged shoppers to buy food products packaged in Cellophane, since "Cellophane protection helps prevent waste, safeguards quality, and helps you conserve food for the whole nation" (inside front cover). If a cellulose wrap led off the food waste campaign, ads for waxed paper, which *could* be purchased for the home, were just about neck-and-neck with it, and considerably more frequent. In the May 1942 *Ladies' Home Journal*, Cut-Rite explained how to use its product to preserve the freshness of fresh vegetables, and, in the following month's issue, how to wrap leftovers in waxed paper before refrigerating them. On July 27, 1942, Cut-Rite devoted its ad in *Life* to the best ways to wrap both raw and cooked meats, and on October 12 it once again gave instructions for conserving leftovers, but with a slightly different text and some new ideas. Another food storage product, Pyrex Oven Wear, put an original spin on the how-to's of cutting down food waste, a spin eminently suited to a singular feature of its products. In *Ladies' Home Journal* for April 1944, Pyrex described how considerable waste occurs when food is transferred from the utensil it was cooked in to the serving dish, with more waste when the leftovers are moved from that dish to a storage container for the refrigerator. Pyrex, the ad pointed out, eliminates such waste by the unique oven-to-table-to-fridge capability of all its cookware.

Ads urging food conservation while selling a product were few compared to those that didn't sell anything as they explained the need to stop food waste or gave specific, practical tips for doing it. Quite a few ads by commercial advertisers borrowed either or both of the slogans from the government's food waste drive, "Food Fights for Freedom," and "Produce, Conserve, Share, and Play Square." And unlike the short-term "blitz" food conservation campaign typical of the Ad Council, which wound down early in 1944, the commercially sponsored ads continued well into 1945. Their advice is rather different from that in ads helping people cope with rationing. In fact, rationing is rarely mentioned in food waste ads.

In *Life* on December 20, 1943, the American Meat Institute's ad picturing a family at dinner (the husband in a coat and tie, even at home) struck a quasi-religious (and certainly patriotic) note in its headline "We waste *not* the Meat" that continued into the copy: "Waste not the food of war. With proud and thankful hearts let's give our fighters the meat to fight on," after which it switched to more prosaic language while still being fairly general about conservation: "That's why women are learning to prepare with new glamour the cuts available from day to day [. . .] That's why all of us are learning to relish every single bit of meat" (64). An ad for Jell-O in the same issue of *Life* was primarily commercial, giving recipes for four different desserts made with Jell-O products, but at the bottom was a box containing a picture of popular singer and radio personality Kate Smith (whose radio sponsor was Jell-O) with a message from her cutting right to the heart of the need for food conservation: "Folks . . . you and I and all of us, are just plain wasting too much precious food! Now of course nobody *means* to do that . . . not in war time, when our boys need all we can send them! Yet Uncle Sam tells us that we waste enough food in a year to feed most of our armed forces both at home and overseas! Well . . . now that we know . . . let's DO something about it! We can go easy on *scarce* and *rationed* foods! We can be careful to buy and to *cook* only what we need! AND we can think up smart ways to use left-overs. Our government has a name for this! 'FOOD FIGHTS FOR FREEDOM!' Let's get behind that slogan and make it *work*! Produce—and Conserve! Share and Play Square!" (51). This copy was a hybrid between ads that simply urged food conservation and those packed with practical advice. Very likely it got the attention of those who read it since it came from Kate Smith. She was not just a popular but also an influential wartime celebrity who not long before the ad had sold nearly $40 million worth of War Bonds during a sixteen-hour radio broadcast on September 21, 1943 (Perrett 299).

More typically, motivational ads to end waste concentrated almost entirely on reasons to do so. Typical is the Pillsbury ad in the *Post* on January 22, 1944: "The less food you waste, the harder you hit the Axis and the more you, personally, do to end the war" (82); from the Crosley Corporation in *Life* on June 19, 1944: "Going! . . . Twice as much food to the fighting fronts this year . . . because there are twice as many men to feed [. . .] It's everyone's job to conserve, avoid waste, play square and starve the black market" (99); and from Canada Dry in *Collier's* on

July 14, 1945, under a picture of a boy at dinner holding up a spotlessly clean plate: "This is today's new improved model Jack Sprat. He licks his platter clean, fat *or* lean, because he knows wasting food is like handing a loaded gun to a Jap. He knows we must take on our plates only what we can eat — then eat every bit — and *waste nothing!*" (70).

The ads offering practical solutions to food waste had to have been more useful to housewives and other consumers than the motivational ones because of the specificity of their suggestions. Before the joint government/Ad Council campaign got going in mid-August 1943, the Frigidaire Division of General Motors — with nothing to sell since it was making armaments, not refrigerators — mounted its own mini-campaign between May and August with at least four different ads in *Life*, *Farm Journal*, and *Ladies' Home Journal*, each discussing a different aspect of proper food storage. One concentrated on "How to Keep Meat." Another specified what foods must be refrigerated, what ones may be refrigerated, and what needed no refrigeration at all, with the aim of making as much room as possible in one's refrigerator. The others laid out ways to fight waste in foods from melons to eggs. The advice in each ad was specific and precise: "Ground meat should be cooked within twenty-four hours after purchase, or frozen when you get home. Before freezing form it into cooking portions. Avoid unnecessary handling" (*Life* May 10 1943: 81; also in the May *Ladies' Home Journal* and *Farm Journal*). The big meat packers, Armour and Swift, *did* have something to sell (in rationed quantities of course), but both companies were strongly represented in food waste advertising, the only selling relegated to a list of some of their products at the end of their ads. In the June 1943 issue of *Ladies' Home Journal* Swift placed a wonderful ad with the headline "Save ¾ lb. on a 4 lb. roast by roasting at 325°," aimed, as the ad suggests, at women who were cooking their roasts at 450° and thereby losing 1½ pounds to shrinkage (47). After that very helpful ad, however, Swift appears to have dropped out, leaving food waste ads to Armour between November 1943 and April 1944. Armour's five ads in this period covered a lot of territory, from rules to remember when buying meat and ways to extend butter to two different ads on appetizing ways to use leftovers, one amusingly titled "How to make a roast taste good all week" (*Life* 7 Feb. 1944:10; also in the February *Farm Journal*). Other products and companies that gave practical ways to avoid food waste were Jell-O and Taylor Instruments, the latter a maker of meat thermometers — not available during the war—among many other things. The Taylor ad in *Business Week* on April 4, 1944, contained some genuinely funny art and included a few unique tips found in no other ads: "Don't make your guests eat more than they want! If you don't like leftovers, try cooking a little less the first time!" and, under a cartoon of a husband presenting a huge case of scallions to an alarmed-looking wife, "Don't load up on 'bargains' unless you have a cool place to store them" (59).

Two different kinds of ads aimed to help the home front cope with rationing. The first was what might be called "philosophical" advertising designed to help people come to terms with rationing through understanding the rationale for it; the second gave practical advice on how to cope with the day-to-day realities of rationing, primarily though not exclusively of meat. Ads addressing the nitty-gritty of coping were far more numerous than the philosophical ones, but those too tried earnestly to help lift people's morale about the one regimen of home front life that affected them most tangibly and persistently.

Reduced to its one essential concept, the philosophy of rationing is that rationing is sharing. Most Americans initially viewed rationing as being *deprived* of things they formerly could have in copious amounts. To counter this outlook, the philosophy articulated by both the government and the ads was that rationing ensured everyone on the home front an adequate supply of what they needed, rather than the greedy few hoarding all they could while the unfortunate many had to do without.

The only food rationing operative during 1942 was the "uniform coupon rationing" of sugar that began on May 5 and of coffee that started on November 29. All eligible persons received a coupon allowing them to buy the same set amount within a certain time frame; coffee, for example, was set at one pound per person every five weeks. Just prior to the onset of "point rationing" in which people received booklets of ration coupons to "spend" as they chose (along with currency) on different goods requiring different numbers of "points," *Life* on January 11, 1943, published a richly informative seven-page photo essay describing this new, more complicated kind of rationing. But before explaining how point rationing would work—blue points for processed foods, red points for meat and related products—at the very start *Life* gave the government's two reasons for instituting it: "1) to make the most effective use of American food in winning the war, and 2) to make sure that what is left over for civilians is fairly divided among all," the latter an explicit statement of rationing as sharing.

Yet half a year before the article in *Life* and the start of point rationing, one national advertiser was already promoting sharing during wartime—not sharing of rationed merchandise, to be sure, but of such durable goods as one neighbor might own but another was unable to buy because of war production. The Hoover Company's ad in *Life* on June 29, 1942, on this theme is even oddly affecting. In very big type, the headline declared "The Neighborly Spirit of Sharing," under which was a large illustration of a young, attractive housewife handing her vacuum cleaner over the backyard fence to her equally pretty next-door neighbor. Before getting down to such practical ideas as one household that owned a washing machine but did laundry just once a week offering neighbors without one the use of it on other days, the ad began with words on sharing suggesting that it promotes national unity on the neighborhood level: *"These are days when many good, old-fashioned virtues are coming back into their own—Neighborliness . . . Sharing what we have [. . .] A great cause has made America a nation of neighbors again"* (55). The case for sharing both rationed and unrationed goods was made, by negative example, much later in a Jell-O ad in the November 1944 *Ladies' Home Journal* titled "There's one in every neighborhood." The ad included four genuinely funny cartoons, each depicting a woman "who isn't willing to 'share and play square' like other folks!"—such as a wife innocently saying to her livid husband over dinner, "Why, Henry! I thought you'd be glad I finally found a good black market" (64).

Between the advent of point rationing and the appearance of the Jell-O cartoons, companies and products as diverse as SKF Ball and Roller Bearings, Calvert Reserve Whiskey, Ethyl, Canada Dry, and Budweiser devoted occasional magazine advertising to explaining rationing as sharing, typical of which was this line about a housewife from the SKF ad in *Newsweek* on January 11, 1943: "She knows that only by a fair-and-square, democratic dividing up of the national supply will her family get its share" (72). But just as Exide Batteries essentially made the thoughtful buying campaign its own, rationing as sharing became the special province of Hiram Walker & Sons' Imperial Whiskey, with no fewer than ten different ads variously in *Life*, *Time*, and *Newsweek* between August 9, 1943, and September 11, 1944. Pointed and intelligent, these ads are also gorgeous. Each one features a full-color painting of barnyard animals or wildlife dominating more than half the page; in most of the ads one big selfish creature makes getting at the food supply tough for some little ones. A huge turkey scares three ducklings away from a feed dish, a Canada goose chases small birds from a grain field, or a squirrel in a park, arms loaded with peanuts spilled from a bag, looks guilty while two other squirrels that have none glare at him (see fig. 42). Just as the art in each Imperial ad is different, so too is the copy, some ingenious copywriter finding more ways to express the concept of rationing as sharing than one might think imaginable, as in two extracts: "No one can have a lot in these times of little—or someone else will most certainly get less than he needs. And that's why rationing of essential and vital things is a national 'must'—for if all are to have what they need, a few can't have all they want" (*Life* 15 Nov. 1943: inside back cover); " . . . we accept rationing of essential things in good spirit. Everyone must get his share. And self-restraint is our weapon against want. This goes also for things less vital which are not rationed. Let your sense of fairness help spread these as well" (*Newsweek* 24 Jan. 1944: 60). There is no way to measure whether such ads helped consumers who normally got all they wanted feel better about the restrictions of rationing, but it's safe to assume that ads giving detailed ways of coping with it had far greater impact.

Somewhere between those kinds of ads was another that must at least be mentioned briefly—ads helping people cope with the shoe rationing that began on February 9, 1943. Shoe rationing was really a thing unto itself, and so were the ads trying to make people feel better about it. All but a handful of such ads were by shoe manufacturers, the others by the makers of Shinola shoe polish and O'Sullivan's replacement heels and soles. The way shoe rationing worked was simple. Every man, woman, and child in the United States was issued three ration coupons or stamps each year that entitled them to buy precisely three pair of shoes during that year, no more. How much people chose to spend on their shoes (within ceiling price limits) was entirely up to them, but in order to buy shoes at any price the consumer had to present one of his or her three yearly coupons. The ads helping people cope with shoe rationing were equally simple, most having two more or less equal parts. Whether the shoes were Florsheim, Bostonians, Walk-Over, Roblee, or Red Cross (changed to Gold Cross for the duration), one part of each ad promoted the advertiser's product as the shoe to buy during rationing because of its fine leather, durability, classic style, or other qualities that would make the

This need for dividing up

There has to be a national dividing-up when needed things are scarce. What we have must be so distributed that all get a like share and none gets a lion's—too many would go without if too many could have too much.

That's the simple reason for letting each have only so much—the reason for rationing. None can have abundance while another lacks enough—and certainly nothing could be fairer or more essential.

With that same viewpoint of fairness, certain purchase-limits have been placed on IMPERIAL—for every distillery in America is making war alcohol, and the present supply of whiskey must last for a longer period than any of us had foreseen.

That is why you may be asked to limit your purchases of this famed "velveted" whiskey to one bottle at a time. But without such limiting—it might soon be *none*.

BLENDED WHISKEY, 86 proof. 70% neutral spirits distilled from fruit and grain
Hiram Walker & Sons Inc., Peoria, Ill.

IMPERIAL

REG. U. S. PAT. OFF.

..."velveted" for extra smoothness

FIGURE 42

shoes last longest: from Walk-Over shoes for women in *Life* on March 29, 1943: "Buy fine quality. Remember, only good shoes can take resoling. Walk-Over quality is backed by 69 years of know-how" (68); from Florsheim in *Life* on May 15, 1944: "Our single responsibility, under rationing, is to build shoes that will outlast any you've ever worn before" (10); and from Gold Cross for women in *Life* on September 29, 1943: "Perhaps it's no coincidence that 'ration' rhymes with 'fashion'" (95). The second part of each ad gave reasons why civilians should feel good about shoe rationing, and, invariably, the appeal was to one thing and one thing only— people's patriotism. From Roblee in *Life* on March 29, 1943: "Our soldiers are on the march—through jungle swamps, across desert sands, over the frozen wastelands of the Subarctic. Wherever they go, their shoes must be ready. That's why shoe rationing at home is an essential sacrifice" (10); and from Florsheim in *Life* on April 19, 1943: "On every battlefront of the globe, someone is fighting in *your* shoes. If he is to have his share of leather, you must be satisfied with less" (13).

Shoes aside, the largest number of ads designed to help the home front cope with rationing were those devoted to food, since this hit people the hardest on an almost daily basis. As a nation of eaters who enjoyed good food in ample quantities, it was tough for Americans to come to grips with the reality that, in the initial estimate of the Department of Agriculture, each person would have to make do with "less than 2 lb. of meat per week; less than ¼ lb. of butter; about 2 oz. of cheese; perhaps 10 or 11 oz. of edible fats and oils" (*Business Week* 13 March 1943: 14). Small consolation perhaps, but fish, poultry, eggs, and milk (except for canned milk) weren't rationed, though there were shortages from time to time.

Point rationing of processed foods (canned goods, etc.) began on March 1 and of meats on March 29, 1943. But in 1942 when the only rationed food commodity was sugar, ads offering suggestions for dealing with this were harbingers of things to come. One General Mills ad suggested putting syrup instead of sugar on one's morning bowl of Cheerioats (*Look* 25 Aug. 1942: 38), and the ads for such products as Brer Rabbit Molasses and Royal Pudding were jam-packed with detailed *recipes* for cooking and baking using less sugar or no sugar at all. Once point rationing began and even slightly before, with few exceptions the "recipe ad" became the primary coping device for food rationing, presenting, among other things, interesting and tasty ways to prepare less familiar (and often tougher) cuts of meat than the most desired and scarcest roasts, steaks, and chops with their higher red point values.

Before turning to the recipe ads in more detail, a mixed bag of other coping ads should be noted. Most but not all such ads were by food processors or canners making suggestions for using their products within the scheme of rationing. Both Del Monte and Libby's devised ads recommending substituting in recipes one of their canned fruits or vegetables for another when the grocer is out of the one the shopper came to buy. A&P Super Markets suggested beating canned food rationing problems by buying fresh produce instead, as did the Erie Railroad: "Thanks to American railroads, you can leave your food ration coupons at home when you go shopping for fresh fruits and vegetables" brought by rail to grocers and supermarkets all over the country (*Collier's* 18 Sept. 1943: 42). Vimms brand of multivitamins placed numerous ads about taking its product to make up for any vitamin deficiencies caused by rationing. An ad in *Life* on September 13, 1943, showed a woman mixing something with an eggbeater; above her were the words, in small type, "*To make the most of ration points . . .* " followed by, in screamingly large letters, "**START WITH BREAD!**" (75). The copy explained that "Plentiful and unrationed, modern enriched white bread is one of your best standbys in times when many food items are scarce," describing how bread needn't just be served *with* meals but could be used in recipes as a meat extender and so forth. The advertiser wasn't a commercial baker selling a product like Wonder Bread. In small letters in the bottom right corner of the ad appears "P.S.—most good bread is made with Fleischmann's Yeast." And in a truly unique ad in the December 1943 issue of *Farm Journal*, the Peters Cartridge Division of Du Pont suggested that sportsmen should kill more deer in order to supply themselves and their neighbors with limitless, unrationed, "tasty" venison (12).

But ads about more conventional red meat far outstripped all others when it came to giving people straightforward, detailed, and creative ways of coping with rationing. Recipe ads didn't even wait for meat rationing to begin in late March of 1943. In January, around the time the government began preparing the public for the new red point rationing, a small ad for A-1 Sauce in *Collier's* on January 2, 1943, offered a recipe for "A-1 Pan-Fried Fish" since "Meat rationing doesn't include fish. Try this easy recipe, and nobody'll mind *two* Fridays in a week" (65), and on February 1, in *Life*, the American Meat Institute covered a full-page ad with numerous practical ideas for "Extending Meat" (17). But it was right around the time meat rationing began that recipe ads started to appear in ever-increasing numbers, reaching something of a sustained crescendo during the summer and fall of 1943 but continuing to appear in *Life*, *Look*, and, primarily, *Ladies' Home Journal* well into June 1944. In addition to the American Meat Institute—the meat packers' trade association—advertisers publishing recipes for rationing in their ads included Swift & Company, Frigidaire, Hormel, Green Giant, and Armour and Company, which led all others with at least eleven recipe ads between March 1943 and June 1944. Most recipe ads were Double-Barrelled, the advertisers promoting their own meat products, but in the last analysis that didn't much matter since they were all rationed anyway. A typical recipe ad contained between three and six recipes, sometimes as many as a dozen or more. Some advertisers like Frigidaire and Armour also offered free ration-oriented cookbooks containing, on average, about eighty recipes. Even Lysol, which had nothing to do with food preparation except cleaning up the kitchen afterwards, offered its free "Victory Cook Book" of eighty-one recipes with every purchase of the disinfectant (*Ladies' Home Journal* June 1943: 123). The Armour ads, however, are the most interesting, not just because of their numbers and frequency, but because of the "specialized" content of each ad. Armour made it clear in its ads that all the recipes were "worked out in Armour kitchens by home economists who know your problems and know all about cooking every kind of meat" (*Ladies' Home Journal* March 1943: 14). Each ad focused on a particular kind of meat cookery using various cuts of meat. Some of these ads' self-explanatory titles were "Stews take little meat" (*Ladies' Home Journal* March 1943: 14); "Meat Pies make meat go a long way" (*Ladies' Home Journal* May 1943: 14); "New Ways to Stretch Beef Pot Roast" (*Look* 2 May 1944: 41); "Look what you can do with Armour Cold Cuts" (*Ladies' Home Journal* Aug. 1943: 14); and "A week's delicious dinners with meat points to spare" (*Ladies' Home Journal* June 1943: 14). In all advertisers' recipe ads the recipes weren't just easy on the ration points, but also easy to prepare, an absolute plus for busy women on the home front.

As a dedicated foodie and home cook by avocation, I read most of the recipes for rationing and even made a few of the dishes. The more than satisfactory results led me to conclude that if housewives and other cooks on the home front followed such recipes, people would have found little in food rationing to complain about. From a purely historical perspective, the hundreds, perhaps thousands, of recipes in ads designed to help cope with food rationing paint a rich culinary landscape of the way we ate (or at least should have eaten) on the American home front.

"THE HAND THAT ROCKED THE
CRADLE RULES THE WORLD"
WOMEN IN WAR WORK

Some gorgeous advertising art in July 1942 and an amusing cartoon ad in March 1945 define the changing roles of women over the course of the war. The two ads also reveal how perceptions of women changed from one end of the war to the other. The venerable fragrance and cosmetic maker Coty placed the gorgeous ad in *Life* on July 6, 1942. The art depicted the head and gloved hand of a woman both glamorous and elegant, and, in shadow off to the reader's right, the partial profile of a man in military dress. Except for the company name, the entire copy was "His duty to serve—Hers to inspire" (79; see fig. 43). To some twenty-first century minds the message may smack of sexism, but it did nothing of the kind in the war years. Then "His duty to serve—Hers to inspire" embodied the same spirit of romance, charm, and gallantry that permeated such hit wartime songs as "I'll Get By," "I'll Be Seeing You," and "I'll Walk Alone" (see Jones 26–27 and Chapter 11). The ad's directive for women to give moral support to their GIs was a constant throughout the war. What changed as time went by was that more and more women would also operate drill presses or drive buses for their own men in the armed forces and to help free all eligible men for military service and alleviate the persistent manpower shortage.

In *Newsweek* on March 19, 1945, *Ladies' Home Journal* placed a full-page cartoon ad headed "Never Underestimate the Power of a Woman!" that shows how far women had come since the 1942 Coty ad. A man in business attire stares in amazement at a sign next to an open manhole reading "MEN AT WORK" with "WO" scrawled in front of "MEN" (63; see fig. 44). If anyone ever wondered where *Ladies' Home Journal* stood on the question of women taking jobs in industry or what were called "essential civilian services," this cartoon provides a ready answer, vividly underscoring the kinds of nontraditional jobs women took to aid home front efficiency and the war effort.

FIGURE 43

FIGURE 44

Early in the war other advertisers weren't terribly enlightened or forward-looking. The first ads showing women involved in the war effort depicted them only in volunteer work, not wage-earning jobs. Some of these ads—for example, Chicken of the Sea Tuna in the November 1942 issue and Tavern Home Products in the April 1943 *Ladies' Home Journal*—made a point of noting that the *maid* left domestic service for better paying work in a war plant, leaving each housewife fairly helpless until she discovered the timesaving virtues of the product being sold. The Chicken of the Sea housewife also did volunteer work, which made her time constraints even greater. These early ads presupposed that readers of this prestigious woman's magazine would not wish to get their hands dirty doing a "real" job. But all that changed rapidly as 1943 moved along—yet in some cases only to a degree. A more traditional or conservative woman's magazine's philosophy of women doing war work, or at least of their joining one of the women's services, is encapsulated in an ad placed by *McCall's* in *Newsweek* as late as August 28, 1944. The first part of the copy is an encomium to homemakers: "Today, the first responsibility of every American woman is to America and we can well be proud of the magnificent job millions of homemakers are doing. For, by maintaining the home, rearing children, preserving *and* conserving the fruits of the land, they serve and reaffirm the strength of the partnership [with men]" (60). The ad then shifts to an appeal for women to join the WACS, but only a qualified appeal, singular among all appeals for women to do war work, military or civilian: "In time of war, it is the privilege of women *without home responsibilities* to serve at the side of our men—in the Women's Army Corps" (emphasis added). War or no war, the *McCall's* homemaker's place was still very much in the home.

But the vast majority of national advertisers didn't think so. Or at least they didn't think a woman's place was *exclusively* in the home during a national emergency. When advertisements talked about "work," many meant it in its broadest possible sense—everything from volunteering a few days a week at the Red Cross to enlisting in the WAVES or making a living wage in a munitions factory. Work meant doing on a regular basis whatever one could do to help the war end a little sooner. And yet, not all war ads depicting women at work or in the service were truly ads *about* women in war work. Rather, art and/or copy frequently included a female factory worker or a servicewoman solely for the purpose of selling hand lotion or life insurance. Consider one of the earliest ads depicting a woman at work in a war plant, placed by the Easy Washing Machine Corporation in the December 1942 *Ladies' Home Journal*. In the top panel of an eight-panel half-page ad, we meet the woman war worker: "When her husband enlisted, plucky Helene Bremer of East Aurora, N.Y. hung up her apron for a job at Curtiss-Wright" (132). But observe how quickly the ad copy switches gears; without missing a beat it goes on, "That job has taught her a lot besides how to build planes. For one thing, she's discovered why proper care of any precision machine, like her Easy Washer, is so important." And in the next six frames Mrs. Bremer proceeds to give the reader advice on the care of washing machines. In this ad, as in nearly all ads like it, a male factory worker or serviceman could replace the woman without altering the message or intent of the copy. Such ads can't really be classified as being *about* women in war work and are not discussed further. All authentic ads concerned with women doing war work fall into one of just two types—those paying tribute to women already doing it, and those appealing for more of them. Hence, after a few words about housewives and volunteers, this two-type format governs the remainder of this chapter.

Uncommon Housewives and Others

Whereas the *McCall's* ad suggested that every American woman who was a homemaker should remain *nothing but* a homemaker for the duration, most ads praising homemakers or housewives went way beyond the *McCall's* vision of women "maintaining the home, rearing the children," to catalogue what housewives or stay-at-home moms not only could do but did do to support the war. From mid 1942 through mid-1944, national magazines ran about a dozen ads collectively honoring *all* American women. The best ads of this type were in a series sponsored by the Eureka Vacuum Cleaner Company, which boasted that 70% of its own war plant employees were women. Necessarily, ads covering women engaged in all manner of activities couldn't say too much about any one group, but the Eureka ads effectively hit the high points for each one of them (and differently in each ad), as seen in an excerpt from the *Post* on June 26, 1943: "YOU, TOO, are fighting this war, Mrs. America. Fighting with your kitchen skillets—and your shopping lists. Fighting with War Stamps and Bonds for which you are bleeding the last pennies from your budgets. Fighting in the uniform of the Army and the Navy and the Red

Cross and the Volunteers. Fighting in slacks on the assembly lines of ten thousand factories" (77).

Ads singling out housewives alone for special praise were even fewer than those saluting all women, but the copy was able to spend more time with these women's strengths and contributions to the home front. The sponsors of these ads were diverse, ranging from two makers of bed sheets, Pequot and Pacific Mills, to Budweiser, *Ladies' Home Journal*, United States Rubber, and, once again, in two particularly striking ads, Eureka. That these ads could take their time giving reasons the American housewife deserved special praise is evidenced by the copy in the United States Rubber ad in *Life* on November 29, 1943, that consisted entirely of a seventeen-point list of what housewives did to keep the home front humming, such as "You're the woman who has learned how to do without! Without help, without certain foods. [. . .] You save scrap, you save fats and money. [. . .] You do without the men of your family. And you can take that, too—if it is necessary" (24). That last point, near the list's end, packs quite a wallop, but for sheer eloquence nothing matches the two Eureka ads, partly because of their specificity. The ad in *Collier's* on July 3, 1943, was a salute to mothers of boys overseas: "She's still the same sweet-faced mother her son kissed goodbye . . . but now there's *steel in her heart* and a fierce determination to back up her boy with every ounce of strength and courage she's got! [. . .] And if she's cut expenses to the bone to buy War Bonds, if she's put up the car, if meat is scarce, if she's taxing her strength to the utmost at the Red Cross . . . no hint of it creeps through to him [in her letters]. He knows only that she's backing him to the limit, and working in her own quiet way to bring him home again, and soon!" (69). The Eureka ad in the *Post* on January 29, 1944, is equally strong but almost impossible to excerpt since most of it is a rather rambling monologue by a young mother to her infant son. The ad pays tribute to the strength and endurance of mothers with young children whose soldier-husbands were overseas. In *Life* on August 2, 1943, Pacific Mills praised a single character trait in home front mothers, wives, and other women and girls: "Smiling goodbyes. Cheerful letters. Ears closed to rumor. Lips sealed to gossip. An uncomplaining spirit. Waiting. That's the gallantry of wives and mothers . . . of sweethearts and sisters" (5). There's that word again—gallantry—and clear proof that during the war it was not a male-only, gender-specific quality. Finally, an ad placed by *Ladies' Home Journal* in *Newsweek* on June 14,

1943, lightened things up a bit with a wry, nearly humorous approach to saluting housewives, here for their ability to manage things on their own, including home repairs. The art shows a little girl in a dress and pinafore at the front door of a neighboring young housewife, who looks down at her. The child says (in the ad's heading), "Here's our pipe wrench, Mrs. Smith—and mother says can we please borrow a No. 3 oil can, your wire cutters . . . and a cup of flour?" (65).

If what they did around the house—such as plumbing and electrical repairs—was pretty unusual for the time, some of the things housewives and other women did in their wartime volunteer work were downright amazing. Certainly they swelled the ranks of Red Cross workers, Nurse's Aides, USO Canteen hostesses, and other traditionally feminine volunteer assignments. But women—many of them housewives—were also uniformed drivers for the Red Cross's Motor Corps, plane spotters for the Air Warning Service or Civilian Defense, and pilots in the Civil Air Patrol, in fact 2,000 of them, comprising a full 10% of CAP's 20,000 pilots. Detailed lists of some traditionally male activities performed by the volunteer women of the British-American Ambulance Corps, the Motor Corps of Women's Voluntary Services, and the National Security Women's Corps appeared in a Camels ad on the back cover of *Life* on September 7, 1942. The ad also gave descriptions of the ladies' uniforms that read like the narrator's script for a fashion show, and, of course, told why these active women, plus a Hospital Aide in the American Women's Hospitals Reserve Corps, all smoked Camels. The small amount of selling can be overlooked in light of the splendid photographs of the volunteers and the descriptions of their duties.

Women engaged in purely voluntary activities saw ads praising their efforts throughout the war. The praise was never perfunctory, as seen in the lavish remarks of Norge Household Appliances in *Life* on August 23, 1943: "Vigilance and resolution in the face of peril have characterized American women since early pioneer days. But now, instead of scanning field and forest for bands of marauding savages, our women's eyes sweep the skies for still more savage foes. To learn what is required of them in Civilian Defense, they have studied long and diligently. To perform their duties they are giving up valuable time from household and business responsibilities, as well as precious hours of leisure. And they are doing all this without thought of recompense other than the satisfaction of serving their neighbors and their country. In every sense of the word, they are truly representative of American womanhood. We at Norge, completely in war work, salute the women of America for the vital services they are rendering their homes and their country" (123). While much briefer, what General Electric had to say about women in volunteer services is a healthy corrective to *McCall's* totally insular picture of the ideal housewife: "She Knows What Freedom Really Means . . . And she has the time and youthful energy to fight for it. Mrs. America is stepping out *for Victory*! You may catch a glimpse of her dressed in the trim attire of the Red Cross Motor Corps—or handing out sandwiches down at the Canteen or doing any of a dozen 'extra duty' jobs. And meanwhile the daily routine of her home runs on with perfect smoothness" (*Ladies' Home Journal* June 1942: 58).

Such tributes to women volunteers were fairly common in national magazines, but appeals for them to volunteer were not. The reason? Because most women volunteered near home, making ads in local newspapers the most effective recruiting tools. But magazine ads saluting women volunteers still served as tacit appeals by inspiring women readers to become as involved as those in the ads.

To the Ladies!

It took a war to make it happen, but by going to work in war industries or what were officially called "essential civilian services," millions of American women, many holding a job for the very first time, learned new marketable skills and capabilities. What's more, the huge influx of womanpower into the workforce gained for women a new kind of respect and prestige in the eyes of men and women alike. The public's awareness of the variety and extent of women's war work came largely from newspaper and magazine photos and articles about "Rosie the Riveter" and her millions of sisters, but advertisements saluting these women also helped increase and publicize their newly elevated stature during the war. War ads recognizing women engaged in paid employment were considerably more numerous than those saluting volunteers. These ads variously praised women in the women's branches of the armed forces (including nurses), in industrial war work, and in "essential civilian services." The last took in every kind of job from taxi driver to secretary, waitress, elevator operator, and store clerk, or just about the entire home front support system for war production and the stateside military except the entertainment industry. Over the four years of the war, about sixty tributes to women in one or another kind of war work appeared in leading national magazines. Around forty focused on women in war industries, only five or so on women in civilian support, and, rather surprisingly, fewer than fifteen on women in the armed services, even though women in the army, navy, coast guard, and marines were an almost unheard of novelty during World War II, even more of a novelty than women in heavy industry.

★ ★ ★ In most ads saluting women in all phases of war work the tribute comprised only part of the ad, the remainder either selling a product or giving information about a company's role in war production. This does not mean that the tribute portions were perfunctory or, worse yet, insincere; quite to the contrary, the ad copy almost always reflected genuine admiration for women at work, both in the military and in civilian jobs. A short but clearly sincere salute was an early one to the members of what was originally the Women's Auxiliary Army Corps (WAAC) from its inception on May 15, 1942; later in 1943, the "Auxiliary" was dropped and the Corps became known as the more familiar WAC. In any event, in *Life* on November 9, 1942, and *Newsweek* on November 16, Mimeograph devoted just a few lines to WAACS, but the ad is important not just for its apparent sincerity but for being one of the first to strike a theme that would continue throughout the war in appeals for women to work or enlist. Titled "The Lady in Khaki," the copy next to a large picture of a WAAC reading something from a Mimeograph duplicator was "She's ready to serve her country with her head, heart, hand, and soul. Because she is serving where she is, one more soldier can serve where the battle calls him. A nation salutes you, member of the WAAC" (*Life* 28; *Newsweek* 1). In advertising appeals and recruiting campaigns, releasing men for active duty became a primary reason given women for taking either military or civilian jobs. The rest of the ad, in much smaller type, is a fairly long description of the role Mimeograph machines were playing in the armed services and war production.

Not that there were no perfunctory tributes, some existing merely as a lead-in to a sales pitch. A notoriously bad example is the Milky Way ad in *Collier's* on October 10, 1944. Headed "MAKING GOOD WITH THE MARINES," the copy began "Women, too, now serve with glory in the oldest branch of the armed services . . . And like the men, they enjoy the treat of a Milky Way candy bar in off-duty hours" (41). The rest of the ad just rhapsodized on the yumminess of the candy bar. (Apparently, too, the copywriter was asleep at the switch when he wrote "women, too, now" are in the Marines, since the Marine Corps Women's Reserve was instituted a year and a half before the ad, in February 1943.)

Few as they are, the rest of the salutes to women in the military are quite varied, from Camels in *Life* on April 3, 1944, and Du Barry Beauty Preparations in *Life* on May 1, 1944, each singling out for praise a specific and apparently real Woman Marine and WAVE, respectively, to Canada Dry's toast in the *Post* on October 11, 1944, and the March 1945 *Ladies' Home Journal* "To the Ladies," *all* of them in the four women's services plus the Cadet Nurses thrown in for good measure (*Post* 76; *Journal* 104; see fig. 45). But of all the women in or allied to the services, nurses received the most lavish, heartfelt, and oftentimes genuinely emotional recognition in tribute ads: "Her uniform may be mud-draggled, her face smudged and lined with fatigue, but no glamour girl ever looked so heavenly to the pain-shocked men served by this most loyal army nurse" (Greyhound, *Collier's* 27 May 1944: 67). The most remarkable of such copy was in an ad by United States Rubber in *Life* on March 26, 1945, an ad that ultimately wound up explaining why women could not buy certain shoes made largely of rubber for the duration. But before that was a large illustration of a nurse in helmet and fatigues kneeling over a wounded soldier lying on the ground on a stretcher, apparently awaiting evacuation. The soldier's thoughts did the speaking in the ad: "I remember you . . . you are the girl with flying feet who led the way to laughter . . . you are all the girls I ever liked who brightened a fellow's life . . . You didn't always wear muddy boots. Once you raced over summer lawns in bright, skylarking shoes . . . a flash of shining brown bare legs . . . sunshine on wind-tossed hair . . . I even remember the things you said. You are the same girl, aren't you—you, there in your muddy boots? The gay companion I needed then—that was you. The angel of mercy that I need now—still you. You grew up, didn't you?" (24). One would be hard pressed to write a more impassioned and personal tribute to the Army Nurse Corps.

★ ★ ★ Some inspired copywriting of a very different kind is the most distinctive feature of the handful of ads paying tribute to women working in essential civilian services. Given how workaday and humdrum some of these jobs were, it's a tribute to the ad agencies that they could

To the
Ladies

These gallant young women are dedicated to the service of our country. WAVE, WAC, SPAR, Marine, Cadet Nurse—they know that every ounce of work and loyalty is urgently needed now. They and millions of other Americans are putting all their hearts and energies into the fight for Victory. To them, Canada Dry, "the Champagne of Ginger Ales," an old family friend, says: Keep up the good work!

Just as soon as conditions permit, we hope to be able to fully meet the ever increasing demand for Canada Dry Ginger Ale... and again make "The Champagne of Ginger Ales" available to you in the handy 5¢ individual bottle.

SO DELICIOUS, SO PURE,
SO REFRESHING ...
ENJOYED THE WORLD OVER!

CANADA WORLD FAMOUS DRY

"The Champagne of Ginger Ales"

FIGURE 45

come up with copy that was sincere, ingenious, and even entertaining. Only one of these ads, by the way, saluted employees just at the advertiser's own company. An ad in *Life* on May 15, 1944, acknowledged the special wartime service of the "Harvey Girls," the waitresses in Fred Harvey restaurants across the country who *every day* collectively served ten thousand or more troops traveling by train from one camp or base to another, not to mention the usual civilian customers. Occasionally, in other ads an advertiser's product was associated with the work of the women singled out for recognition, but the tribute was meant for all of them, no matter what company they worked for. "No uniform adds glamour to her job. There's no publicity, no medal . . . she's just in there slugging" began the first of two Smith-Corona typewriter ads in *Life* two and a half months apart honoring the good work of the country's secretaries, especially considering the extra burdens placed upon them because of war production. That first ad concluded with "a word of tribute because we know it is richly deserved. Here's to a girl doing one grand job . . . your own private 'secretary of war'" (15 March 1943: 64). The second Smith-Corona ad, on May 31, 1943, depicted two executives crowning a secretary with a laurel wreath and was written as a "Citation to the American Secretary" (43). In ads naming very diverse real women, Du Barry honored a skilled professional woman who replaced a man in the service as photo editor of a press syndicate (*Life* 3 July 1944: 63) and another who seemingly had never worked before taking over for a man as a toll collector on the George Washington Bridge (*Life* 17 Apr. 1944: 75). Both ads also sold cosmetics. The cleverest tribute to civilian workers was Canada Dry's in the *Post* on November 20, 1943, and *Collier's* on December 11. A young mother in a very smart uniform is giving her son a snack of cookies and (what else?) Canada Dry Ginger Ale. The copy began with a string of questions: "What service is she in? WAVE? WAC? SPAR? MARINE? No . . . none of these. No parades. No bands. But because of this woman — and others like her — America keeps on running. What is she? A taxicab driver — formerly housewife, manicurist or debutante . . . now in the service of her country. She and thousands of others like her are *doing something* about the manpower shortage" (*Post* 101; *Collier's* 9). That last sentence demonstrates how a tribute ad could also function as an implicit appeal for women to go to work.

The most apparent idiosyncrasy about the tributes to women in actual war industries is that close to half of the ads — seventeen out of thirty-eight—specifically and exclusively honored women working for the advertiser's own company. Most of those companies were prominent, with such nationally recognized names as General Electric, North American Aviation, Northrop Aircraft, RCA Victor, and Chrysler Corporation, as well as the Erie, Pennsylvania, Southern Pacific, and Santa Fe railroads. There was certainly nothing wrong with a company singling out only its own women for recognition. No firm was so chauvinistic as to suggest that *its* women were better workers than another company's. Nor is there even an implicit pitch in these ads to hire more women at a given firm. Instead, the strategy of paying tribute to one's own female employees seems to have been an ingenious variation on the goodwill institutional advertising discussed in Chapter 3 that kept a company's name or product before the public while the advertiser was making only war materiel.

These company-centered ads mostly focused on the workingwomen themselves. Striking for its detail is a two-page spread by General Electric in the *Post* on August 29, 1942, in which mini-biographies of six actual women at GE—along with a photo of each—described their work, their lives, and their reasons for taking a war job. One group of three began with just one worker, a former model turned draftsman for bombers at North American Aviation: "The lovely girl at the drawing board is Jackie Maull, onetime model for John Powers. She is one of many career women—former secretaries, singers, milliners and others—whose new careers are at North American. Other women employees were housewives—and good ones, too. Here you will find wives, sisters, sweethearts (and a few widows) of men who are fighting for freedom. They are proud of their men—and every woman here can be proud of her own contribution to the winning of the war. America, you owe a lot to women like these" (*Life* 9 Oct. 1942: 57; *Collier's* 24 Oct. 1942: 43). Railroads devoted nearly a full page of small print copy to praising women who took a multitude of different nontraditional jobs from conductors and ticket agents to oiling steam engines and working on track repair crews.

Tributes to women in war work beyond the advertiser's own company weren't much different. A Veeder-Root ad in *Newsweek* on December 12, 1942, began with "Here's a salute to the thousands of American women who have cheerfully deglamourized themselves (during working hours) to tackle the really tough jobs in industry" (10); an Armco ad in *Time* on

April 10, 1944, compared female war workers to pioneer women helping to win the West, concluding that "The modern girl, with millions of her sisters, is meeting this war's emergencies with the same pluck" (85); and an Oldsmobile ad in *Time* on June 5, 1944, praised at great length the first woman service instructor for Airacobra fighter planes, who went on to teach Army Air Force flight mechanics at Camp Bell. The lavish encomium began, "A WOMAN'S PLACE in wartime *is where she can be of greatest service to her country*! So reasoned Elsa Gardner of Buffalo, who had been a merchandising stylist before the war" (5). *Ladies' Home Journal* twice tackled the question of the proper "woman's place" in wartime through ads placed in *Newsweek* aimed at attracting advertisers to the new kinds of readers of the *Journal* as opposed to the more traditional breed of women's magazines. On April 19, 1943, the *LHJ* ad depicted two feminine-looking young women speaking in odd, coded language with a marine sergeant hardly believing his ears. He finally realizes that this was the shoptalk of "the better part of a big gun crew" at an ordnance proving ground (64). Even more fun and instructive was the second ad on August 9, 1943, in which a grandmother recounts to her young grandson her day's exploits test-driving a General Sherman tank. The ad then extrapolated, "And we can show you pictures of older women firing big guns and sewing and folding parachutes. And of delicate-handed home and office women bucking rivets and driving drills. All of them part of the great army of 18,000,000 women who will answer America's call to industrial and civilian services by fall [. . .] from all walks of life, they have brought their own feminine backgrounds and tastes and interests right along on their new jobs" (69). Clearly, *LHJ* believed a woman's wartime place was practically anywhere *but* in the home, yet still maintaining her femininity. And, just as clearly, some other advertisers agreed, a few including parts of the expression "The hand that rocks [or rocked] the cradle rules the world." In the eyes of Thermos in *Time* on November 23, 1942, it became "Hands that might have rocked a cradle now hold a rivet gun. America's womanhood has 'gone to war'" (62), and, in the May 1943 *Farm Journal* John Deere put it quite succinctly: "The hand that rocked the cradle . . . *is the hand that is beating the Axis*" (51). But perhaps the most eloquent tribute to women in war work was absolutely wordless—John Maxwell's handsome drawing titled "Miss America, 1943" above the unrelated Philco copy in the *Post* on November 6, 1943 (see fig. 46).

Miss America, 1943

DRAWN FOR PHILCO by JOHN MAXWELL

Copyright 1943—Philco Corporation

WHEN PHILCO speaks of the future and the rich legacy which war research will leave to the peacetime world, they do not forget that without victory there can be no peace and no future for free men.

So the one thing that the men and women of Philco are thinking of today is the only thing that matters for us all ... *winning the war*. Their total effort is devoted to the making of weapons for our fighting men—radio and communications equipment, ordnance and storage batteries.

But all this research and production for war creates new

John Maxwell makes this contribution to the series being drawn for Philco by America's leading editorial cartoonists, depicting the significance of America's productive might. While available, a full size reproduction of the original drawing will be sent, free, on request to Philco Corporation, Philadelphia, Pa. Ask for Cartoon No. 67A.

knowledge, new ideas, new skills. Men of science see their dreams spring to reality. And no matter how much the product of their brains and labor may be destroyed in battle, *their ideas live!* When victory is won and peace made secure, those ideas will survive for the happiness and good of all mankind.

This is the basis of Philco's post-war planning. In this, the picture grows clearer each day of the peacetime miracles which will appear under the famous Philco name ... in radio, television, refrigeration, air conditioning and industrial electronics.

PHILCO CORPORATION

FIGURE 46

★ ★ ★ Regrettably, much that women gained during the war years—financially, in job training and experience, and in their heightened stature based on their abilities in the working world or military service—proved to be only temporary. Valued as women workers were during the war, as it came to an end several things combined to unceremoniously dismiss most of them from industrial jobs. The widespread union rule of "last hired, first fired" worked against many women. Plants needed fewer workers when they returned to peacetime production at the same time that millions of veterans needed jobs. Even the doctrine of equal pay for equal work adopted by numerous manufacturers and enacted into law by several states worked against women factory workers since many employers, still prejudiced in favor of male workers, could once again hire large numbers of men for the same wages women had received during the war. Finally, some advertising helped spread the myth that most women employed in war work were eager to "get back in the kitchen." In an ad by the Southern Pacific Railroad, an apparently actual Mrs. Blanche Tuttle, a soldier's wife who supervised women track crews in California, says "I wanted to get into war work and do my bit, [. . .] The railroads must run, and this means railroad track must be kept in good condition. I'll stay in my S. P. job until my husband comes home," implying she'd go back to being a housewife, not seek a different job (*Collier's* 4 Sept. 1943: 41; *Time* 13 Sept. 1943: 59). But according to surveys by the Women's Bureau of the Department of Labor, "75% to 80% of new women industrial workers want to continue in or return to plant jobs they held during the war" (*Business Week* 29 Dec. 1945: 92). These figures corroborate the results of earlier surveys of working women, including one that found 70% of "married women want postwar jobs" (*Business Week* 11 March 1944: 49). Still, despite the mass layoffs at the end of the war, women's success in the wartime workplace gave them a taste of what they could eventually achieve, a vision that lasted well beyond August 1945.

"The More Women at War — The Sooner We'll Win"
Tribute ads played a key role in raising and sustaining the morale of the women war workers they saluted and also helped make the general public, including women not engaged in war work, realize how vital the role of women was in war production, the armed services, and keeping the home front running efficiently. Still, such tributes were more public re-

lations than advertising, having little to do with advertising's prime mission since time immemorial of selling a product. Appeals for women in all varieties of war work fell into this mainstream function of advertising and were more immediate and urgent than the tribute ads. Just the numeric breakdown of the classes of such ads is revelatory: twenty appeals for women to enlist in one of the women's armed services, thirteen of them in 1944; thirty-two appeals for nurses of all types and levels of experience, nineteen in 1945 when battle casualties were rising and more wounded GIs were coming home; twenty for women to take jobs in essential civilian services, mostly in 1943; only five for women just in war production, split between 1943 and 1944, and sixteen for women both in war industries and civilian services, the bulk of them coming in 1944. The largest numbers of appeals occurred when the need for woman-power specified in them was greatest.

That need was critical at various points during the war. According to *Business Week* on May 16, 1942, "The Bureau of Labor Statistics estimates that a shortage of 6,000,000 [war workers] is in prospect for late 1943 [. . .] Today, out of an estimated total of 8,500,000 war workers, 1,000,000 are women. By the end of 1943, there will be 20,000,000 or more war workers and 4,000,000 — or one-fifth — will be women. That means that 3,000,000 women will be needed in war plants in the next two years; and at least that many more will be absorbed into civilian industry" (22). By early 1943, things looked even more grim: "Unless industry hires 200,000 women now unemployed and draws 2,800,000 more away from household or school duties in 1943, [. . .] production quotas will have to be revised downward for lack of labor" (*Business Week* 9 Jan. 1943: 72). Another *Business Week* article vividly showed the importance of women at work over the first three years of the war: "In December, 1941, some 12,090,000 were employed [in all occupations], forming 22% of the labor force. By March, 1944, the number had risen to 16,480,000, or 31.5%. Of this 4,390,000 increase, Dept. of Labor statistics show that 2,670,000 women were added in the manufacturing field. By July, 1944, female employment reached a peak of 19,110,000; it dropped to 18, 480,000 in October" (16 Dec. 1944: 90). And an earlier *Business Week* article remarked that advertising must play a major role in recruiting women workers: "WMC [War Manpower Commission] comes out with an estimate of 7,000,000 women prepared to take factory work but it knows that to count on anything remotely like that number it must do a big selling job" (9 Jan. 1943: 74). Advertisers in national magazines performed much of that job.

That the need for women as everything from nurses to factory workers was urgent is revealed by the many multiple appearances of appeals ads in different magazines, usually almost simultaneously, but sometimes weeks or even months apart. The intent of the advertisers was saturation so that their calls for women to enlist or join the workforce would reach as large an audience as possible. The actual appeals in the ads ranged from the entirety of the copy in a full-page ad to one of those perfunctory blurbs the War Advertising Council christened a Plug in a Slug in a sidebar or as a seeming afterthought at the bottom of the page. One is tempted to wonder how committed to helping expand womanpower the advertisers were who used such plugs, or how seriously they perceived the labor shortage to be. But at least they were committed enough to say *something* by way of recruiting women into the workforce. Many appeal ads incorporated into the copy the slogan said to have been created by the War Manpower Commission, "The More Women at War— The Sooner We'll Win." And too, the very character of appeal ads demonstrated advertising's stated aim of helping to achieve universal participation by all Americans to make the home front an efficient support system for the war industries and armed forces.

★ ★ ★ Incentives for women to join one of the women's armed forces went from one extreme to another. Seven appeals included some variation of the patriotic duty they would perform by freeing for combat some man already in the service, while a few ads recruiting specifically for the WAVES and/or SPARS offered as an incentive that women in those services got to wear the "smartly trim uniform designed by Mainbocher," one of the most fashionable fashion designers of the day (Adel Precision Products, *Collier's* 5 Aug. 1944: 40). But mainly the straightforward copy of most full-length enlistment ads was packed with the kind of matter-of-fact information a woman might hear from a recruiting officer. The Libbey Glass Company more than any other advertiser took up the cause of women's enlistment, with separate ads for the Marines and the WAAC, and a joint ad for the WAVES and SPARS. From the WAAC ad a woman could learn that "pay is the same as soldiers'—$50 to $138 a month— and all medical and dental care, meals and quarters are furnished. You have full opportunity for advancement—all officers come up from the ranks" (*Time* 17 May 1943: 2). Each ad also informed the woman reader of the requirements for enlistment, as in the Libbey ad for the Marines in *Time* on June 14, 1943: "You must be a citizen, in good health, height at least 5 feet, weight at least 95 pounds, single or married (except to a Marine) and with no children under 18" (7), followed by the differing educational requirements for enlisted women and officer candidates. Only the Libbey ad for the WAVES and SPARS got a bit personal, and rather amusingly so: "You live in pleasant surroundings—room, board and medical care paid for—and can have dates and leave" (*Time* 26 Apr. 1943: 7). All these ads gave information about where to write or go for further information and to actually enlist.

Aside from such mainstream recruiting pitches and the occasional Plug in a Slug in ads largely doing something else, some advertisers took creative or oblique approaches to enlistment appeals. Paralleling its ad honoring uniformed volunteers mentioned earlier, Camel Cigarettes ran a handsome one titled "first in Fashion" with photos of WACS, WAVES, SPARS, and Women Marines in their dress uniforms (each, of course, with a Camel in her hand). Built into the paragraph about each of the women's services, with the curious exception of the WAVES, was an implicit recruiting appeal such as this one for the SPARS: "That job you take over *at a desk* means another Coast Guardsman free to fight *on deck*" (*Life* 1 Nov. 1943: back cover). This ad typifies saturation advertising; in addition to *Life*, it ran in *Time* on the same date, in the December 1943 *Ladies' Home Journal*, and, most likely, in other magazines not considered here. There was also an occasional emotional appeal such as International Sterling's in *Life* on September 11, 1944. The art shows a WAC on the deck of a ship, looking over the rail (unlike women in the other services, some WACS saw overseas duty). In the copy she recalls how, after her husband enlisted, she "proceeded to be as miserable as a girl can be, who's left empty-handed and empty-hearted. I'm not sure when it dawned on me that I was behaving badly. I don't remember what started me thinking about joining the Women's Army Corps. But I do know it was the wisest thing I ever did. I'm truly happy now, the way a woman is when she's busy and useful. And I feel close to Fred . . . knowing we're working together for all the things that will ever matter to us" (75).

★ ★ ★ If the number of advertising appeals is any indication, the need for more nurses both at home and at the war's battlefronts was as proportionally great as the need for women workers in war industries and civilian support jobs. In fact, the need was so great that in 1943 the federal government established one of the most remarkable yet less remembered programs of the war years—the U.S. Cadet Nurse Corps. Under the aegis of the United States Public Health Service, the Corps provided nursing education and training for all qualified young women between the ages of seventeen and thirty-five who were at least high school graduates, with the students becoming certified registered nurses at the end of the program. Girls accepted into the Corps could choose where to take an accelerated nursing course from among nearly a thousand accredited schools of nursing across the country and, what's more—the most remarkable part—the government provided the Cadets completely free tuition, room, board, hospital and street uniforms, and a monthly cash allowance for personal expenses during the entire time they were enrolled. With the Corps begun only in 1943, it's hardly a coincidence that at least seven full-page ads appeared in the leading magazines between January and June of 1944 urging young women to apply. More ads followed later that year and in 1945. That the need for new nurses-in-training was critical is attested to by ads sponsored by Kodak in May and Kotex in June 1944 mentioning that "65,000 high school graduates, from 17 to 35, are needed *now* to help replace nurses who are serving our fighting men [by] joining the U. S. Cadet Nurse Corps" (*Ladies' Home Journal* June 1944: 66). And the need didn't let up for the remainder of the war. An ad undoubtedly written for Canada Dry before the war was over but not published until August 18, 1945, in the *Post* still stated that "60,000 Cadet Nurses are needed this year!" (67). The Corps and its attendant educational benefits for the Cadets continued into 1948.

Other numbers in other ads brought home the urgent and increasing need for nurses of all kinds and at all levels of experience as the war went on. According to a Commercial Solvents ad in *Newsweek* on May 15, 1944, there was a critical shortage of nurses on the home front because so many registered nurses had enlisted in the Army Nurse Corps for overseas duty. This impelled the Red Cross to call for 100,000 more volunteer Nurses' Aides in stateside hospitals "to make beds, take temperatures, assist with treatments, and perform many other services" so that the shorthanded nursing staffs would be free to perform those duties that only skilled professional nurses could (1). Housewives, students, and other women could become Nurses' Aides by taking classes only three days a week for seven weeks. The numbers were equally critical regarding those registered nurses. A Sanka ad in *Life* on March 5, 1945, declared that the Army Nurse Corps (ANC) would need "10,000 more graduate registered nurses by June!" (44), and by April 15, the need had increased to 16,000 in the words of the U.S. Army Surgeon General, Major General Norman T. Kirk, in an ad sponsored by Westclox in the *Post* (1). Not only did the ANC need ever more RNs for front line duty but also in home front Army hospitals as more and more wounded or ill veterans returned to the United States. In all, eight ads appealed specifically for RNs to join the ANC, nearly all in 1945. Inexplicably, there were no ads appealing for Navy nurses.

But eleven ads, all in 1945, sent out a joint call for nurses with all degrees of experience, or even none. In a few cases, the appeal was a perfunctory Plug in a Slug, but the majority of advertisers set aside selling in favor of a full-page plea for nurses. Nothing indicates that the War Advertising Council had a hand creating these ads, yet nearly every one of them contained an almost identical summary statement of who was needed and what their qualifications should be, sometimes in full, sometimes abbreviated. Even if this oft repeated information didn't reach ad agencies via the Council, the likelihood is that it one government agency or another, most probably the OWI, released it to the advertising industry. A representative full version of the statement occurred in the Jergens Lotion ad in the *Post* on May 26, 1945: "If you are a graduate registered nurse—join the Army Nurse Corps immediately. If you are a senior cadet nurse—serve your final six months of training in an Army hospital. If you are untrained— (1) join a WAC Hospital Company; or (2) take a Red Cross Nurse's Aide or Home Nursing Course. There is a place for every woman to help" (85). Wherever this statement was published there appeared an address to which interested women could write for more information and an application or, frequently, a mail-in coupon for them to fill out with their name, address, and level of experience.

The appeals for nurses were serious business and mostly as matter-of-fact as those for women to join the armed forces. Yet occasionally they took on a different tone, if only momentarily. After describing the winter and summer uniforms of Cadets, the Kodak ad in *Life* on January 24, 1944, continued playfully and parenthetically, "(When you feel you just must slip into something frilly and feminine for a school dance, you can)" and, later, "And don't think you're closing the door on romance.

There will be time for dates of an evening, and occasional weekends off duty" (31). Clearly this copywriter knew all the angles to play to entice young women into Cadet Nurse Corps training. The Cadet appeal in the Sanka ad in *Life* on May 1, 1944, took a comic approach. A girl's "Old Fuddy-Duddy" doctor (her words) won't pass her Cadet physical because of her jangled nerves and bad temper and finally recommends Sanka coffee to this overcaffeinated damsel. When she returns to see him in her Cadet uniform he reminds her that when she completes the course she can have a lifetime career as an RN (38). The emotional and sentimental also found their way into appeals for nurses. In the Bryant Chucking Grinder Company ad in *Time* on February 19, 1945, a GI who lost a foot on D-Day recounts in a long narrative how a nurse saved his life (95). And brief passages such as this lead-in to the appeal for ANC nurses in the Prudential ad in the *Post* on February 3, 1945, and *Life* on February 12, appeared fairly often: "Ever since woman first comforted a suffering creature against her breast, man has carried a grateful reverence for her in his heart. Whenever he is wounded—in spirit, mind, or body—he turns to the tender magic of that touch for which there is no substitute. Today, when men are suffering more than ever in history, their need for her help and comfort is even greater—it is *desperate*" (*Post* 99; *Life* 22). Desperate was not too strong a word. The power and immediacy of the appeals for nurses along with their frequent, repeated appearances in several magazines reflected the desperate need for nurses of all kinds. Such urgency was matched only by the ad campaigns for War Bond drives (see Chapter 9).

★ ★ ★ This is not to say that there was little or no sense of urgency in advertising appeals for women in all kinds of war work. The approach was just different from calls for nurses. Although appeals for nurses most often stressed the immediacy of the need by citing very specific facts and figures, the calls for women in war industries and essential services more often than not appealed to women's patriotism. Each workingwoman's contribution would help the war end sooner, giving her personal satisfaction in the job she was doing. A few ads in 1943 cited the well-publicized need for eighteen million women to be at work by the end of that year, but, by and large, the ads took a more personal approach.

Like appeals for nurses, ads for women in war work almost universally included a statement of where they could find out about job opportunities in their local communities, always in the same or nearly same language. The "canned" quality of this statement, even in abbreviated forms, suggests it was something the government, again most likely the OWI, sent to ad agencies to include in their copy. A fully fleshed-out version appeared in a Westinghouse ad in *Collier's* on October 2, 1943: "Look at the Classified Advertising Section of your newspaper to see the kinds of jobs open in your locality. Then go to your local United States Employment Service for advice. The U.S.E.S. is in the phone book. This is your government's own employment agency. No fees—No favorites" (7). Full or abbreviated, the blurb gave women enough information to start hunting for a job in a war industry or civilian support.

The few ads appealing for women in just war industries were very general; none specified what types of industries needed women workers the most. Also, since few women wanted to pull up stakes and move to where war work was happening, these ads had little relevance to women who wanted to work close to home unless there happened to be a war plant, shipyard, or airplane factory in the immediate vicinity. Aside from one appeal each by Chesterfield and Prem (Swift's answer to Spam), industries doing war work placed all the other calls for womanpower. On the other hand, of the larger number of appeals for women in essential services, a fair number sent out very specific calls. In two different ads about a year apart, Mimeograph issued a plea for teachers to fill the gaps left by those who had gone into the service or war work. Appropriately, the Statler Hotels asked women to fill numerous kinds of jobs in hotels and restaurants—desk clerk, waitress, elevator operator, maid, and cook. Libby's, the canned fruit people, in one ad stressed the urgent need for women in food processing and packing plants, and in another recommended women seek employment with their local grocer. Smith-Corona appealed for secretaries, and Drano, to show the range of jobs for women, included in one ad photos of a teacher, waitress, laundry worker, and taxi driver, explaining how each job performed an essential service. But for the most part appeals for women in civilian services were as general as those for war workers.

Only twice did the War Advertising Council's name appear on an appeal for women in war work of any kind. Both ads appeared in *Life*, and both were sponsored by Tubize, on September 20, 1943, calling itself the Tubize Chatillon Corporation, and on April 17, 1944, the Tubize Rayon Corporation. The first ad noted it was "Prepared in cooperation with the

War Advertising Council and the O.W.I." (85), the second, "Prepared in cooperation with War Advertising Council, War Manpower Commission, and Office of War Information." Of all the appeal ads, these two were uncharacteristically extreme and strident. Under a large illustration of women playing cards, the first ad's heading was "Will it take a BOMB to break up the afternoon bridge game?" with the copy continuing, "*Must bullets whine and the sirens shriek before* all *American women realize that the time is here.* The time for them to get out and drive a truck, load a freight car, carry a waitress's tray, work in a day nursery, operate an elevator? It isn't pleasant, no! But neither is war. And the *war won't be won* unless our men abroad, *fighting,* are backed up by our women at home, *working.*" After that, the ad calms down and prints the canned information about reading want ads and going to the Employment Office — assuming the reader wasn't too paralyzed with fright to do so. The second ad featured a picture and some words of Edith Cavell, a British nurse during World War I who helped hundreds of Allied soldiers escape from Belgium into the neutral Netherlands, for which she was tried and executed by the German army. The picture showed Cavell, a priest, and a German officer the night before the nurse's execution. Her last words to the women of England were "Tell them that in time of war, Patriotism is not enough!" The rest of the ad expands on this theme and then, once again, provides the by now familiar job-seeking information seen in other ads. Granted, these ads have a certain power, but one can't help wondering if this was the general tone of ads prepared in conjunction with the War Advertising Council. If it was, that might explain why the Council is conspicuously absent from the large majority of successful war ads in national magazines.

Usually the tone of ads appealing for women for both war plants and civilian services was much more reasoned. Kleenex ran an exemplary series of four ads answering women's specific questions about taking a wartime job that appeared variously in *Life, Collier's, Ladies' Home Journal,* and the *Post.* In a series of illustrated panels, each ad addressed a different concern: "What to tell your husband if he objects to your getting a war-time job" (*Life* 14 Feb. 1944: 13); "But I've Never Worked Before! — what kind of war job could I do?" (*Post* 4 March 1944: 84; *Collier's* 1 Apr. 1944: 4); "I know I'm Needed — but how can I get a war job?" (*Life* 10 Apr. 1944: 20); and "Housework's the Only Job I Know — what could I do in a war job?" (*Ladies' Home Journal* May 1944: 68). An ad sponsored by the Hoffman-La Roche pharmaceutical company in *Life* on August 21, 1944, is typical of the reasoned quality of most appeal ads, even when confronting grim subjects: "How many [GIs] will be lost? No one knows. But this is certain: the more women who join those already at work— take a war job, enlist in the armed services—the better chance these men will have to live. For the truth is this: we cannot allow war production to lag without paying a fearful price in casualties. The serious shortage of manpower in war plants and necessary civilian work threatens the success of our military forces" (8).

Strongly emotional copy was not altogether absent from appeals for women in war work, as seen in another Hoffman-La Roche ad, this one from July 10, 1944, in *Life*. The drawing is of a young woman on a residential street, seen from the back; walking toward her perhaps half a block away is a thin, clearly despondent older woman: in the young woman's words, "Yesterday I met her for the first time since we heard that Tom was killed. Poor woman! She looked so much smaller . . . seemed more frail . . . had a tightness in her face. We stood there talking. Trivialities. What *can* you say to a mother who has lost her only son? 'If only there was something I could do,' I finally blurted out. Her eyes took in my slacks, the lunchbox in my hand. Her smile was real . . . like I remembered his. 'You're doing it, my dear,' she said. 'God bless you, child, and thank you'" (2). The rest of the ad details how to find a job, but I would guess that readers of the ad, men and women alike, would have been most struck by that powerfully emotional copy. In the next chapter we shall see how often and how successfully the ad industry enlisted the service of equally intense emotion and sentiment for appeals to the home front to give blood, buy War Bonds, and make other personal contributions to fighting and ending the war.

"DIG DOWN DEEP" GIVING BLOOD AND BUYING BONDS

Of all the appeals by wartime advertising to achieve the home front's universal support of the fighting front, none were more direct, personal, and persistent than those for buying War Bonds. Or, indeed, more numerous—about five hundred just in the ten leading national magazines, and that doesn't include the numerous ads that merely appended a "Buy War Bonds" Plug in a Slug to otherwise unrelated copy. As important but with much less frequency, other ads encouraged giving blood or contributing to war-associated charities. In the same ten magazines only thirty or so ads asked people to give blood, but their urgency made up for their scarcity. Appeals for donations to social service and relief agencies numbered a mere eleven. Still, these causes appealing for funding were needed for the war effort, so a few words about them are in order before turning in more detail to ads for giving blood and buying bonds.

"The Greatest Mother in The World" and Friends

To the federal government during the war, people paying their income tax in full and on time was as important as their buying War Bonds. By the early 1940s paying one's taxes was an automatic exercise for most people, so not many ads encouraged them to meet what was then the March 15th deadline. Still, this timely influx of revenue was of enough concern by 1942 that, at the bidding of Treasury Secretary Henry J. Morgenthau Jr., Irving Berlin wrote the song "I Paid My Income Tax Today" that told people to be proud their tax dollars helped build war materiel (see Jones 200). In the *Post* on March 6, 1943, the Stewart-Warner Corporation took out a two-page ad on a similar theme. The ad didn't urge paying taxes on time but contrasted free Americans with people's oppression elsewhere. It took the tack that "WE ARE PRIVILEGED to pay— and to work and earn and have what others of the earth only dream of having. [. . .] the privilege of paying is so small a price for the right to live in safety" (51). This was the sole ad devoted exclusively to the wartime rationale and importance of income taxes.

Community Chest—forerunner of the United Way—was once the agency in many cities that collected and disbursed funds for various philanthropies and service organizations. The brainstorm of a priest, two ministers, and a rabbi in Denver in 1887 as a way to deal with the city's welfare needs, Community Chest got its name in 1919 in Rochester, New York ("United Way"). By World War II there were close to a thousand local Community Chests, but no national organization. The war prompted a spin-off of Community Chests variously known as the National War Fund and the Community War Fund that collected and allocated funding for nineteen war-related service agencies including War Prisoners' Aid, the USO, and the American Red Cross, even though the latter two did much of their own fundraising. Two ads soliciting money for the War Fund appeared in the leading magazines, both in *Time*. A month after its striking War Bonds ad in October 1943 (see below), New York's Waldorf-Astoria hotel ran an ad on November 15 with just the words "NATIONAL WAR FUND / *Match Their Gallantry With Your Giving*" (80). With more copy and a drawing of an American POW reading in a Nazi prison camp, the American Seating Company on October 23, 1944, urged contributions to the Community War Fund by describing the workings of agencies it supported, primarily War Prisoners' Aid, which "provides text books, courses of study and other comforts that strengthen the hope of those who are cut off from the pursuit of American ideals" (77).

Also providing comfort to GIs away from home, but usually under less strained circumstances, was the United Service Organizations, universally known just by its initials USO. Established only months before the United States entered the war, in February 1941, this nongovernmental organization depended for funding on corporate and individual donations. The USO quickly became best known for sponsoring entertainment for GIs far and wide and for serving coffee, donuts, and camaraderie in its canteens stateside and abroad, but USO services for the military extended much more broadly. Although the USO's activities, indeed its very existence, depended wholly on private giving, only one ad soliciting contributions appeared during the war in the national magazines. In the *Post* on November 25, 1944, Hart Schaffner & Marx pointed to the loneliness of servicemen away from home and how "You can help them. You can give them a Happy Thanksgiving and Merry Christmas, warm with lights and laughter, familiar food and friendly voices. For their home-away-from-home . . . the U. S. O. . . . has done a really great job in this war and deserves your whole-hearted support, personal, as well as financial" (99).

In 1881 nurse Clara Barton founded the American Red Cross and headed it up for twenty-three years thereafter. From the caption for artist A. E. Foringer's compassionate 1918 poster of a larger-than-life Red Cross nurse cradling in her arms a wounded soldier, stretcher and all, the Red Cross became known as "The Greatest Mother in the World," well into World War II in at least one of the handful of ads reaching out for donations. That ad, incidentally, was placed not by a commercial advertiser but by the Red Cross itself in *Newsweek* on March 3, 1944. While best known on the home front for its blood donor centers and for delivering the processed blood plasma to base and field hospitals, this particular ad emphasized other wartime activities of the Red Cross, mostly describing how "every week the Red Cross will carry to [each American prisoner of war] a carton of food. Yes, eleven full pounds of real American food, the kind you used to give him at your own table. And real American cigarettes and tobacco!" (103). The operative and carefully chosen word in that statement was "carry," for as we learn from a Red Cross appeal placed by the White Motor Company in *Time* on April 9, 1945, while "to send these packages requires millions of dollars," the "contents of the food parcels are paid for by the U. S. Government" (63). Still, since the Red Cross was an independently funded relief agency, those millions of dollars had to come from somewhere, and that somewhere was the American public.

Among the remaining few Red Cross appeals was a tribute to Elizabeth Schuller, one of the first American Red Cross workers to hit the beach at Normandy, placed by Avon Cosmetics on page 106 of *Ladies' Home Journal* for March 1945. Two other ads detailed in words and pictures the kinds of assistance the Red Cross gave GIs and their families both during the war (American Cyanamid Company, *Newsweek* 1 Feb. 1943: 55) and after the boys returned home (Commercial Solvents, *Time* 27 Nov. 1944: 91). Nearly all Red Cross ads contained some variation of the message "Keep Your Red Cross at His Side," but the most vivid slogan, one that could have served as the banner for all personal giving campaigns throughout the war, appeared at the bottom of the White Motor ad: "THE MOST WE CAN GIVE IS THE LEAST WE CAN DO." Despite so few national advertising appeals for funds, nothing suggests that a lack of contributions kept the Red Cross, USO, and other agencies from carrying out their missions in support of American servicemen and women at home and overseas.

While purely conjectural, one or both of two things might help explain the paucity of such ads for donations. First, since the Red Cross and the rest worked mostly through local chapters, they may have found that direct mail solicitations and advertising in local or regional, rather than national, print media, were most effective. Second, they knew that whereas a donation to the Red Cross or the USO was an outright gift, buying a War Bond was an investment, a loan the government would pay back with interest, as discussed more fully below. Accordingly, they may have thought it futile to try diverting people from putting large sums of money into interest-bearing bonds. The only return these agencies could offer on a gift was the personal satisfaction of knowing one had helped them help American GIs.

"From Your Heart to His"

Personal satisfaction was also the only positive return one could get for giving blood to save wounded GIs, something ad agencies traded on when encouraging people to do so, with such phrases as "Think of it as from your heart to his" and "send some of yourself to the front" (Tobe Deutschman Corp., *Time* 6 Mar. 1944: 101; Philco, *Time* 31 July 1944: 8). Though the ads articulated the need, most appeals for giving blood were comparatively bloodless, lacking the passion and intensity of the majority of ads for War Bonds or recruiting women into the workforce. The earliest such ads late in 1942 were matter-of-fact "scientific" explanations of how blood was collected, transformed into stable plasma, and reconstituted for transfusions. Some were brief: "The life-saving part of the blood you give is called plasma. It is used for the treatment of the gravest complication of war wounds . . . shock. Science has discovered how to preserve plasma and ship it to the battle fronts of the world" (Carrier Corporation, *Post* 12 Sept. 1942: 72; *Time* 21 Sept. 1942: 81). Other explanations were lengthier, such as that by Parke, Davis & Company in *Life* on December 28, 1942, which filled two full pages with copy and illustrations that included information explaining the advantages of plasma over whole blood transfusions: "This dried plasma can be 'reconstructed' into wet plasma suitable for injection almost immediately. It needs no typing. It needs no refrigerating. And it can be administered anywhere . . . even directly behind battle lines" (41). The Parke, Davis ad further described the process by which plasma "is separated from the blood cells, frozen, and then dried" and packed into vacuum-sealed containers for transportation to the front. It also listed the twenty-four cities with blood donor centers where one could go to give blood (the number rose during the war to thirty-five). But nowhere in the two-page spread was anything like an impassioned appeal for giving blood. By and large, the same held true as the number of blood donor ads swelled during 1943 and 1944 to just about a dozen each year.

About the most personal or emotional tone in blood donor appeals occurred in such words as those following a picture of two medics carrying a wounded soldier on a stretcher captioned "EIGHT MINUTES BETWEEN LIFE AND DEATH": "*You* can help bridge that time-and-blood gap between life and death. At this very moment, perhaps your son or your brother—or the kid who delivered the morning papers—is in that gap. Here's how you can help tide him over" (Telechron Electric Clocks, *Collier's* 30 Oct. 1943: 60). But most often the ads appealed more to intellect than emotion, using such reasoned arguments for giving blood as "*Plasma*, plus the sulfa drugs, *has reduced the death rate of wounded men from the World War figure of 7% to 1% or less*" (Telechron, *Collier's* 15 May 1943: 41). Many ads reassured readers that almost anyone could give blood and that doing so was quick, painless, personally rewarding, and patriotic: "There is no risk, no pain. It takes about 45 minutes and is one of the most humanitarian and satisfying acts you can do" (Owens-Corning Fiberglass Corporation, *Newsweek* 4 Oct. 1943: 71; *Time* 11 Oct. 1943: 57); "You can donate blood—as patriotic thousands are doing—five times during a year" (Tobe Deutschman, *Time* 6 Apr. 1944: 101).

The majority of blood donor ads were sponsored by less generally familiar companies engaged in war production, including some such as Penn Automatic Controls, Commercial Solvents, York Refrigeration, and Taylor Instruments that manufactured equipment used in the processing, storage, or transportation of blood plasma. Also, counting ads published in more than one magazine, fourteen blood donor appeals—more than a third of the total—appeared in *Time*, *Business Week*, and *Newsweek*, publications with a large readership in business and industry. By comparison, the general interest magazines *Collier's* and the *Post* each ran only seven such ads, *Life* six, and *Look* only two.

The dispassionate tone in blood donor ads was not entirely universal. One sponsored by Munsingwear in *Look* on January 11, 1944, blatantly struck at the reader's sense of guilt. A picture of a simple white cross on some Pacific island captioned "Don't let this be *your* fault" was followed by three paragraphs of copy in that vein (8). More gently, two ads appealed to the feelings of generosity and "goodwill toward man" that millions of Americans annually feel around Christmas, something even greater numbers of War Bond ads also did. The entire copy of the Westclox ad in the *Post* for December 25, 1943, proclaimed "THE MOST TIMELY GIFT OF ALL . . . a pint of your blood to save a fighter's life," while a York Corporation ad took a few more words to say, "There is no better time than now, in this Christmas Season to make the greatest gift we mere civilians have ever been privileged to present. When your very own life blood goes to war it does *more* than bring Victory nearer, it helps to bring back to us more of our bravest and best" (*Time* 6 Dec. 1943: 84; *Business Week* 11 Dec. 1943: 4).

A Taylor Instruments ad proved that humor can indeed be found in all things. Placed in an unlikely venue for levity—*Business Week*—on March 3, 1945, the ad's lightheartedness effectively conveyed its serious message. (This ad was also only one of two blood donor appeals in the leading national magazines during what would prove to be the final year of the war.) In the first of four frames of this cartoon ad, a husky blue-collar worker first in line at a blood bank says to a top-hatted plutocrat behind him, "Imagine me giving a loan to a bank!" (89). "It ain't nothing to lend *dough*. I'm doin' that too, in war bonds, all I can afford. But there ain't no satisfaction like lendin' a pint of blood to the blood bank. You'll get it all back a million times if you save just one kid's life!" In the second frame the working stiff is having his temperature and blood pressure taken, remarking, "Why they even pay you . . . with a free physical examination that would set you back three bucks in any doctor's office." Next, he's lying on a table with a nurse prepping him to have his blood drawn, and our hero utters the ad's funniest line, "And then if them swell looking nurses ain't raised your blood pressure too much, you go on and make your blood donation," this prefatory to his sales pitch for blood donors, "It's so easy you don't even know you're doin' it, hardly. All you do is lay there and rest—and wonder why *everybody* don't do it!" In the final frame, he's back home showing off his blood donor button to his wife and three kids, saying, "I figure sendin' a pint of my blood overseas is the nearest thing I can do to goin' myself!"

The Taylor Instruments ad wasn't the only one to equate giving blood with buying bonds. Revere Copper and Brass ran a fairly extensive series of ads featuring the photographs and stories or words of actual disabled veterans. Most of the series urged buying War Bonds, as will be seen in the next section. But an ad in the series on July 10, 1944, in *Newsweek* appealed for blood donors by telling the story of Platoon Sergeant James H. Hearn who "had 15 blood transfusions . . . so far" after losing the use of both arms to Japanese gunfire (69). At the end of Sgt. Hearn's narrative, the copy concluded with a strong, thought-provoking analogy between giving blood and buying bonds: "*If we offer blood for plasma, nature gives it back. If we lend money for Bonds, Uncle Sam pays it back. It doesn't seem like too much that these men [combat soldiers] are asking us to do compared to what we ask them to give.*"

"Back the Attack"

Tommy Dorsey's 1942 jukebox hit "Dig Down Deep" with vocal by Frank Sinatra and the Pied Pipers encapsulated the message, if not the wording, of the huge number of ads asking the home front to buy War Bonds (see Jones 198–99). Even without the ads on the radio and in newspapers and other print media, bond ads in just the leading magazines comprised the largest body of war ads asking for personal support by civilians. To do full justice to the role in the war effort of this large group of ads and their techniques and strategies for performing that role would require a full-color album of several hundred such ads with descriptive notes and commentary for each one. Since this is impossible, we will have to make do with a rather more summary yet still detailed account of War Bond ads. But first a few words about the bonds themselves, both to help explain the function and methods of bond ads and to clarify any erroneous notions or misconceptions about War Bonds among twenty-first-century readers.

In 1917 and 1918, the government issued Liberty Bonds to help pay for America's involvement in World War I, and after the fall of France in 1940, the Treasury Department promoted its new Defense Savings Bonds to the public to help fund increased defense production (Perrett 71). (The name Defense Bonds, incidentally, hung on in some bond ads in the first year of World War II.) But the money raised between Liberty Bonds and Defense Bonds was little more than the proverbial small potatoes compared to the huge sums Washington asked for—and got—from the home front over the four years of the war.

According to historian Ronald H. Bailey, the war cost the United States over $330 billion in military and related expenses (all figures are in terms of the dollar's face value at the time). *Minute Man*, the monthly magazine that the Treasury Department's Savings Bonds Division distributed to its "field force," published data showing that enormous sum was significantly aided by Americans buying about $185.7 billion worth of bonds, nearly $131 billion of that bought by banks, insurance companies, and other big corporations. But Mr. and Mrs. Home Front and their kids accounted for close to $40 billion by buying lower denomination Series "E" War Bonds and War Stamps (January 1946: 18). Secretary Morgenthau got things going by personally selling the first Series E bond to President Roosevelt on May 1, 1942. I mention the kids since their contribution was not inconsiderable; between what they bought on their own and through drives in schools, America's children purchased over a billion dollars worth of War Stamps and Bonds (Bailey 108, 122). Their doing so did not go unnoticed in wartime advertising.

What is important to remember about War Bonds, how they were often marketed, and what made buying them so attractive to both individuals and corporations is that they were loans, not outright gifts, contributions, or taxes. Accordingly, purchasers would in time—especially upon or after a bond's maturity—receive a substantial return on their investment. These government-issued bonds came in all shapes and sizes. Those bought in amounts of millions, or, at the very least, hundreds of thousands of dollars by banks, insurance companies, and corporations ranged from long-term bonds maturing in twenty-six years and paying 2½%, through a "medium term obligation" 2% bond due in September 1952, down to a ⅞% one-year certificate (*Business Week* 3 Apr. 1943: 104). While the sums of money raised for the prosecution of the war through such financial instruments were tremendous, the bonds sold to the business and banking community are least relevant here since virtually no ads in the leading magazines promoted their sale. In fact, only one ad, the Metropolitan Life Insurance Company's in *Time* on September 6, 1943, even mentioned that large corporate entities bought War Bonds: "Through investment in Government Bonds, your life insurance companies are helping to finance the war effort. Metropolitan, for example, has invested substantial sums for the benefit of its policyholders" (5).

Promotional campaigns to the public were all for the small but mighty Series E Bonds with their face values of $25 to $1000, as well as War Stamps, their little pipsqueak companions that sold for 10¢, 25¢, 50¢, $1, or $5 each. One pasted them into a book and turned the full book in for a $25 bond at the going rate of $18.75. That going rate, which was 2.9% for a bond held to maturity, applied to Series E bonds of all denominations. The bond yielding $25 ten years after its date of purchase became emblematic of the entire bond drive. It was most often mentioned in ads, when any dollar amounts were mentioned at all, with the $100 bond costing $75 not far behind. To help prospective bond buyers visualize the extent of their investment, ads often contained a statement like "For every $3 you invest in War Bonds, you get back $4 at the end of 10 years" (Ipana Tooth Paste, *Farm Journal* Apr. 1943: 49). Even though eighty-five million Americans bought bonds by the end of the war ("Ad*Access"), Series E bonds sold to individuals represented only about 22% of the total revenue from wartime bond sales.

Still, Washington went to great lengths to encourage people to buy them, both in advertising and poster campaigns originating with government agencies, and, primarily, through advertisements sponsored on the radio and in print media by commercial advertisers. With commercial advertisers carrying so much of the burden by paying for radio airtime and advertising space in magazines and newspapers, the government saved enormous sums of money publicizing War Bonds and Stamps. As early as September 1942, when speaking of an exhibit of war ads at the Department of Commerce, Undersecretary Wayne C. Taylor was able to say, "The good effect of such advertising is incalculable. The money it represents is tremendous. For instance, in just one type of advertising shown here—the promotion of war savings bonds and stamps—the Treasury Department estimates that it has received free publicity which would cost $65,000,000 if purchased" (*Business Week* 12 Sept. 1942: 94). And that was just when the United States had been at war less than a year! That advertisers' expenditures for War Bond ads were evidently money well spent was reflected in a mid-1943 survey showing that 82% of the public thought that advertising "has done a good job of selling war bonds" (*Business Week* 19 June 1943: 96). In addition to helping finance the war, Washington saw value in War Bonds as vehicles for giving home front civilians an immediate sense of personal participation in the war effort, patriotism, and their place in national unity. And, most especially, since the public's collective disposable income far outstripped the number and kinds of consumer goods available, the Treasury Department welcomed people's investing in the bonds as a healthy check against runaway inflation.

From the time War Bonds went on sale on May 1, 1942, to the end of the program on January 3, 1946, the home front's men and women, boys and girls, could buy War Savings Stamps and Series E War Bonds whenever and nearly wherever they chose, at banks, post offices, and retailers from department stores to the corner drug store, as well as at booths manned by War Bond volunteers at public gatherings from fairs and sporting events to patriotic celebrations and War Bond rallies mounted, usually in major cities, with considerable frequency. Also, employees of large companies could, and in great numbers did, enroll in payroll deduction plans, the usual deduction being 10%, though many workers opted for higher percentages of their pay to go toward bonds. Payroll deduction was one of the most successful schemes for channeling individuals' money into bonds on a regular, ongoing basis. According to *Business Week* on the early date of October 17, 1942, over twenty million workers were already participating in payroll deduction, and in that September alone their deductions tallied up to $265 million (90).

Yet despite all this activity, the government, chiefly in the person of Treasury Secretary Morgenthau and his crew, mapped out a plan for a series of vigorous War Bond drives in order to further stimulate bond buying by both individuals and large corporate and banking investors. Over the course of the war there were seven such numbered drives (each called a "War Loan") spaced out at irregular intervals, plus a final "Victory Loan" after the war (originally designated the Eighth War Loan before Japan surrendered) to help pay for bringing the troops home, medical care for wounded veterans, and all else needed to wrap up the business of the war. Each war loan had a goal or "quota" of the total amount Washington hoped to see invested in bonds from institutions and individuals combined. Following are the salient data about the seven War Loans and the Victory Loan, most taken from Duke University Library's advertising website "Ad*Access," with a few missing dates filled in from various *Business Week* articles. The figures in the final column represent the amount raised during each war loan just from the sale of small denomination Series E bonds, the bonds at which most advertising was aimed, here rounded off from a table on page 4 of *Minute Man* for January 1946.

WAR LOAN NAME	DATES	QUOTA	TOTAL RAISED	SERIES E
First War Loan	Nov. 30–Dec. 23, 1942	$9 billion	nearly $13 billion	$726 million
Second War Loan	Apr. 12–May 1, 1943	$13 billion	over $18.5 billion	$1.5 billion
Third War Loan	Sept. 9–Oct. 2, 1943	$15 billion	almost $19 billion	$2.5 billion
Fourth War Loan	Jan. 18–Feb. 15, 1944	$14 billion	$16.7 billion	$3.2 billion
Fifth War Loan	June 12–July 8, 1944	$16 billion	$20.6 billion	$3 billion
Sixth War Loan	Nov. 20–Dec. 16, 1944	$14 billion	$21.6 billion	$2.8 billion
Seventh War Loan	May 14–June 30, 1945	$14 billion	$26 billion	$3.9 billion
Victory Loan	Oct. 29–Dec. 8, 1945	$11 billion	over $21 billion	$2.2 billion

★ ★ ★ The many ways of looking at magazine ads for War Bonds all yield productive results about everything from the aesthetic of their art (and even some of their copy) to the strategies ads employed for getting the public to buy bonds to the overall place of advertising in selling War Bonds and Stamps to the home front. To begin, I pruned from my database of roughly five hundred War Bond ads those that included nothing more than an "almost worthless" Plug in a Slug (Wharton 146) like "Buy War Bonds" tucked in an obscure corner of the ad. My pruning reduced to about 287 the number of War Bond ads of some substance; these form the corpus of bond ads for nearly all further observations about them.

A basic way to look at War Bond ads is purely chronologically, in order to see how many appeared when during the war. Year by year for the four years of the war, the number of bond ads in the ten leading magazines forms something close to a perfect, if steeply rising and falling, bell curve: 33 ads in 1942; 106 ads in 1943; 96 in 1944; 48 in 1945. These figures confirm one's initial guess that most bond advertising occurred when the need for revue from War Bonds was most urgently needed, namely, during the two middle years of the war. It is also telling that, except in 1944 when about half the bond ads appeared during War Loan drives, advertisers placed far more bond ads during the rest of each war year than during the drives. This says that commercial advertisers thought putting money into ads urging people to buy bonds at any time was more important than sponsoring such ads during the War Loans themselves since the government would drum up enough hoopla and ballyhoo for its bond drives on its own. Even during 1944 and 1945 when the number of bond ads placed by commercial advertisers during official bond drives measurably increased, the numbers show that there was no let up in year-round bond advertising to offset the extra expense of more fully supporting the bond drives. With respect to seasonal bond sales, each Christmas season during the war advertisers placed specially designed Christmas War Bond and Stamp ads in national magazines to suggest bonds as gifts to family and friends in lieu of the usual presents. Christmas bond appeals occasioned some especially creative art and copy, whether spiritual, sentimental, or just plain cute—all effective approaches to selling bonds.

★ ★ ★ Still looking at War Bond ads quantitatively, but now intrinsically rather than extrinsically, a fair bit can be learned about them and the advertisers placing them by examining the relative amount of space the ads devoted to the actual promotion of War Bond sales. To do this I divided the roughly five hundred War Bond ads according to the categories the War Advertising Council came up with to describe all kinds of war ads plus one category of my own that emerged during my reading of all the bond ads. Starting from the bottom up and as already mentioned, roughly two hundred bond ads were just a Plug-in-a-Slug buried inconspicuously somewhere on the perimeter of an ad. Next up the ladder was the Ad Council's category of the Sneak Punch, in which an advertiser included "a war theme by working it deftly into his product copy" (Wharton 78). The copywriters for International Sterling were especially adept at this, employing it a number of times. In the International ad in *Life* on March 19, 1945, a woman watching people on a city street ruminates about her sweetheart-soldier returning from the war, their getting married, making a home together, and, of course, starting their collection of International Sterling silverware: "When I see two people laughing together, I think someday *we'll* laugh like that. The hats I buy are to make your eyes light up . . . the War Bonds, to bring you back to me sooner. My window shopping is for the house we've planned . . . " and on and on, approaching stream of consciousness, but with War Bonds tucked neatly into the midst of her thoughts. Not nearly so adroit but more typical of the Sneak Punch, an ad by Libby's showed how to economize by stretching meat with Libby's canned fruits and vegetables, and, at one point, how to turn leftovers into bonds: "Using leftovers is an economy too, and economizing is a duty, for every penny you save means that much more you can put into War Stamps and Bonds" (*Post* 13 Feb. 1943: 39). Sometimes a Sneak Punch was tacked on as a sort of afterthought at the end of the main body of the copy. An example from very short copy is the ad for Kayser hosiery in *Life* on October 4, 1943. A stylishly dressed woman says, "I can do without less if it's Kayser because I depend on the quality of Kayser hosiery . . . and buy more bonds" (16). A Sneak Punch closes an ad with much more copy (and art) in a cartoon ad by Sanforized in *Life* on November 1, 1943. A wife carries on a running tirade at her husband about his extravagant shirt-buying habit. He tries to defend himself by pointing out how fast all his shirts shrink. She enlightens him to shrinkless shirts treated with the Sanforized process. He finally says, "I get it — and with the money I save we buy War Bonds. Right? Right!" (1). Twelve such Sneak Punch ads for War Bonds appeared during the war.

In my own category of Space Sharing, the War Bond appeal was more central to the entire copy of an ad than in the previous two types, but it shared its place with appeals for one or more other kinds of citizen support of the war. The Hart Schaffner & Marx ad in *Collier's* on October 9, 1943, urged "We're all in this war together * Let's *redouble* our war effort. * Let's *buy* those extra Bonds we've been thinking of buying . . . *make* that appointment at the blood bank . . . Let's do our own job, and then help out on farms, in factories . . . wherever we can * And let's do it *cheerfully!*" (67). Powerfully effective Space Sharing that for good measure threw in a double whammy at people's Christmas spirit occurred in one of Revere Copper's disabled veterans ads in the *Post* on December 4, 1943. A large photograph of Private Celester Harnden Jr. of Michigan lying in a hospital bed, his bandaged left arm amputated between the wrist and elbow, was captioned "Lend a hand . . . he gave one." The ad asked readers to look in the private's eyes and honestly say they are doing enough to support the war: "If you have to hesitate, then lend a hand! There's so much for us civilians to do. There's plasma needed for the blood bank; salvage has to be collected; the Red Cross needs support; the black market must be stamped out. Always more and more War Bonds must be bought. And if buying War Bonds seems to interfere with your plans for Christmas . . . Remember there is no Christmas on the battlefield" (45). There were thirteen such Space Sharing ads for War Bonds.

The Double-Barrelled ad for War Bonds doesn't require much explanation since we have encountered this type of ad numerous times already, just conveying different kinds of war messages. Such an ad, in the words of the Ad Council, simply contains "a war theme and sells merchandise to boot," and to the Council such ads were "just as effective as the 'All-Out'" (Wharton 78, 146). Advertisers placed forty-two Double-Barrelled ads promoting War Bond sales in leading magazines throughout the war. Finally, there were the All-Outs themselves, those ads in which all of the art and copy was devoted to War Bonds, save for the advertiser's name and sometimes a very brief squib about the company's role in war work. Impressively, 220 of 287 substantive War Bond ads were All-Outs, meaning that 77% of bond ads were paid for by companies concerned enough about selling War Bonds that they didn't sell their own products or even promote institutional goodwill in the same ad.

★ ★ ★ Three aspects of the art and copy of War Bond ads are particularly useful for understanding the ads' role and effectiveness in persuading individual civilian sales of bonds: (1) what the ads were asking or encouraging people to do; (2) what reasons the ads gave them for doing so; and (3) what approaches, strategies, and techniques the ads employed for urging the home front to, in contemporary parlance, "get on the Bond wagon." The first of these is almost as simplistic as it seems, but not quite. Yes, War Bond ads asked people to buy bonds, but even early in the war some also asked people to purchase *more* bonds than they already had, as bluntly stated at the end of the appeal by the Barrett Division of Allied Chemical in the *Post* on November 7, 1942, "Buy more bonds!" (107). The number of ads encouraging people to buy more and more bonds increased as the war went on, as did the intensity of the appeals, reflecting the ever-increasing need for more funding for the war. Most of the ads asking people to augment their previous bond buying came in 1944, such as Studebaker's in *Time* on February 14 urging people to help the Fourth War Loan reach its goal: "Remember, we're only *lending*— they're [our troops] *risking everything*! Let's buy and buy more and more Bonds—and hurry them home!" (13). But it didn't take official War Loans for bond ads to rev up their rhetoric asking folks to up the ante: "How many of us are *doing* something about [the war] by purchasing our *full* share of war bonds—*every week, every pay day—and* ALL *we can possibly afford*?" (Bauer & Black, *Life* 31 May 1943: 64).

In addition to getting people to buy bonds and yet more bonds, from late 1943 until close to the end of the war, magazine ads took up a new, seemingly difficult, and very critical challenge—getting people to hold on to the bonds they already owned and not cash them in to buy necessities or luxuries. As there was more and better news of Allied successes and, especially, just before the fall of Germany until after its formal surrender on May 7, 1945, Mr. and Mrs. Home Front were redeeming their War Bonds at an alarming rate. And we're not just talking about pocket change. On July 28, 1945, *Business Week* reported with some alarm that in the weeks just prior to the start of the "Mighty 7th" War Loan, as it was christened, "E bonds were being redeemed at a rate equal to about 45% of their sales" (85). It didn't sit well with the government that the home front giveth, the home front taketh away, so Washington and commercial advertisers marshaled their forces to encourage people to hang on to their Series E bonds, at the same time continuing to ask them to buy even more. As early as the Third War Loan, in *Time* on September 13, 1943, the Cast Iron Pipe Research Institute urged in big bold type, "**BUY MORE WAR BONDS—*and hold them*"** (82). Appealing to patriotism (and maybe a little guilt) during the Fourth War Loan, the Gruen Watch Company argued, "when you cash any War Bond now, you pull your money out of the fight. You make deserters of your dollars—a coward out of your cash" (*Life* 24 Jan. 1944: 68). And, among the urgent appeals late in the war, in the Glenmore Distilleries ad in the July 1945 *Esquire*, a picture of a rainbow leading to a stack of $100 bonds contained just four unambiguous words: "BUY THEM * KEEP THEM" (19). How much advertising influenced people's retention of War Bonds can't be known, but despite the rush to cash them around the time of Germany's defeat, *Business Week* more happily reported on August 25, 1945, "Thus far, the Treasury reports, more than 84% of all the E bonds sold since May 1941 have remained uncashed" (78).

The reasons advertising gave the home front for buying War Bonds are nearly identical to the earlier mentioned values the government saw in bonds beyond raising money for the war. Some ads incorporated several reasons, others focused on just one. To start with the most abstract or philosophical reasons, a fair number of ads, especially early in the war, sought to get people to buy bonds by invoking their patriotism and/or desire to help ensure the American way of life: "To help preserve those sacred traditions which are so precious a part of the lives of all of us—to help preserve the priceless freedoms of America—will you invest as much as you possibly can in United States War Bonds and Stamps?"

(Westclox, *Post* 12 Dec. 1942: 1). In contrast to this rather matter-of-fact statement, most ads on this theme contained much longer and often emotionally charged or sentimental copy. The art in United States Steel's Christmas ad in the December 1942 *Ladies' Home Journal* depicted a father bending over a crib to look at his sleeping infant son and saying, "While you were sleeping, young John J., I just went out and bought Christmas! Bought the 4th of July, too, while I was about it. And Thanksgiving—and hot dogs—and pink lemonade. I bought those ball games we're going to see together. And the long quiet twilights when you catch fireflies and I cut the grass. I bought a share in the right to continue the American way of life for your lifetime, sonny—and for generations to come. I bought you a War Bond" (119). Long appeals to patriotism and preserving the American way continued on occasion later in the war, possibly no better than in the Caterpillar Tractor ad in *Collier's* on September 9, 1944, featuring an eye-catching color illustration of a farmer looking out over his expansive fields in autumn. The copy, too long to quote in full but on view in fig. 47, began with "This is what a man can tie to" and ended with "*I am protecting my future as an American with every War Bond I can buy*" (57). Also indirectly appealing to people's patriotism and not really needing illustrative examples were ads during the several War Loans urging bond buying to help each drive meet its goal.

Similar to the patriotism/American Way motif, some ads gave as a reason for buying bonds people's heightened sense of participation or inclusiveness in the war effort and their personal place in national unity: "It helps satisfy your emotional longing to do your bit for the cause. It gives the thrill that makes you feel you belong to the War effort—the certitude, the assurance that, multiplied by all other War Bond buyers, yields the indefinable something we call 'Morale'" (P. R. Mallory, *Newsweek* 27 Sept. 1943: 9; *Time* 27 Sept. 1943: 103). Other ads I have come to call "generational" played on the inclusiveness theme almost entirely through art depicting a parent or grandparent and a child together pasting War Stamps into a book. Canada Dry sponsored several such ads. One of the more affecting showed a little girl with her granddad in his American Legion uniform engaged in this activity (*Ladies' Home Journal* Feb. 1943: 132; *Collier's* 13 Feb. 1943: 73; see fig. 48). Other ads showed just a child buying a stamp or bond, with an admonition for adults to do the same. The prime example was the Auto-Lite ad in *Time* on June 12, 1944, and the *Post* on June 24. A snippet of an actual news story reprinted

This is my Birthright!

This is what a man can tie to. No matter how black the casualty lists, or how long victory is in coming; no matter how truth is twisted to selfish ends; no matter how the effort of the nation seems to flounder: *here I will make my stand.*

No power on earth can shake my faith in this land which is my home. Its beauty and its bounty are part of me. I have breathed the free wind that blows across its mountains and prairies, woods and farms. *It has given me liberty to make a life in my own way. To work, to build a home and raise my children, to worship God as I see fit.*

I am sick of all wars, and who is not? I am worried about my fighter sons, and discouraged by long-drawn months of uncertainty. But there is an inner depth of my spirit that has never faltered.

I will keep on and I will do my best. My job, my gifts of blood to the Red Cross, the money I lend to my Government are small things by themselves. But I am not alone. There are millions of others like me—quiet, unimportant people, *willing to give all they have to keep their country free. I am protecting my future as an American with every War Bond I can buy.*

 CONTRIBUTED TO THE WAR EFFORT BY CATERPILLAR TRACTOR CO., PEORIA, ILLINOIS

56

FIGURE 47

Battlefront There it is—on the table—your theatre of war. Those stamps are your bullets—those books are your guns. When you've filled them, they'll speak in tones the whole world will hear—and know that an American home has not failed its sons at the front. As an old family friend and welcome guest in the home, Canada Dry says: let freedom ring—with all the War Bonds and Stamps you can buy.

If sometimes you can't get all the Canada Dry Ginger Ale you want, please don't blame your dealer. Wartime restrictions on bottle caps, sugar, and particularly on fine imported ginger make it difficult for us to keep up with the growing popularity of Canada Dry, "the Champagne of Ginger Ales."

CANADA DRY "THE CHAMPAGNE OF GINGER ALES"

FIGURE 48

in the ad describes the full-page photo of a tiny two-and-a-half year-old girl in North Carolina pouring a torrent of coins on a counter to buy not stamps but a whole $25 War Bond, all of this captioned "LITTLE SANDRA LYNN *has joined the fight . . . have YOU?*" (*Post* 48; *Time* 100).

The few ads devoting any significant space to War Stamps alone or along with bonds all seemed to do so, albeit tacitly, in the spirit of promoting inclusiveness in the war effort. Not just to get children to save their pennies for War Stamps, but, by implication, they invited participation by those adults for whom it would have been a financial hardship to scrape together at one time the $18.75 needed for a $25 E Bond. In its 1943 Christmas ad Hoover added to its listing of the dollar amounts of all the Series E bonds, "Whether you choose the Bond with the picture of Washington, Jefferson, Cleveland, Wilson, or Lincoln, or the Stamp at 10¢, 25¢, 50¢, $1, or $5, you'll find the exact 'size' for the Christmas stocking you want to fit" (*Life* 16 Dec. 1943: 10). In ads in the *Post* sponsored by the Insurance Company of North America on October 30 and November 27, 1943, one showed a child pasting a War Stamp, the other a kid counting out change to buy one. The text of both ads was devoted almost entirely to War Stamps. Headed, respectively, "Mary Jane's quarter won a battle" and "Bill's quarter will save 2000 lives," the copy dramatically demonstrated how even small amounts of money help to fight the war.

Throughout the war a few ads used flat-out urgency as reason enough to buy bonds. Early on, in copy aimed at the nation's farmers, Allis-Chalmers in the August 1942 *Farm Journal* urged, "The time to set the trap [for the Axis] is *now* . . . with WAR BONDS bought every time you take eggs or produce to town" (49), just as late in the war, and addressing a more diverse audience, Ansco film & Cameras cautioned in a Space Sharing ad, "**We must not relax!** Continue to buy all the War Bonds you can! And *keep* them! Continue to give blood! *Don't let down on your paper salvaging efforts!*" (*Life* 16 Apr. 1945: 9; *Post* 21 Apr. 1945: 93). But more ads included specific things about the war to help convince people to buy bonds, such as telling them what their bond money would buy. It was commonplace for ads just to list such things as tanks, planes, and ammunition, but some others were considerably more offbeat or creative. In a plan worked out with the Treasury Department and the War Advertising Council, a great number of War Bond ads were designated "Published in Cooperation with the Drug, Cosmetic, and Allied Industries." A specific member of the industry sponsored each ad, and sometimes different companies placed the same ad in different magazines (see *Business Week* 29 Aug. 1942: 49). One such ad sponsored by Vicks in the January 1944 *Ladies' Home Journal* came up with a most unusual reason to buy bonds: "Forgetting for a moment the tanks, planes, bullets, and bayonets we must send to our men, think of just this one item: SHOES. The millions of pairs of shoes our men must have over and over again" (73). Oldsmobile made vivid a number of instruments of war in small pictures with captions like "You help supply these anti-aircraft guns — and train the men who use them" (*Esquire* Apr. 1943: 3; *Life* 22 Feb. 1943: 5). A very original ad placed by Parke, Davis in *Life* on June 7, 1943, showed in six drawings and accompanying copy how bonds help save American boys as well as kill the enemy: "Training and maintaining Navy nurses and pharmacist's mates take hundreds of thousands of dollars. Approximately $66.00 per month is needed to house and feed each nurse. 42 civilians each investing $18.75 in a $25 War Bond will support one nurse for one year" (45).

Also in the drug industries' group, an ad sponsored by Ipana Tooth Paste in the April 1943 *Farm Journal* brought what bonds buy for the war down to the personal level, with a touch of throat-catchy sentiment thrown in. A farmer stops his truck to give a lift to a neighbor's little girl walking to town to sell a basket of berries she picked. The girl tells the farmer that the store will probably pay a dime for them like yesterday and the day before: "'That's fine, Dot,' I said, 'and you'll be just in time for the movie.' She looked at me, surprised, and said, 'But it's not for the movies, it's for a War Stamp. You get them at the Post Office!' I felt sort of funny. 'That's right,' I said, '— a War Stamp. For Uncle Sam.' 'But it's *not* for Uncle Sam!' she replied, impatiently. 'It's to go for a bond to buy bullets and things for my brother.'" (49). Later in the long copy the farmer and his wife decide to make his overcoat do for another year and buy a $25 bond instead: "It's for Uncle Sam, of course, but especially it's for my nephew in the Navy. You'd be surprised how much better you feel when you do it that way."

Closely allied to showing people what investments in War Bonds bought for the prosecution of the war, and appearing more frequently in ads, was the argument that the more bonds people bought, the more they could help shorten the war. The rationale was that the more funds from War Bonds for building war materiel and training troops, the better equipped American forces would be to bring the conflict to a speedy conclusion. Yet this connection between paying for weapons of war and hastening victory was openly articulated just once, in Hardware Mutuals' Christmas and Sixth War Loan ad in *Time* on December 4, 1944: "The purchase of 6th War Loan Bonds is equivalent to the greatest of all gifts to our friends and loved ones on the fighting front, because it speeds the weapons and materials they need to shorten the grim remaining task" (57). More often, even when an entire ad was about bonds, shortening the war as a reason for buying them was rarely central to the copy but was a stand-alone slogan like "Let's Shorten the War!" or a tag at the end. In a Caterpillar ad in the *Post* on Jan. 15, 1944, an elderly mailman contemplates quitting his job not because he can no longer take all the walking but because it has become too painful for him to watch "white, stricken faces" as people more and more frequently opened an official letter beginning *"The Secretary . . . desires that I tender his deep sympathy . . . "* (50). This emotional copy concludes with, *"Save lives, save hearts—save every cent you can spare from what you earn—in War Bonds and Stamps to speed the end of war!"* Ads giving shortening the war as a reason to buy bonds were numerous from late 1942 until just before American and other Allied forces began to get mired in the grueling Battle of the Bulge on December 16, 1944, but, curiously, even before the Allied troops finally emerged victorious on January 16, 1945, all such ads abruptly ceased.

Some ads offered reasons to buy bonds that were more purely personal than global. Generally speaking, people don't like to spend more money for things than they spent on the same items in the past, whether these are things they need or simply want. Accordingly, advertising that showed how buying War Bonds could help curb the potential for inflation caused by wartime conditions fell upon some willing ears. The big anti-inflation campaign was a joint effort of the War Advertising Council and the Treasury Department, and accordingly, their frequent and widespread magazine ads are beyond the scope of this account of war ads by commercial advertisers. Still, a few companies took up the anti-inflation cause as a reason to buy bonds. In most instances, the brief copy both convincingly and lucidly explained the relationship between buying bonds and inflation: "Many Americans have extra income at their disposal these days. It's money that could be a menace to all of us, for too much spending at a time when civilian merchandise is limited would naturally shove prices sky-high. Fortunately, we have in War Bonds a ready-made device that can stop Inflation. Every dollar you put in this safest of investments is a dollar which you will have for necessary post-war purchases, and a dollar which will no longer help shove prices out of reach" (SKF Ball and Roller Bearings, *Business Week* 2 Oct. 1943: 2); and, even more succinctly, "[Bonds] help hold prices down today by keeping dangerous surplus money out of circulation" (International Nickel, *Time* 5 June 1944: 65; *Business Week* 10 June 1944: 11).

Many on the home front were attracted to buying bonds for the return they'd realize on their investment. Accordingly, numerous ads included this most personal of motives for buying War Bonds. Some of these ads attached buying bonds to people's future ability to purchase brand-name goods that were unavailable or scarce during the war. These will be considered along with other kinds of ads about what I call "future goods" in the epilogue. But even without these ads, many others stressed bonds as investments, briefly or at length: "Sacrificing to buy extra bonds is the *least* we at home can do to back them up. Sacrifice? You'll get $4 back for each $3 invested" (Wickwire Spencer Steel Company, *Time* 19 June 1944: 84); "Your country asks you to dig down deep to invest in United States War Savings Bonds that you may redeem or hold after the War, and on which you receive interest for all the time you hold them. After the War, they will provide for your old-age security, your children's educations, and peacetime pleasures such as travel, vacation, and rest," presuming, I suppose, that one bought a whopping pile of bonds (W. A. Sheaffer Pen Company, *Collier's* 30 Jan. 1943: 9). Most ads touting bonds as investments were more realistic, some even playful. Under the headline "**Look . . . the Smiths are building a new home**," the whimsical art in a General Electric ad shows a whole family (including the cat) shingling a roof with War Stamps and raising walls of War Bonds; the serious copy ends, "Look at it this way. U. S. War Bonds and Stamps are common sense savings . . . Four dollars at maturity for every three invested now. After Victory, your Bond purchases can be used as part payment on the kind of a home you have always wanted . . . *with everything in it that makes a real home*," stopping just short of mentioning GE appliances (*Collier's* 6 Feb. 1943: 41; *Look* 9 Feb. 1943: inside front cover).

Of all approaches to presenting financial gain as a reason for buying bonds, the most prevalent and specific were the detailed lists of the investment features of War Bonds contained in sidebars to all the bond ads prepared for the Drug, Cosmetic, and Allied Industries and sponsored by various member companies. The main body of these ads made the case for buying bonds from various angles, some quite emotional, but the sidebar lists were pure facts. The items varied a bit from list to list, but typical is that in an ad that otherwise tried to get people to buy bonds by blasting complacency and overconfidence about the war (Pepsodent, *Time* 19 July 1943: 6; Hoffman-La Roche, *Life* 8 Aug. 1943: 34):

FACTS ABOUT WAR BONDS

1. War Bonds cost $18.75, for which you receive $25 in 10 years—or $4 for every $3.
2. War Bonds are the world's *safest* investment—guaranteed by the United States Government.
3. War Bonds can be made out in 1 name—or in 2, as co-owners.
4. War Bonds *cannot* go down in value. If they are lost, the Government will issue new ones.
5. War Bonds can be redeemed, in case of necessity, after 60 days.
6. War Bonds begin to build up interest after 12 months.

These lists in the drug industries' frequent ads came closer than any other war ads to advertising's time-honored method of "selling" a "product" by describing its benefits for the prospective customer.

★ ★ ★ If, overall, War Bond ads gave readers about a half dozen different reasons for buying bonds, the artists, photographers, and writers who created the ads employed as many or more strategies and techniques to make their bond messages vivid and persuasive. The simplest was the inclusion of a memorable slogan. Some companies created one that appeared nowhere but in the company's own ads, such as West-clox's "Victory won't wait for the nation that's late" and *Business Week*'s "YOU'VE DONE YOUR BIT . . . NOW DO YOUR BEST," but one slogan eventually superceded all others. Accompanied by two different Axis-bashing cartoons showing Tojo and Hitler being buried by bonds, two Philco ads a week apart plugging the Third War Loan announced, "Beginning September 9th, the battle cry of America's home front is, '*Back the Attack— with War Bonds.*'" (*Time* 30 Aug. 1943: 16; *Life* 6 Sept. 1943: 1). Philco couldn't have been more correct. Shortened to "Back the Attack," this became the rallying cry for bond sales not just for the Third War Loan but all year round at least through the fifth War Loan in the summer of 1944. A dozen or more companies from Exide Batteries and Philco itself to

Three Feathers whiskey and Upjohn made it a prominent part of their War Bond ads. Catchy and to the point, "Back the Attack" also found its way onto posters and into popular songs promoting bond sales.

One technique employed in War Bond ads doesn't readily fall into any specific category but consisted simply of art and usually brief copy combining to make a very compelling statement. The most prolonged and elaborate example of this was a series of fourteen Timken Roller Bearing Company ads in the *Post* between August 1943 and July 1945. Each ad featured a full-color, nearly full-page portrait of a different American admiral or general, some signed by the artist, some not, beneath which were usually just a few words like "SUPPORT GENERAL EISENHOWER—BUY WAR BONDS!" If ever there were war ads "suitable for framing," these were the ones, as may be seen in Dean Cornwell's especially striking painting of Admiral Nimitz on page 83 of the *Post* for January 15, 1944 (fig. 49). This ad differed only slightly from the rest in the series in its comparatively longer copy. Some of the most impressive pairings of exceptional art and copy in individual ads were almost minimalist, one not even mentioning War Bonds directly or depicting anything to do with the war. On October 18, 1943, the ad for New York's opulent Waldorf-Astoria hotel consisted of only a picture of the imposing structure at night with its windows lighted and above it the words "You want them Back— / Back them Up" (78; see fig. 50). Nearly as succinct and just as powerful, the Auto-Lite ad in *Life* on November 11, 1943, superimposed on a grim picture of six GIs carrying a flag-draped coffin the brief text "He didn't count the cost . . . should you? Back the attack with WAR BONDS" (123; see fig. 51). On a warmer note, in *Collier's* for December 25, 1943, the Three Feathers whiskey ad depicted two lit Christmas candles on a mantelpiece and between them three Series E Bonds tied with a bow to look like the feathers on the advertiser's whiskey labels, the only copy, "first among fine Gifts . . . War Bonds" (2).

Speaking of whiskey, such an alliance of art with very brief copy ingeniously turned one distiller's familiar long-running logo from selling booze to selling bonds. Long before the war (and for a long time thereafter), ads for I. W. Harper Kentucky Straight Bourbon Whiskey featured a picture of a consummate gentleman in frock coat, ruffled cuffs, and walking stick, bowing slightly at the waist, tipping his top hat in greeting, and saying, " . . . *it's always a pleasure*." But starting on July 26, 1943, always in the pages of *Life*, with understated gentility the I. W.

Admiral Nimitz is Banking on You

American fighting men by the millions are expecting us at home to turn out war equipment and to buy War Bonds to the very limit. When you buy Bonds you help pulverize the enemy—yet make a sound investment and get your money back with interest. Buy an extra War Bond today.

The Timken Roller Bearing Company, Canton, Ohio

FIGURE 49. Reprinted by permission of the Timken Company.

FIGURE 50

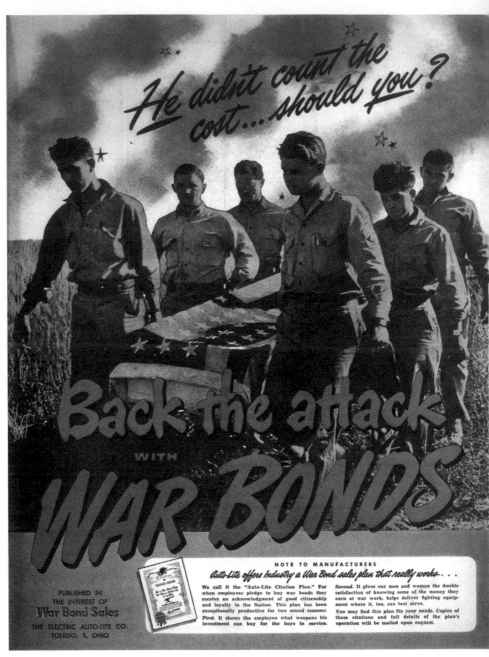

FIGURE 51

Harper man began saying politely, first, " . . . *may I suggest you buy more U. S. War Bonds today?*" then for Christmas that year, "*may I suggest the best gift of all, U. S. Bonds,*" and later " . . . *may I urge you to hold on to all the War Bonds you buy,*" all the way to June 5, 1944 (inside back cover; see fig. 52). Certainly a genteel, low-key bond campaign, but likely an effective one given the high recognition value of the I. W. Harper man.

★ ★ ★ One specific strategy admen occasionally used to sell war bonds was to tap into people's wartime feelings of fear and/or guilt. Some of these, mostly by the Stewart-Warner Corporation, bordered on scare tactics, but to the credit of its ad agency, like all Stewart-Warner ads on many topics throughout the war, their art and copy were always riveting and powerful. Three of the Stewart-Warner ads unabashedly used fear to motivate buying bonds. In the earliest and most innocuous, in *Collier's* on October 10, 1942, a Polish immigrant factory worker gives a long harangue to his co-workers, saying, among other things, "If you had no letter from *your* family in three years, I think you would buy bonds! [. . .] We have it so fine in America. The poorest of us are rich here, because we are safe—to sleep at night and do our work and eat well. But *they* can come *even here*. And if they do—you will know how beasts can kill and laugh. And then you will learn to hate—*when it is too late*" (51). Another ad, also in *Collier's*, made even more vivid the prospect of the enemy invading the United States. The illustration showed a Japanese soldier barging into an American home, a young mother cowering behind the door with her daughter clinging to her. The long copy didn't mince words: "Would you rather wait until *you* hear the whistle of bullets before you *loan* money to buy guns . . . to keep the skies clear of hostile planes . . . to keep the filthy hands of the Axis off your wife or daughter?" (27 Feb. 1943: 63).

If Stewart-Warner had a monopoly on selling bonds through fear, an array of other prominent national advertisers played on people's guilt to get them to buy bonds, the number of such ads exponentially increasing as the war went on. Stewart-Warner itself placed four such ads between September and December 1942, three in *Collier's* and one in the *Post*. Each was set in a public place like a hotel lobby, the club car of a train, or a country store, in which a righteously indignant character similar to the Polish-American factory worker above becomes enraged by someone's remark like "I'll be damned if I spend another dollar for bonds or anything else," and launches into a tirade that would stir guilt in anyone

*. . . may I urge you to hold on to
all the War Bonds you buy.*

it's always a pleasure

I. W. HARPER

the gold medal whiskey *since 1872*

Distilled in peace time and Bottled in Bond
under the supervision of the U. S. Government.

Kentucky Straight Bourbon Whiskey, Bottled in Bond, 100 Proof. Bernheim Distilling Company, Inc., Louisville, Kentucky

FIGURE 52

short of Ebenezer Scrooge (*Collier's* 19 Sept. 1942: 77). By 1943 guilt-tripping became more concise. Even Coca-Cola, its ads usually pretty benign, declared on the back cover of *Life* on April 5, 1943, "And no matter what anybody is doing to help (this doesn't go for fighting men) nobody is doing his full share if he's not buying U. S. War Bonds and Stamps regularly. Are *you* buying them?" By 1944 Revere Copper and Brass repeatedly poured it on in some of its disabled veteran ads: *"How's your conscience? A few more war bonds, some blood donations, extra war work might make it easier"* (*Business Week* 4 March 1944: 87); and, accompanying a photo of Pfc. Charles Gvozdich, who lost an eye in combat, *"What has it cost you so far to do YOUR part?"* (*Life* 14 Aug. 1944: 78). Arguably the most vivid guilt ad was General Tire & Rubber Company's in *Collier's* on June 16, 1945. Under a nearly full-page photo of an exhausted marine resting during the battle for Peleliu Island, the entire copy just asked, "Could you tell him you're tired of buying WAR BONDS?" (10; see fig. 53).

Jumping into the wrangling about what properly constitutes "sacrifice" discussed in Chapter 7, some bond ads argued that nothing the home front did could be called a sacrifice compared to what combat GIs were willing to give up in order to win the war, while still urging people to give till it hurts when it came to buying War Bonds. Yet other ads, related to guilt ads, openly used sacrifice to motivate bond buying. Most of these ads were in the group prepared for the Drug, Cosmetic, and Allied Industries that had the blessing, if not direct copywriting input, of the War Advertising Council and the Treasury Department. Their methods varied but their message remained the same. One sponsored by Pepsodent in *Life* on April 19, 1943, specifically addressed the girls back home—the fiancées, wives, and sweethearts of GIs—reading in part, "You're going to make sacrifices—real ones—aren't you? You're going to give up many things you've dreamed of—that lovely coat—that cute little hat! And with the money you save—you're going to buy *U. S. War Bonds!* Your bonds will help *your* sweetheart! They'll help to put a machine gun in his hands—a gas mask in his pack" (6). The Ex-Lax ad in *Life* on November 8, 1943, ended powerfully, "How are *your* ethics today? Anything less than your complete and willing sacrifice is, in plain talk, sabotage" (18), and the Hoffman-La Roche ad in *Life* on July 3, 1943, concluded, "If you're buying as many War Bonds as you can conveniently fit into your budget—you're not buying enough. For war isn't a matter of convenience—but rather of sacrifices" (20).

*Actual photograph of
tired Leatherneck on Peleliu Island*

Could you tell him you're tired
of buying WAR BONDS?

★ ★ ★ THE GENERAL TIRE & RUBBER COMPANY • AKRON, OHIO

FIGURE 53

★ ★ ★ The three primary art and copy techniques that informed most War Bond ads were the same ones movies, popular songs, and radio programs employed to keep the home front emotionally connected to the war—moving dramatic narrative, humor, and, perhaps above all else, sentiment. None of these, of course, was the private property of bond ads alone. Dramatic narrative, for instance, was the heart blood of the chaplains' heroic exploits in Hammond Organ's series of ads and, in institutional ads, in stories by rubber companies telling how one of their bullet-proof rubberized gas tanks allowed a fighter pilot to safely land his bullet-strafed plane. The difference between these stories and those in War Bond ads lay in their function, the latter used to stir people to buying bonds. Since most "war stories" in bond ads are far too long to bear full quotation here, a brief one told by Chief Signalman Willard A. Murphy in one of Revere's disabled veteran ads in *Time* on June 19, 1944, will have to serve as an example: "I count myself lucky. I just lost a leg. There were eighty of us. I'm one of four who survived. That's paying at the rate of 95%. When the Japs can do that with just one shell, you've got to agree they're not as cross-eyed as some folks make out. Take it from me, they're tough! Thank the Lord they lack our imagination and initiative. We can't have too many ships, ships with a great big wallop behind them if we want to win soon. The Navy can deliver that wallop—but *you* have to provide it" (64). The ad wrapped up with just two short sentences: "*They gave 95%. Is 10% for War Bonds too much for you to give?*"

Humor may seem an odd device for selling bonds, but evidently a number of national advertisers didn't think so since they took the comic approach in not just one but several of their War Bond ads, all of them cartoon style except for Borden's. At least two of the Borden Double-Barrelled ads were funny on behalf of both bonds and dairy products. In the funniest, in *Life* for November 27, 1944, Elsie the Cow tried to console her always-grumbling husband Elmer the Bull after he flunked an army physical and was told by the doctor to "stay home and buy War Bonds" when all he wanted to do, he said, was "to shoot Japs . . . lots of Japs!" (10). Very early in the war, when War Bonds were still called Defense Bonds, buying them shared center stage with Pepsi-Cola in an almost wordless three-panel cartoon by O. Soglow. In the first panel four people are running like mad from right to left toward an outstretched arm holding a bottle, the unseen vendor crying "PEPSI-COLA." All that is visible in the second panel is another arm, this one holding a bond poster, its owner out of sight on the right yelling "DEFENSE BONDS." In the final frame the same four people are running back from left to right, with a Pepsi in one hand and a wad of money for bonds in the other (*Look* 24 Feb. 1942: 6). One ad in Sanka Coffee's Double-Barrelled series that combined spreading war messages with selling decaf took on buying War Bonds and did so with a comic vengeance. As in the other Sanka cartoon ads, the anything but subtle War Conscience berates a woman for buying a hat instead of a bond—no, not just berates her, forcibly yanks the hat from her head right in the shop. War Conscience doesn't let up until the lady is convinced to switch to Sanka and buy bonds not just during bond drives (*Life* 20 Aug. 1945: 60).

More than any other companies, two advertisers repeatedly placed humorous War Bond ads—Gripper Fasteners and Gem Razors and Blades. Before the war Gripper was a leading manufacturer of the little metal snaps that, among other things, held up men's underwear shorts. Gripper's war work made the snaps unavailable and that in turn inspired some clearly off-the-wall cartoonists and writers to have fun selling War Bonds. Most of the rhymed copy was hilarious and the cartoon art outrageously silly. In each ad a funny little man gets distressed that his shorts keep falling down because the ineffectual wartime buttons pop off. To solve this, he starts buying War Bonds to bring home our GIs and Gripper Fasteners for his droopy drawers. Between March 1943 and March 1945, Gripper's silliness appeared in nearly twenty different ads in the *Post*, *Esquire*, and *Collier's*, two of which may be seen in fig. 54, the ad on page 87 of the *Post* for March 15, 1944, and the one on page 33 of *Collier's* for October 16, 1943. Although other cartoon ads for bonds employed multiple frames, those sponsored by Gem Razors and Blades consisted of just a single panel, in the manner of most cartoons in magazines like the *New Yorker*, *Collier's*, *Esquire*, and the *Saturday Evening Post*. In fact about half of the Gem cartoons were drawn by noted *New Yorker* cartoonist Peter Arno, and the others, some unsigned, and some by Herbert Roese, who followed Arno's distinctive, more than slightly risqué style. Always at the center of the proceedings was a girl, very busty, very big-eyed, and very flirtatious. Gem used these repeated characteristics in cartoons for selling both War Bonds and razor blades, which, thanks to some ingenious copy and the fun in the art, the ads did simultaneously, as seen in the Roese cartoon on page 6 of the *Post* for June 30, 1945 (fig. 55).

FIGURE 54A

FIGURE 54B

FIGURE 55

★ ★ ★ Since the value placed on sentiment during the war years was so much higher than it is today, sentimental copy and art figured large in War Bond advertising in order to touch readers' emotions. As in many bond ads that opened with a dramatic narrative, the copy in a lot of ads employing sentiment is too long to quote in full, and its impact depends on reading the whole thing. But the quality and tone of the sentiment in many others can be seen from brief excerpts or summaries. For Christmas 1943, Hamilton Watches employed a kind of "split-screen" effect in which a flyer on the left and his young wife in a nurse's uniform on the right are reading letters announcing their presents to one another. The flyer reads, in part, "To Tom (wherever your Christmas is) — For wanting to go . . . and not wanting to leave me. For the goodbye you didn't say . . . and the 'see you soon' you said. For the silly, solemn will you made . . . and the 'beloved' before my name." The nurse reads, "For understanding why I had to go. For that last day we had together. For the laughs in all your letters . . . and the love between the lines. For running a home without me . . . and a hospital ward besides." Both letters lead up to the husband and wife saying that their Christmas gift to each other is a War Bond (*Esquire* December 1943: 14; *Life* 29 Nov. 1943: 65). In a Eureka ad in *Life* on April 1, 1944, a letter from a GI to his wife employed at Eureka, judging by her uniform, embedded bonds directly into his sentimental words to her: "Here's something I want you to do, darling. I want you to buy an extra War Bond and put both our names on it. And when you've bought that extra bond . . . I want you to buy yourself a dress . . . something soft and something blue. Because *out here* that's how I think of you — and thinking of you I think of all the fun we'll have together when I come home . . . buying things for the most wonderful house in the world . . . our house, the house I'm going to build for you" (63). Easy Washer's Christmas ad in *Collier's* for December 26, 1942 (it hit the newsstands earlier), has a young wife looking adoringly yet a bit tearfully at the partial profile of her husband, telling him in fairly long copy that although she always used to cry when she opened her Christmas gifts from him, "Know why I didn't cry this time? When I unwrapped the War Bond, with your sweet note pinned to it, I was so proud of you I couldn't *remember* to cry" (57). She then re-reads his note, thanks him for the practical gift in times like these, tells him what she plans to do with it when it reaches maturity after the war, and ends by saying, in the ad's charmingly sentimental ending, "O, darn! Where's my hanky? I *am* going to cry!" (57).

Judging from the number of them, bond ads including children were a surefire guarantee of effective sentiment. In an ad placed by Clark Grave Vaults in the October 1944 *Farm Journal*, a returned GI carrying his pigtailed daughter piggyback up the stairs to bed replies to her saying "It seems, now, like you were home all the time, Daddy," with a long list of the ways he was really always "home" with her even when away at war, finishing with "Yes, I was with you, *all the time*. For a person is where his *heart* is, Sally. And a soldier's heart is home" (55). A totally separate bond appeal followed. Similar, and with truly delightful art, was the Studebaker ad in *Time* on June 26, 1944. In the picture another returned GI is met at the garden gate of his home by a happy cocker spaniel and a very little boy saying, "ARE YOU MY DADDY?" to which he replies, "Yes, sonny boy, I'm your daddy—the daddy you don't remember because you were just a few months old when I left for war" (7; see fig. 56). The copy picked up from there to discuss the preservation of the American home and American values and the role that buying bonds had in doing so. Quite the opposite of these cheerfully sentimental ads was one placed in *Time* by the Bryant Chucking Grinder Company on June 11, 1945, that definitely came down on the grim side of sentimental. The genuinely creepy art titled "*LOST*" was a drawing of a tiny boy and even tinier girl holding hands as they walked through a forest of menacingly tall trees, just a few shafts of sunlight cutting through the ominous shadows. The copy in its entirety read, "We are all the boys and girls whose fathers have been killed at war . . . and will never come home again. We who are lost ask only this of you: Please, please buy another bond. Buy it and keep it—for our sake" (103). Between ads depicting the joy of children whose fathers returned from the war and the utter desolation of those whose fathers would never come home, yet more children with fathers still at war played a pivotal role in ads asking people to buy bonds to help bring our boys home sooner. Two of these were truly memorable, one with long copy, the other with almost none. The advertiser that placed the first must have known how effective it could be, since the Chesebrough Manufacturing Company, maker of Vaseline brand products, placed the same ad three times in 1944, on page 12 of *Look* for November 28, page 6 of *Collier's* on December 9, and page 4 of *Life* on December 11. Promoting the 6th War Loan and titled "When?" the ad's art showed an anxious looking boy and girl peering out the window of a house displaying a service flag with a single Blue Star. The copy was

"ARE YOU MY DADDY?"

"Yes, sonny boy, I'm your daddy — the daddy you don't remember because you were just a few months old when I left for war."

War is heartless, little man. It doesn't give much heed to family ties. But, along with millions of other men and women in uniform, your daddy is certainly doing everything he can to keep another war from starting when you're grown up and have children of your own.

* * *

None of us in civilian life can match the sacrifices that fathers away from home and fireside — and many others in uniform — are making for us on the fighting fronts.

But this much we all *can* do . . . we can make sure that the America they're fighting for stays strong. We can help them protect the way of life they left behind by putting every dollar we can spare into U. S. War Bonds.

It's more than good Americanism to invest to the limit in War Bonds . . . it's good business. Let's buy more Bonds than we planned, now during the 5th War Loan Drive . . . *and let's keep on doing so!*

THE STUDEBAKER CORPORATION

Builder of Wright Cyclone engines for the Boeing Flying Fortress . . . multiple-drive military trucks . . . other vital war matériel

FIGURE 56

FIGURE 57

about equally divided between a catalogue of all the children have missed since their father has been away and a declaration of how bond buying could help bring him back sooner. The second ad was placed by Auto-Lite on page 51 of *Time* on February 7, 1944, and page 56 of *Collier's* on February 12. As seen in fig. 57, the ad could serve as a case study for both understatement and how sentiment can be engendered visually as well as verbally, the entire ad consisting simply of the close-up full-page photo of an irresistibly adorable yet very sad little girl, and, beneath it, just six words of copy: "Please help bring my daddy home" plus, at the side, "Published in the interest of the 4th WAR LOAN."

Reading this, someone is probably thinking "I feel manipulated," now that sentiment has been devalued and manipulation has only a negative meaning for people who object that devices in plays, TV shows, and movies elicit emotions in them they'd rather not admit having. Yet emotional manipulation has always been a part of playwriting and fiction. And of advertising, too, where it has perhaps its most legitimate place since ads exist to "manipulate" people to do or buy something. With buying bonds just about the most important thing people could do for the war effort, it was only natural for admen to pull out every manipulative stop in their repertoire to sell them. What could be bad about *that?*

★★★ **EPILOGUE**

THE WORLD OF TOMORROW

Throughout the war, creative civilians like songwriters and admen showed they had a better grasp of wartime psychology than did Washington bureaucrats. As early as July 1942 the OWI began a campaign to steer Tin Pan Alley away from writing "boy-and-girl roseate stuff" and "peace-and-ease songs of the future" as "the kind of drivel that might handicap the fighting and winning of the war" (*Variety* 15 July 1942: 3; see Jones 10–12, 289–92). But the songwriters ignored the OWI, and civilians and GIs alike embraced such songs as hits since people needed uplifting, personal goals in their minds and hearts to sustain their morale during a long and difficult war. Later, the War Finance Committee gave public voice to its own mission as killjoy. In the words of *Business Week* on June 9, 1945, "The War Finance Committee is taking precautions against advertising copy that urges bond-buying now merely as a vehicle for temporary savings to be used in postwar family buying programs. The 'buy bonds now and use them to finance your post war plans' theme [. . .] is frowned on because enough war bonds are being cashed without further encouraging such a trend" (69). Admen were about as deaf to the WFC as songwriters to the OWI.

Jumping the Gun

Not a common word today, but during the war "reconversion" was nearly as familiar to the average American as to the industrial and business community, to which it meant the conversion of industry from the manufacture of war materiel back to making products for peacetime. To Mr. and Mrs. Home Front, reconversion had the connotation of things simply getting back to normal.

Even granting it takes time to retool from making tanks to making refrigerators, some advertisers jumped the gun to promote goods and services for industrial reconversion long before an Allied Victory was assured. News magazines in late winter and early spring of 1944 show that Americans knew that in the not-too-distant future there would be an Allied invasion of Europe of much greater magnitude than those that began in Sicily on July 9 and in Italy on September 9, 1943. But, of course, no one but some government and military officials knew just when or where this would occur. As invasion was in the air, so was reconversion. Industrial ads were full of it long before what became D-Day on June 6, 1944.

About two months before that fateful day, in *Business Week* for April 8, 1944, under a picture of its distinctive building on Wall Street and a Plug in a Slug for War Bonds, Bankers Trust Company ran an ad of just three lines: "Loans to Business and Industry / for war-work, reconversion / and post-war programs" (1), even though no one could forecast when the postwar period might begin. Under the headline *"Today's Production Needs! Tomorrow's Reconversion!"* in *Time* on June 5, 1944, the Louden Machinery Company detailed what its "Overhead Material Handling Systems" had done to facilitate war work: "Where Louden serves today . . . will be the scene of rapid reconversion and plant rearrangement tomorrow. It is not too late to meet the needs of today and the demands of tomorrow with flexible, adaptable Louden Overhead Handling" (100). And the Johnson Bronze Company in *Time* on September 25, 1944, headed its ad "BE PREPARED FOR RECONVERSION." The copy described how proper "sleeve bearings" would be critical for reconversion from war work to peacetime production and how Johnson Bronze could supply all that any industry might need (87). While these advertised financial services, industrial equipment, and supplies were no doubt legitimate components of industrial reconversion, the ads came along too early, during a wave of premature home front optimism about an end to the war. As proof, fewer and fewer reconversion ads appeared as the war lingered on until August 1945.

The Future Lies Ahead

This deliciously absurd platitude immortalized by trenchant satirist and stand up comic Mort Sahl aptly describes certain ads promising American consumers what they could have after the war—ads that still read more like fiction than fact. The advertisers were all prominent national firms, so there's no question that they were trying to hoodwink the public with false promises. In fact, the reason not just to ignore these fanciful, futuristic ads is to show that the advertisers must have believed that postwar prosperity would make their products accessible to middle-class Americans *immediately*, not in some distant, foggy future. Most such ads were by companies involved with the aviation industry. But the earliest, in *Life* on October 19, 1942, came from Revere Copper and Brass, touting the use of copper in urban or, to be precise, suburban planning. The ad showed a young, well-dressed, middle-class couple looking from a height down on suburban homes and a larger building in the distance. Explaining this, and forming most of the ad's long copy, was a quotation from Lawrence B. Perkins, a partner in the Chicago architectural firm of Perkins, Wheeler, and Will. Clearly *not* referring to inner city dwellers on the one hand or residents of today's retirement communities or affluent "gated communities," Perkins said, in part, *"What a single family cannot possibly afford, a group of families can easily possess. After the war we will make the discovery of what this can mean for happy living. Neighbors can have a swimming pool, a gymnasium, a little theatre, a hobby shop with power tools, in a community building within walking distance of tomorrow's home"* (109), as well as meeting rooms, library, and other amenities seen in a blueprint and drawings throughout the ad. Except for YMCAs, Jewish Community Centers, and similar facilities typically funded by nonprofit organizations in urban areas, such centers of community life have yet to emerge on a grand scale across the suburban American landscape.

Aviation company ads promised both luxury public air travel and private aircraft ownership. In *Life* on January 8, 1945, Martin Aircraft told how its huge Mars transports—the biggest planes in the sky—could be converted to peacetime air travel: "Operating as a fleet of luxury liners, 20 Mars transports could afford complete living facilities for 1600 passengers on non-stop flights of 24 hours duration" (83). The ad's "complete living facilities" conjures up a vision of each passenger having something like a compartment on a Pullman car or small cabin on a cruise ship. Needless to say, it never happened.

Nor did several companies' vision of a private plane in every garage— or at least on a neighborhood landing strip and as common as the family car. The Consolidated Vultee Aircraft Corporation was fairly matter-of-fact about the American family's flying future in *Life* on November 6, 1944, describing how a new version of a small utility plane the army nicknamed the "Flying Jeep" would be available for civilian purchase after the war. Under a picture of mom and daughter in the family convertible waving to dad landing their plane, the copy began "Your postwar 'Flying Jeep' may not look exactly like this. But you can be certain it will be safe, easy to fly, and an economical family plane" (73). Other companies, including normally tough-talking Stewart-Warner, fairly waxed poetical about not just the joys but the reality of family planes. In *Time* on June 26, 1944, under a picture of a husband at a plane's controls and his wife in the co-pilot's seat, the copy ran "That's you in the driver's seat of your 194X family airplane. You're off for the weekend with the wife and kids. There are still 300 miles to go and the gas gauge says 'half full.' Your stomach says 'empty.' So, you drop down at Middletown for gas and a bite of lunch. As casual and commonplace as that! [. . .] Look forward to the days of peace when you and your family can take to the air . . . and travel far and fast in a bright, safe, new world" (73). Referring to a 194X plane, not, say, a 195X model or later, the ad confirms that manufacturers were projecting immediate realities, not vague future possibilities.

Cessna Aircraft Company, builder of light planes, was even more rhapsodic—and certain. In *Time* on June 26, 1944, Cessna claimed "most progressive communities are planning air parks" or landing strips for owners of private planes. But the real fun lies in the ad's headline "Scrapple for breakfast in Philadelphia / Then pompano for dinner in New Orleans," the ensuing copy stating that this isn't a "gourmet's dream" but "a personal transportation reality in your Cessna Family Car of the Air" (64).

"Buy War Bonds Today—an Electric Kitchen Tomorrow!"

Aviation's flights of fancy were relatively rare compared to the larger field of future goods advertising in which over two hundred ads for postwar products made more realistic promises of almost immediate fulfillment after the war. These ads divide into two broad types about equal in number and differing in only one key essential. The first type promised what consumers could once again have, whether waffle irons, automobiles, or improved telephone service, often describing how better products would result from what was learned during war production. The second type was virtually identical but intrinsic to the copy was a pitch to buy bonds as a way of saving for the advertiser's postwar merchandise.

To begin with the ads that factored War Bonds into buying future goods, a small and interesting group actually talked about consumer products generally, not just the advertiser's own brand. Five early General Electric ads attached bonds to people's dreams of better postwar living without being brand specific, running variously in *Collier's*, *Look*, and *Life* between early March and late May of 1943. Typical was one in *Look* on April 6 headed "*That dream home on* BOND STREET *will come true*": "You'll like living on Bond Street. Cool, green lawns, and children's laughter in the twilight. Tall, friendly trees, sheltering a houseful of happiness. You can start plans *today*. Stamp by stamp, bond by bond, you can build a home with comforts and conveniences far beyond your fondest dreams. For all those wondrous aids to Better Living that seem just fantasies now, will be *realities* tomorrow. [. . .] The War Bonds you are buying today are your Bond Street Building Fund. Invest all you can, all the time" (39). An ad by the J. G. Wilson Corporation, a manufacturer of steel doors for industry, is interesting since the firm didn't make any of the items mentioned in its ad in *Business Week* on March 20, 1943. Central was a two-column list headed "**A $1000 WAR BOND PAYS FOR:**" the "NOW" column citing several items of war materiel and the "AFTER THE WAR" column including "An extra plot of ground next to your house. A new roof. An extra bathroom. Extra finished rooms in the attic. New floors or floor coverings" (105). But overall, brand-specific future goods advertising held sway.

Almost all brand-specific advertising envisioning what people could buy after the war was published in *Life*, which was sound advertising sense and strategy. *Life* had both the largest circulation of any popular national magazine and a readership primarily of the kind of affluent, middle-class Americans who most likely would contemplate buying the sorts of big-ticket consumer goods generally featured in such ads. For a time in *Life* and occasional other magazines, two of the giants of the home appliance industry, Hotpoint and General Electric, seemed to be racing to see how many ads each could place about better electric living through buying War Bonds. In five ads from late June 1943 through early May 1944—all in *Life* except for one in *Look*—GE linked buying bonds with purchasing General Electric appliances, sometimes briefly, as in *Life* on June 28, 1943: "After Victory General Electric will go back to the job we know so well—*equipping homes for better living*—with even finer appliances. To make *your* wish come true . . . buy War Bonds—to the very limit of your ability" (49). At other times GE went into great detail, as in *Life* on November 8, 1943, when it described in minute particulars the features of GE's new electric dishwasher and garbage disposal and the pleasures to be derived from each (49). Hotpoint's "War Bonds for appliances" ads started on October 12, 1942, in *Life*, with nine more continuing through July 1943 when its last ads on the subject appeared, not in *Life*, but in *Ladies' Home Journal* and *Farm Journal*. The theme of the first Hotpoint ad was echoed in all the rest with just necessary changes in language or point of view: A woman says, "Every dollar I spend for War Bonds gives me a great big thrill of satisfaction! I figure I'm not only helping win the war but hastening the day when I'll be able to own the kitchen I've always dreamed about—a Hotpoint Electric Kitchen like Jane's" (9). Each Hotpoint ad also included the stand-alone slogan, with just slight variations, "BUY WAR BONDS TODAY—AN ELECTRIC KITCHEN TOMORROW." Although the Hotpoint copy—and there was a lot of it—remained similar from ad to ad, each ad included a different and very inviting picture of what a postwar Hotpoint electric kitchen could look like, as on page 17 of *Life* for December 7, 1942 (fig. 58).

Quite a few other makers of major appliances also ran ads promoting buying War Bonds to buy their postwar merchandise, but less frequently than GE and Hotpoint. Among these were Blackstone washing machines, Philco, Arvin small appliances and metal dinette furniture, Tappan gas ranges, Duo-Therm fuel oil heaters, Gibson ranges and refrigerators, and Stromberg-Carlson radio-phonographs. The approaches in these companies' ads and the ads of makers of other generally expensive merchandise varied considerably, some of it emulating the distinctive tone or personality of an advertiser's other ads. In *Life* on May 8, 1944, a middle-aged man with a cat on his lap is listening to the radio: "To Mr. Potter, music is relaxation from war work . . . To the girl whose husband has gone to war, music is a companion. [. . .] Tomorrow, all the richness of great music . . . all the elusive tonal qualities . . . will come to you through the postwar Stromberg-Carlson. [. . .] Your War Bonds will buy nothing finer!" (53). And International Sterling maintained the romantic quality of all its ads when, in *Life* on March 8, 1943, the young wife of a soldier talks about moving back in with her mother to cut down on expenses for the duration, putting her and her husband's things into storage: "yes, everything except the few pieces of International Sterling we got when we were married. I know it's silly of me to keep them out—but they mean something pretty special to me somehow. Not just because fine sterling is so lovely in itself. But because—well, that sterling silver is a kind of a promise of the home we'll have again when the war is over, when the money from our War Bonds will complete our set and buy the other things we've always talked about having" (48). The most

FIGURE 58. Reprinted by permission of General Electric.

elaborate presentation came from Universal household products. Its ad in *Farm Journal* for May 1944 and *Look* on October 17, 1944, proposed a plan for making postwar household purchases that began with reviewing the ad's list of thirty types of merchandise made by Universal and the range of their 1941 prices (e.g., Carving Sets $2.95–14.95)—the list covering washing machines to lunch kits. After tallying up the "estimated values" of what one wanted, one was to "put that sum into War Bonds" and take the checklist to a Universal dealer who would put him or her on a priority list for postwar purchases but with no obligation to buy (*Farm Journal* 65; *Look* 18).

Such specificity was an exception. Most advertisers contented themselves with including in their ads what I call "short takes" about buying bonds to buy their products, whether as a stand-alone blurb or incorporated into the more extensive copy of the add as a whole. All manner of manufacturers, not just those of big-ticket items, used these short takes. Accompanying a drawing of a happy family having breakfast around a metal-chrome dinette set, Arvin prclaimed, "**BUY WAR BONDS NOW . . . So You Can Buy This Later**" (*Life* 24 Aug. 1942: 108), and Duo-Therm Fuel Oil Heaters had a man in line at a War Bond booth saying, "Give me a Duo-Therm's-worth of War Bonds!" (*Farm Journal* Feb. 1943: 5). Other representative examples of this quick, snappy approach to encouraging buying one's material future with bonds included "For us it's . . . BONDS TODAY—*A TAPPAN tomorrow!*" (Tappan Gas Ranges, *Ladies' Home Journal*, Feb. 1943: 146); "SAVE WAR STAMPS AND BUY A ROADMASTER AFTER THE WAR" (Roadmaster Bicycles, *Life* 8 Nov. 1943: 128); and "Buy U. S. War Bonds Today—Tomorrow command your own Chris-Craft" (*Life* 31 May 1943: 119). Such bold, unambiguous equations between buying War Bonds now and buying generally high-priced goods later were likcly enough to rattle the War finance Committee to its very bones.

Happiness Is . . .

The other large body of future goods ads shouldn't have given the WFC much to lose sleep over since they didn't suggest buying bonds now to save for buying consumer goods after the war. Of course, readers of these ads probably also read those that did make that suggestion and acted accordingly. Many of the advertised items in this group were the same as in the other—big-ticket household appliances—and included some of the same advertisers, most prominently Gibson and GE, as well as a number of other major makers of stoves, refrigerators, and the like—among them Frigidaire, Westinghouse, Norge, Kelvinator, and Crosley. The copy in these ads is remarkably similar, with two themes prominent in most of them. First was the idea that what the manufacturer learned during the war will benefit consumers through better peacetime products: "Here at Kelvinator, when Victory is won, all the new strengths, the new abilities and skills born of war, will be turned to production for peace. That means Kelvinator will build even more and finer refrigerators, electric ranges, home freezers, and electric water heaters to make the kitchens of America the truly enchanted places they can be" (*Life* 9 Oct. 1944: inside front cover). But one ad stands out for its outlandishly hilarious art and caption (see fig. 59). On page 65 of *Collier's* for May 29, 1943, and page 49 of *Farm Journal* in June, Norge placed an ad captioned "This is how a NEW 1943 NORGE would look in your kitchen" accompanying a picture of a young married couple taken aback—to put it mildly—to see in the place their refrigerator should be a fully equipped revolving gun turret, complete with helmeted gunner, his sights and two huge guns trained on them. This was a funny and graphic way to say that Norge was now fully engaged in war work, but the rest of the copy was serious and straightforward, much like that in the other ads in this group: "When the guns are stilled, you can be sure that Norge thinking and Norge skill, stimulated by the stern school of war, will bring you even greater satisfaction, greater convenience than you have enjoyed before."

The second theme shared by this group of ads could be reduced to something like "Happiness Is . . . the latest appliances." Far beyond hyping their utilitarian functions, advertiser after advertiser stressed how such miracles of modern manufacturing "add so much to our American way of life" (General Electric, *Look* 28 July 1942: 29): "Westinghouse makes a pledge to a woman and her dreams . . . that some day, not too far distant, her life shall be richer and happier because . . . new electric products, appliances, equipment, shall bring her greater comfort and leisure in the days of peace to come" (*Life* 9 Aug. 1943: 41). Each Kelvinator ad featured a woman's lengthy reverie about her all-electric, all-Kelvinator, home, describing in almost poetic luxuriousness the joys of each individual appliance, and concluding, typically, "Oh it's easy to see how happy we'll be . . . when our days are filled with the peace of being together in our very own home . . . forever and ever," after which Kelvina-

FIGURE 59

tor added in its own voice, "This will be our part in the building of a greater, a happier nation" (*Life* 16 Apr. 1945: 57). In two ads specifically addressed to farmwomen, one naturally enough in *Farm Journal*, the other interestingly in *Life*, GE wrote of how "it's right and natural that they should dream of an easier, happier, more leisurely life in the days to come. Such a life *can* be theirs with all the work-saving, time-saving advantages of General Electric's home appliances" (*Farm Journal* March 1945: 62), after which each ad catalogued the kinds of happiness to be derived from five different GE products.

Other advertisers never made the "Happiness Is . . . " claim that was endemic in the ads of major appliance manufacturers, but instead were just descriptively matter-of-fact in announcing their postwar goods and services. Over a picture of six of its ranges and oil-burning heaters, the Florence Stove Company just noted that "as rapidly as the war permits, Florence will again produce all of these types of appliances. Take a peek!" (*Farm Journal* Apr. 1945: 75). A bit optimistically, considering the date of the ad, Wear-Ever Aluminum declared in *Life* on November 12, 1944, "The WEAR-EVER Aluminum You're Waiting for . . . will soon be homeward bound again. By the time this message reaches you, we hope production of Wear-Ever utensils will be only a few weeks away" (71). And Mobilgas let drivers know in *Life* on May 15, 1944, "After Victory— the same aviation power ingredients of 'Flying Horsepower' which have made possible the tremendous power output of airplane engines—will be made available to motorists in Mobilgas" (62). Like Mobilgas, Pullman and Bell Telephone concentrated on improvements in already existing services. In a number of ads, Pullman described sleeping cars newly designed to accommodate private "Duplex-Roomettes," in which "you'll lounge in comfort through the day and sleep in comfort through the night. [. . .] You'll have your own dressing quarters. Your own washing and toilet facilities. Your own individually controlled light and heat and air conditioning" (*Life* 28 Feb. 1944: 75). More simply, in *Farm Journal* for May 1945, and similarly in other issues, Bell Telephone promised a wide extension of rural telephone lines: ". . . as soon as conditions permit, many new devices and methods will be used to further improve and extend farm telephone service" (10).

Much less vocal about what consumers could expect from their postwar production were the nation's automobile manufacturers. Their ads were few, and they generally said the least of all future goods ads. Nash

Motors was one of the more voluble automotive firms in describing its postwar cars: "When Victory comes, Nash will go on once again to production for peace . . . from the building of engines of war to the making of two great new cars designed to be the finest, biggest, most comfortable, most economical, most advanced automobiles ever produced in their respective fields . . . the new Nash Ambassador in the medium-priced field, and the new Nash '600' in the low-priced field" (17).

One automobile ad, striking in its simplicity, is of genuine historical interest. As detailed at length in Chapter 3, throughout the war the Ford Motor Company never placed ads about its war production in *Life* as it did in *Collier's*, *Look*, *Newsweek*, and the *Saturday Evening Post*. If Ford acknowledged its war work at all in its rare ads in *Life*, it was only in a throwaway line such as "Ford assignments are now military," near the end of an historical narrative about the company or its founder that comprised the rest of the ad (*Life* 9 Oct. 1944: 22). Yet Ford chose to launch the national advertising campaign for its new postwar cars in *Life*, most likely on the advice of the new ad agency Ford brought on board in mid-1944, the almost legendary J. Walter Thompson. For the campaign, the J. Walter Thompson agency created a slogan that grew to almost mythic proportions in its familiarity. After appearing only locally in the *Detroit Times* on November 6, 1944, the nation at large first saw on page 11 of *Life* for December 11 the ad that was simply an upturned hand holding a crystal ball and, written across it, "There's a Ford in your future!" (see Lewis 382–83, 544 n. 25). In later ads the crystal ball showed a happy family picnicking or taking the car for a spin, but Ford's succinct slogan, arguably one of the most effective in wartime future goods ads, remained constant long after the war. In the annals of commercial advertising, that slogan was one of the few to achieve something like immortality.

Back Again!

On May 6, 1945, one day before the German surrender and two days before what officially became V-E Day, the War Production Board "picked the industries which will get first priorities assistance to speed reconversion." On May 25, *Business Week* published a list of seventy-one such industries prefaced by the explanation that manufacturing firms to receive such government assistance were "those which, by and large, undertook the greatest amount of conversion from normal peacetime production and will require the greatest amount of change to return to it again" (16).

Most items were listed under General Industrial Equipment, Machinery (Construction), and Plumbing and Heating, but Consumers' Durable Goods listed twenty-three types of products including domestic electric ranges, mechanical refrigerators, electric fans, photography equipment, flatware, domestic vacuum cleaners, clocks and watches, lawn mowers, small appliances, fishing tackle and reels, bicycles, and pianos. The list was a clear signal that such consumer goods would be back on the market before too long.

Yet not until after the Japanese surrender on August 14 did ads begin to appear in the leading national magazines announcing the new or renewed availability of these kinds of products and others, heralded by the Hoover ad in *Life* on August 27 proclaiming in large letters like those stenciled on packing crates, "NOW IN PRODUCTION" followed by "The *New* HOOVER CLEANER" and "Uncle Sam has given us the green light to manufacture and sell new cleaners" (91). This copy, like that in other such ads mostly in fall and winter, resonated with a kind of euphoric, celebratory mood worthy of a Victory parade—a mood, no doubt, that advertisers and their copywriters hoped would infectiously catch on with the buying public. Typical among such jubilant copy was Western Electric's "NEW TELEPHONES FOR YOU! *Full speed ahead on our biggest peacetime job!*" (*Life* 8 Oct. 1945: 14); Smith-Corona's "There'll be a few for Christmas!" writ large over a huge picture of the company's new portable typewriter (*Life* 3 Dec. 1945: 65); and Cannon Hosiery's ad featuring popular singer Ginny Simms perched on a ladder trimming a Christmas tree and saying, "What a thrill! Nylon stockings back in time for Christmas!"—something that probably delighted more American women than all the other ads combined (*Life* 10 Dec. 1945: 21). Ads like these proclaimed that what had been the future was now present, proudly offering the return of desired consumer goods as the home front's justly deserved reward for its patience, cooperation, personal effort, and financial generosity in helping win the war,

And yet, for all the advertising world's rejoicing over consumer goods coming back, a few companies celebrated something yet more precious—the safe return of millions of servicemen and women from overseas. No ad did this more delightfully than the Chesapeake and Ohio Line's on page 92 of *Newsweek* on December 24, 1945, and a week later on page 47 of *Time* on December 31 (see fig. 60). Captioned "Together Again!" the large illustration featured Peake the cat returned from the

Together Again!

Millions of loved ones are now back home, taking up the pursuits of peaceful living. And the hope of all of us is that never again will they—or another generation—need to be separated from us by war. For the part that it was our privilege to play in speeding this reunion, we of the Chesapeake and Ohio are truly grateful.

Right now, as we welcome back our personnel who have been serving their country, we are going full steam ahead in a program to provide you with the finest of travel accommodations.

So that some day soon—after we have helped speed many more people in uniform on their way home—we can again suggest that you travel by the road on which you "sleep like a kitten."

The illustration above is from the new 1946 Chessie calendar. If you want one free of charge, better write and reserve yours now. We're printing only a limited number.

CHESAPEAKE AND OHIO RAILWAY

3312 Terminal Tower • Cleveland 1, Ohio

FIGURE 60

war with a souvenir Japanese battle flag like many other GIs, his right front paw bandaged from a shrapnel wound and showing off his two medals and four service ribbons to his beloved (though, as usual, sleeping) Chessie, and their two adoring kittens, Nip and Tuck. The following copy pretty well encapsulated what most Americans truly wanted most after the war: "Millions of loved ones are now back home, taking up the pursuits of peaceful living. And the hope of all of us is that never again will they—or another generation—need to be separated from us by war."

This brief glance at wartime future goods ads suggests that admen used these ads to "reconvert" advertising back to its traditional role of selling, which it began again almost exclusively in the postwar world. Yet in a very real sense even the most dedicated war ads had never abandoned selling at all during the war, they just modified it. Admen shifted from selling products and services *to* the American public to selling home front Americans on ways for *them* to support the war. In doing so, the advertising industry was never self-congratulatory about the role it played during World War II. Yet the range and number of war ads in just the ten national magazines examined here paint a vivid picture of advertising's central place in *creating* the very efficiency and universal participation it promoted among the home front to work with the military in fighting and winning the war.

★★★ BIBLIOGRAPHY

"Ad*Access/World War II." http://scriptorium.lib.duke.edu/adaccess/
wwad-history.html [cited as "Ad*Access"].

Allen, Frederick Lewis. *Since Yesterday: The Nineteen-Thirties in America,
September 3, 1929–September 3, 1939*. New York: Harper, 1940.

Bailey, Ronald H. *The Home Front: U.S.A.* Chicago: Time-Life Books, 1978.

Blum, John Morton. *V Was for Victory: Politics and American Culture During
World War II*. New York: Harcourt Brace Jovanovich, 1976.

Bork, William. "Massacre at Republic Steel." http://www.kentlaw.edu/ilhs/
republic.htm.

"Canned Foods on Ration List." *Life* 11 January 1943: 21+.

Clark, Blake. *The Advertising Smoke Screen*. New York: Harper, 1944.

De Lange, Edgar (lyrics), and Sam H. Stept (music). "This Is Worth Fighting
For." New York: Harms, 1942.

Flink, James J. "Ford, Henry." *American National Biography*. Ed. John A.
Garraty and Mark C. Carnes. Vol. 8. New York: Oxford UP, 1999. 226–35

Fox, Frank W. *Madison Avenue Goes to War: The Strange Military Career of
American Advertising 1941–1945*. Charles E. Merrill Monograph Series in the
Humanities and Social Sciences. Provo, Utah: Brigham Young UP, 1975.

Girdler, Tom M., in collaboration with Boyden Sparkes. *Boot Straps: The
Autobiography of Tom M. Girdler*. New York: Scribner's, 1943.

Hart, Sue. "Madison Avenue Goes to War: Patriotism in Advertising During
World War II." *Visions of War: World War II in Popular Literature and Culture*.
Ed. M. Paul Holsinger and Mary Anne Schofield. Bowling Green, Ohio:
Bowling Green U Popular P, 1992. 114 126.

Honey, Maureen. *Creating Rosie the Riveter: Class, Gender and Propaganda
during World War II*. Amherst: U of Massachusetts P, 1984

Iacocca, Lee. "Henry Ford." *Time 100: Builders & Titans*. New York: Time Books,
1999. 7–9.

Jones, John Bush. *The Songs That Fought the War: Popular Music and the Home
Front, 1939–1945*. Lebanon, N.H.: UP of New England/Brandeis UP, 2006.

Jordan, Louis, Anthonio Cosey, and Collenane Clark. "Ration Blues." New
York: Leeds Music, 1943.

Jordan, Louis, and Sam Theard. "You Can't Get That No More." New York:
Leeds Music, 1944.

Lewis, David L. *The Public Image of Henry Ford: An American Folk Hero and His Company*. Detroit: Wayne State UP, 1976.

Lingeman, Richard R. *Don't You Know There's a War On?* New York: Putnam's, 1970.

Marchand, Roland. *Advertising the American Dream: Making Way for Modernity, 1920–1940*. Berkeley: U of California P, 1985.

Marchand, Roland. "Suspended in Time: Mom-and-Pop Groceries, Chain Stores, and National Advertising during the World War II Interlude." *Produce, Conserve, Share and Play Square: The Grocer and the Consumer on the Home-Front Battlefield during World War II*. Ed. Barbara McLean Ward. Portsmouth, N.H.: Strawbery [sic] Banke [sic] Museum, 1994. 117–39.

"Marketing Terms Dictionary—American Marketing Association." http://www .marketingpower.com/mg-dictionary-view1555.php.

Martin, Hugh, and Ralph Blane. "Have Yourself a Merry Little Christmas." New York: Leo Feist, 1944;

Perrett, Geoffrey. *Days of Sadness, Years of Triumph: The American People 1939–1945*. New York: Coward, McCann & Geoghegan, 1973.

Stolberg, Benjamin. "Big Steel, Little Steel, and C. I. O." *The Nation* 31 July 1937: 119–23.

Sutton, Antony C. *Wall Street and the Rise of Hitler*. Cutchogue, N.Y.: Buccaneer Books, 1976.

"Texas Advertising." http://advertising.utexas.edu/research/terms.

"Things That Are Not in the U. S. Constitution." http://www.usconstitution .net/constnot.html [cited as "Things"].

United Way. http://www.uwtb.org/subpage.asp?navid=44&id=45 [cited as "United Way"].

Wallace, Max. *The American Axis: Henry Ford, Charles Lindbergh, and the Rise of the Third Reich*. New York: St. Martins, 2003.

Wharton, Don. "The Story Back of the War Ads: How the War Advertising Council got started and what it has accomplished." *Advertising & Selling* June 1944: 49+.

WWII-Posters.com. www.wwii-posters.com.

★★★ INDEX

efficiency, 124–35; morale ads focused on, 183–84; premature optimism, 25–29, 27 fig. 9, 86, 256, 283; railroads and, 141–46; rumor control, 135–38; and sacrifice, 186; shortages of goods, 196–205; travel and accommodations on, 140–49. *See also* Morale; Victory Gardens

Home Front: U.S.A., The (Bailey), 2

Honey, Maureen, vii

Hood Rubber, 197

Hoover (vacuum cleaner company), 107, 114, 210, 260, 294

Hoover, President Herbert, 2

Hormel, 22, 215

Hotpoint, 286–87, 288 fig. 58

Humor, 54, 79, 122, 124, 181, 210, 223, 247; cartoons and, 13, 32, 273; in music, 196; as sales device, 8, 273–74; sentiment and, 8, 173

I. W. Harper Bourbon whiskey, 265–69, 270 fig. 52

Iacocca, Lee, 66

Income taxes, 193, 242–43

Industrial accidents, 78

Inflation, 32, 188, 189, 191, 192–93, 251, 262–63

Inland Steel, 5

Institutional / informational ads, 4, 19, 64–85, 87, 92, 185, 273; art and copy in, 5, 11, 12 fig. 3, 13, 45, 67, 85; and the farm front, 69–74; in popular magazines, 5, product messages mixed in with, 5–7; wartime brand consciousness and, 65–69

Insurance Company of North America, 260

International Harvester, 90–91, 98, 112

International Sterling, 22, 235, 253, 287–89

"I Paid My Income Tax Today" (Berlin), 242

Ipana Tooth Paste, 130, 261

Ivory Soap, 132

J. G. Wilson Corporation, 286

Jell-O, 207, 208, 210

Jenkins Valves, 88

Jesus Christ, 55 fig. 12, 56

Jimmy Dorsey Orchestra, 56

Jockey Underwear, 165, 202–3

John B. Stetson Company, 136–38, 138 fig. 28

John Deere, 91, 230

"Johnny Doughboy Found a Rose in Ireland" (Twomey & Goodhart), 162–63

Johnson Bronze Company, 283

Johnson & Johnson, 154

Johnson's Wax, 121

Jordan, Louis, 196, 205

Jordan, Lt. Benjamin R., 175

"Junk Ain't Junk No More" (Croom-Johnson & Kent), 118

Kaiser, Henry J., 135

Kalamazoo Stove & Furnace Company, 113–14

Kayser hosiery, 254

Kaywoodie Briar Pipes, 164

Keds and Kedettes (sneakers), 197

Kellogg's cereals, 81, 127

Kelvinator appliances, 290–92. *See also* Nash-Kelvinator

Kendall Refining Company, 59, 60 fig. 13

Kenwood blankets, 198

Kenyon & Eckhardt (ad agency), 53

Kesten, Paul W., 30

Kimberly-Clark Corporation, 37, 124

Kirby, Rollin (editorial cartoonist) 69, 70 fig. 16

Kirk, Major General Norman T. (U.S. Army Surgeon General), 237